2000

Assessing

Testing

Graduating

What Do I Do When...

The Answer Book on Assessing, Testing and Graduating Students with Disabilities

Assessing

Testing

Graduating

Susan Gorn

Assessing

Testing

Graduating

Publications

LRP Publications
Horsham, Pennsylvania 19044

This publication was designed to provide accurate and authoritative information in regard to the subject matter covered. It is published with the understanding that neither the author nor the publisher is engaged in rendering legal, accounting, or other professional service. If legal advice or other expert assistance is required, the service of a competent professional should be sought.

Library of Congress Cataloging-in-Publication Data

Gorn, Susan, 1954-
    What do I do when-- : the answer book on assessing, testing, and graduating students with disabilities / Susan Gorn.
        p. cm.
    ISBN 1-57834-015-2
    1. Learning disabled--United States--Examinations. 2. Learning disabled--Services for--United States. 3. Learning disabled--Legal status, laws, etc.--United States. I. Title.

    LC4705.G68 2000
    371.9--dc21

                                                                                    00-025098

About the Author

Susan Gorn is a legal writer with a strong interest in law concerning persons with disabilities. As a member of LRP Publications' Education and Disability Law Group, she co-authored, with Melinda Maloney and Vicki Pitasky, *Special Education Regulation: Annotation and Analysis (1995)*. Ms. Gorn also is the author of the 1995 Supplement to Patricia Morrissey's *Survival Guide to the Americans with Disabilities Act*, three pamphlets in LRP's *Elder Law Practice Guide Series* and *Qualified Retirement Plan and IRA Distributions: A Guide for Practitioners*. She also has served as managing director of LRP Publications' newsletter *Serving Elderly Clients*. She is co-author of the *Special Education Regulation: The A-Z Guide to Part B* and sole author of the 1996 and 1997 supplements thereof.

Among Ms. Gorn's numerous editorial accomplishments, she is also the author of LRP's Answer Book series — *What Do I Do When . . . The Answer Book on Special Education Law*, first, second and third editions, *The Answer Book on Individualized Education Programs*, *The Answer Book on the Family Educational Rights and Privacy Act, What Do I Do When . . . The FERPA Answer Book for Higher Education Professionals*, and *What Do I Do When . . . The Answer Book on Section 504*. She also authored *What Do I Do When . . . The Answer Book on Discipline*.

Before joining LRP, Gorn spent five years practicing in a mid-size law firm, where she concentrated her practice in the areas of health law, employee benefits, and business planning and taxation. She received her Juris Doctor degree with honors from the Temple University School of Law in Philadelphia, Pennsylvania.

Table of Contents

Table of Questions

Chapter 1. Testing Accommodations, Generally

Chapter 2. Identifying Students with Disabilities Who Require Testing Accommodations

Chapter 3. Testing Accommodations and Services for College-Bound Students with Disabilities

Chapter 4. Measuring Progress and Assigning Grades For Students with Disabilities

Chapter 5. Regular Education Report Cards and IEP Report Cards for Students with Disabilities

Chapter 6. Participation of Students with Disabilities In General Statewide Assessments

Chapter 7. Alternate Assessments

Chapter 8. High School Exit Examinations

Chapter 9. Graduation and FAPE

Chapter 10. Pomp and Circumstance

How to Use The Answer Book

Overview of the Book

What Do I Do When . . . The Answer Book on Assessing, Testing and Graduating Students with Disabilities concerns the federal laws addressing one of the most unsettled policy issues facing today's educators: how should schools educate and accommodate students with disabilities participating in the general curriculum while preserving districtwide standards for all students? Long-standing challenges involve identifying, testing, grading and graduating students with disabilities that affect learning. In this book we review in detail the controlling directives of both the Individuals with Disabilities Education Act and Section 504 with some confidence that the guidance we provide about these issues is based upon fairly well-settled federal law.

The opposite is true, however, when the participation of students with disabilities in general statewide or districtwide assessments is at issue. The controlling requirements of the IDEA are new, vague and untested. The backdrop — the role of assessments in standards-based education — is itself roiling. For that matter, the current lively public debate about how to improve educational results for all students is unprecedented. Regrettably, it is also outside the narrower focus of this book — federal laws governing assessments of students with disabilities.

The answers in this book are based upon a variety of sources. Federal statutes and regulations are, of course, primary sources. In addition, we rely on judicial decisions interpreting those laws. Administrative interpretations of the IDEA, Section 504 and the ADA by the Department of Education are discussed, as are the decisions of state administrative decision-makers, such as special education due process hearing officers. Thanks to the wonders of the Internet, we are also able to bring to your attention pertinent policies and pronouncements of state departments of education. When addressing inclusion of students with disabilities in general assessments, we compensate for the paucity of controlling law by digesting for your consideration scholarly research and reports concerning assessment policies.

Naturally, the amount of authority of a particular source varies, as does the amount of deference that a particular reader should accord it. In many instances, court and administrative decisions are cited for their illustrative, rather than precedential, value. We are limited in our ability to address state law and policy. But we urge our readers to always consider their impact.

Citation to Authorities

For the readers' convenience, court and state educational agency administrative decisions, as well as OSEP Policy Letters and Memoranda and OCR Memoranda and Letters of Findings, are cited to LRP Publications' Individuals with Disabilities Education Law Report® (IDELR) or, when appropriate, the Early Childhood Law and Policy Reporter (ECLPR).

Citations to the IDEA are made, in most instances, to the pertinent section or sections of the Part B Regulations (34 C.F.R. Parts 300 and 301), rather than the statutory provision under which the regulation was promulgated, even in those instances when the regulation essentially repeats the statutory language.

Abbreviations and Terms

Special education law employs a number of abbreviations and acronyms that may appear throughout this book. The following is a list of some of those commonly used.

ADA	Americans with Disabilities Act
ADD/ADHD/AD/HD	attention deficit disorder/attention deficit hyperactivity disorder
BIP	Behavioral Intervention Plan
Chapter 1	State Operated or Supported Programs for Handicapped Children, authorized under Chapter 1 of Title 1 of the Elementary and Secondary Education Act.
DSM IV	Diagnostic and Statistical Manual of Mental Disorders-Fourth Edition
ED	emotional disturbance/emotionally disturbed
EDGAR	Education Department General Administrative Regulations
EHA	Education for the Handicapped Act (now known as the Individuals with Disabilities Education Act)
ESY	extended school year
FAPE	free appropriate public education
FBA	Functional Behavior Assessment
FERPA	Family Educational Rights and Privacy Act
IAES	Interim Alternative Educational Setting
IDEA	Individuals with Disabilities Education Act
IEP	individual education program
IEU	intermediate education unit
LD	learning disability/learning disabled
LEA	local educational agency
LOF	letter of findings
LRE	least restrictive environment
OCR	Office for Civil Rights
OSEP	Office for Special Education Programs
OSERS	Office of Special Education and Rehabilitation Services
Part C	Part of the IDEA (Infants and Toddlers with Disabilities Program) (formerly Part H)
SEA	state educational agency
Section 504	Section 504 of the Rehabilitation Act of 1973
Section 1983	42 U.S.C. Section 1983 of the Civil Rights Act
SLD	specific learning disability

The term "district" or "school district" is used throughout this book as an abbreviation for local school district, and to the extent indicated by the context, any other public agency within a state involved in the education of children with disabilities.

The terms "handicap" and "handicapped" may appear in the text. Prior to 1990 (for the IDEA) and 1993 (for Section 504) the term "handicapped" was used in the statutory texts and resulting regulations, court decisions, administrative rulings and the like. This terminology has not been updated in direct quotations from pre-change materials and documents. The masculine gender is used when referring to an individual who could either be a man or woman, boy or girl. This is just a convenience.

Chapter 1

TESTING ACCOMMODATIONS, GENERALLY

1. Does Section 504 require school districts to make changes to in-school (teacher-made) tests for students with disabilities?

Yes. Because Section 504 and Title II of the ADA prohibit discrimination on the basis of disability in providing education services to students with disabilities, school districts must provide appropriate test accommodations.

The purpose of testing modifications is to provide for students with disabilities equal opportunities to demonstrate their abilities and compensate for their deficits in the testing situation. *See, e.g., Yorktown Cent. Sch. Dist.*, 16 EHLR 771 (SEA N.Y. 1990). An often-used articulation of purpose equates academic testing to athletics: Modifications are provided in order to "level the playing field."

In *Southeastern Community College v. Davis*, EHLR 551:177 (1979) the Supreme Court interpreted Section 504 as limiting a covered educational institution's obligation to the provision of "reasonable" accommodations. As a general principle, accommodations are reasonable when they provide students with disabilities an equal opportunity to participate without lowering or fundamentally altering the district's otherwise validly established standards or procedures.

2. When is a regular education classroom test accommodation considered reasonable, for purposes of Section 504?

Academic tests should reflect a student's achievement or aptitude in the subject area tested rather than reflect a disabling condition. A reasonable accommodation modifies the conditions under which a test is administered so that the student's performance reflects his skills, abilities and mastery of the curriculum, not the impact his disability has on his ability to comprehend the questions or formulate responses.

Extrapolating from that basic principle, there are two types of circumstances when a test accommodation is always unreasonable, as a matter of law. In both instances, the legal principle is easy to understand, but its application in particular instances is tricky, thus keeping litigators' earning prospects bright.

- An accommodation that is not required because of the student's disability will never come within the ambit of a school district's obligation under Section 504. *See, e.g., Letter to Anonymous*, 25 IDELR 632 (OSEP 1996).

For example, a student with a disability is not entitled to extended test time unless the disability impacts his ability to take the test within the allotted time. See Question 6. This is the same principle governing grading of students with disabilities: Section 504 protections and procedural safeguards may be extended only when a student's poor academic performance is related to his disability.

- An accommodation, or modification, that lowers or substantially changes academic standards is not reasonable.

The Supreme Court made it clear in *Southeastern Community College v. Davis*, EHLR 551:177 (1979) that Section 504 does not compel the lowering of academic standards in deference to the intellectual, or other disability-related, limits of a student with a disability. As the Seventh Circuit Court of Appeals ruled in *Brookhart v. Illinois State Board of Education,* EHLR 554:285 (7th Cir. 1983) with respect to high school minimum competency tests:[1]

> Altering the content of [a test] to accommodate an individual's inability to learn the tested material because of his handicap would be a 'substantial modification' as well as a 'perversion' of the [test's] requirement. A student who is unable to learn because of his handicap is surely not an individual who is qualified in spite of his handicap.

EHLR 554 at 288.

Sometimes it is easy to apply the Court's ruling to a particular situation. It is clear that the student's disability has no relation to whatever competence or knowledge is being tested, or has only an incidental relationship. A student who cannot write or use a keyboard should be permitted to dictate his answers when his subject matter knowledge is being tested.

But if, instead of a physical disability and a test of subject matter knowledge, you may be dealing with, for example, a student who has a learning disability and a test of cognitive abilities, as well as subject matter knowledge, then there are no truly clear answers to questions of what is, or is not, a reasonable accommodation. And that is the case from both a legal and pedagogical perspective.

The National Research Council warned educators about thinking that there are easy answers in its 1997 report, *Educating One and All: Students with Disabilities and Standard-Based Reform.*

> Accommodations are intended to correct for distortions in a student's true competence caused by a disability unrelated to the construct being measured. ...

> Many approaches to the assessment of individuals with disabilities, particularly assessment accommodations, assume that disabilities are not directly related to the construct tested. Case law indicates that rights to accommodations do not apply when the disability is directly related to the construct being tested. In other words, a student with a reading disability might be allowed help with reading (the accommodation) on a mathematics test, since reading is not in the construct being measured, but would not be allowed help with reading on a reading test, since the disability is directly related to the construct of reading.

> However, the groups of students with clearly identifiable disabilities (such as motor impairments) that are largely unrelated to the constructs being tested constitute a small number of the identified population of students with disabilities. Most students with disabilities have cognitive impairments that presumably are related to at least some of the constructs tested.[2]

A good illustration of the miasma courts enter into when a student with cognitive deficits collides with a test of cognitive skills is *Wynne v. Tufts University School of Medicine,* 3 NDLR ¶ 121 (1st Cir. 1992). That decision involved the rejection of the claim of a medical student with dyslexia that his disability placed him at an unfair disadvantage in taking written multiple-choice examinations and that the medical school had an obligation under Section 504 to design an alternate format by which to test his mastery of biochemistry. An evaluation buttressed the student's assertion that his disability resulted in difficulty interpreting the type of multiple choice questions characteristic of medical school examinations. The student had requested administration of an oral examination in which he could respond in his own words to the questions posed.

Many would think what the student proposed sounded even harder than the standard test. And, in any event, what is really critical is the student's knowledge of biochemistry, isn't it? Well, no. Not according to Tufts. At a hearing the school presented credible evidence of its legitimate belief in (as opposed to its pretextual rationalization of) "the unique qualities of multiple-choice examinations as they apply to biochemistry." In so doing, it demonstrated to the court that deviation from its test format would substantially alter its medical program, lower academic standards, and even "devalue Tufts' end product — highly trained physicians carrying the prized credential of a Tufts degree."

The decision also confirms the challenges faced by educators when defending rejections of requested accommodations in situations where, as the medical school in *Wynne* appeared to concede, there is no clear "right" or "wrong." In that regard, the court's decision is instructive for school districts and parents. It well illustrates what the body of published decisional law reveals: courts and OCR generally defer to school districts that can "demythologize" their reasoning, consider requests for testing accommodations in a reasoned, professional manner, and present a rational explanation of why the requested accommodation would lower academic standards or fundamentally alter the test. In other words, its refusal to provide the requested accommodation was a "reasoned, professional academic judgment, not a mere *ipse dixit*."

To conclude, please do not allow yourself to become paralyzed by the complexity of this issue. Decisions have to be made every day for individual students with disabilities whose parents are requesting — maybe even demanding in no uncertain terms — specific accommodations in order to take particular tests. To that end, we review published legal decisions and guidance addressing a range of specific accommodations in Questions 3 to 7.

3. Under what circumstances is use of a "spell check" device a reasonable test accommodation?

Published decisions illustrate two lines of reasoning under which it is not appropriate to allow a student with a disability to use "spell check" when taking tests.[3]

When spelling is the precise skill being tested, a student who has a learning disability that impacts his ability to spell may not use a spell check device. For example, in *Texas Education Agency*, 18 IDELR 280 (OCR, Region VI 1991) OCR supported the state agency's denial of use of an automated spell check device as an accommodation for students with dyslexia and attention deficit disorder taking the state's academic skills program (ASP) test for college entrance. OCR found that the evidence supported the agency's claim that spelling was a tested skill.

Requests for relaxation of requirements for correct spelling in tests — or an exemption from being graded on such a basis altogether — involves the same analysis as a consideration of whether a disabled student should be permitted to have a spell check at the ready in a test situation. The review officer in *Yorktown Central School District*, 16 EHLR 771 (SEA N.Y. 1990) did a good job of placing a dispute about testing the spelling of a student with a spelling-related disability in the larger context of a school district's obligations under Section 504 to offer test accommodations. In the process, he supported a school district that seemed to have bent over backward to allow a student's true merit to shine through.

In *Yorktown* the parent of a 15-year-old honor roll student with a learning disability in spelling wanted the district to limit spelling tests to a predetermined number of non-cumulative words each week. The district was willing to exempt the student from being penalized on the basis of his spelling errors in all examinations and other graded work, except actual spelling tests. It also agreed to allow the student extended time on spelling tests. But it refused to grant the parent's request to limit the number of words on which the student would be tested. An impartial hearing officer upheld the district's testing modifications, and the review officer upheld that ruling.

The review officer recognized that achievement in English involves far more than spelling for older students. The main concern was to relieve the student of pressure to succeed in an area where his disability frustrated his potential, thus allowing him to continue to function well in his regular classes and succeed in other areas to the extent commensurate with his overall high intelligence. To that end, the review officer agreed with the proposed provision of all the accommodations, including relief from grading, proposed by the school district. But he drew the line precisely where the school district did.

1 : 3

Given the severity of this pupil's spelling disability, petitioner's son should only be given spelling tests in an individual, separate setting, with extended time for completion of such tests. However, there is no basis for granting petitioner's request that her son be held accountable for only a limited, non-cumulative number of spelling words. Despite this student's spelling disability, he continues to be an honor's student in his mainstream English class. Therefore, I find that his current educational placement is not only least restrictive, but one designed to enable this student to benefit from his educational program. Consistent with its purposes, the [IDEA] neither contemplates special education that maximizes a student's potential nor one that inflates a student's grades by lowering academic standards. Because I find such a request goes beyond the purpose of testing modifications contemplated by the Act, petitioner's request that her son be tested on a modified spelling list must be denied.

16 EHLR at 772 (citations omitted).

As an additional consideration, when use of a spell check program masks a disability for which the school district should be providing remediation services, its use in testing situations can be a denial of FAPE. Two recent administrative decisions illustrate this point: *Board of Education of the Arlington Central School District,* 30 IDELR 313 (SEA N.Y. 1998) and *Dare County Public Schools,* 27 IDELR 547 (SEA N.C. 1997)

The IEP proposed by the school district in *Dare County* for a ninth-grade student with dyslexia did not provide remedial instruction for the student's acknowledged disability-related spelling difficulties. Instead, the student was given a "spell check" program to use for assignments and tests. Because the district failed to provide instruction to remediate basic spelling skills the school district denied the student a FAPE.

The same type of approach to serving a student with a learning disability affecting spelling was labeled an attempt by the district to "escape" its obligation to provide services in *Arlington Central School District.* In that instance the district's IEP for a ninth-grade student addressed deficits in spelling by providing that his poor spelling would not be held against him in grading his tests or assignments. The IEP made the student "spelling exempt." Because this approach did nothing to improve the student's spelling skills, which were on a second grade level, the student was denied FAPE.

4. Under what circumstances is use of a calculator a reasonable test accommodation?

These days calculator use seems accepted in many testing circumstances for both students with disabilities and nondisabled students. The author's review of the LRP Publications' database of special education decisions revealed no dispute concerning whether a student with a disability could use a calculator in the course of a regular education classroom test.

Notwithstanding the above, calculator use by students with disabilities continues to be a lively controversy in connection with statewide or districtwide proficiency examinations that are "high stakes" tests. In these circumstances the Section 504 limitation on provision of accommodations that change the fundamental nature of the test comes into play. If calculator use compromises the nature, content, and integrity of the test, then its use is not a reasonable accommodation under Section 504. The test-giver, a state or district, can bar use by students with disability-related deficits in computational skills. The state department of education in *Nevada State Department of Education,* 25 IDELR 752 (OCR, Region X 1996), for example, could bar the use of calculators for the math portion of its state proficiency examinations because an essential purpose of the testing was assessment of basic computational skills. Similarly, in *South Carolina Department of Education,* EHLR 352:475 (OCR, Region IV 1987) OCR held that the state did not violate Section 504 by refusing to permit disabled students to use calculators in statewide tests. In that instance, a significant aspect of the tests was assessment of students' understanding of basic arithmetic operations. The Alaska DOE seems to go further, making a blanket statement that use of calculators by students with disabilities, when nondisabled students are not permitted to use them, should be "avoided."[4]

5. Can reading aloud test questions be a reasonable accommodation for a student with a learning disability?

A reasonable accommodation for a student with a reading disability may be having test or examination questions read aloud. The one clear exception would be when the purpose of the test is to evaluate the student's reading comprehension.

OCR takes the position that reading test questions to students with disabilities related to the ability to read may be a reasonable accommodation under Section 504.

> To measure the competencies of a reading-disabled student in areas other than reading, it may be necessary to administer a test orally, to provide a reader, to allow extra time for the student to complete the test, and/or to provide other accommodations. Such adjustments ensure that a student who is proficient in other areas of competency does not fail the test because of his/her reading problems.

Hawaii State Dep't of Educ., 17 EHLR 360, 362 (OCR, Region IX 1990).

But when reading is the competency at issue, a student with a reading disability will have to do the best he can unaided. In *Birmingham Board of Education*, 20 IDELR 1281 (SEA Ala. 1994) a hearing officer affirmed the right of an 11th-grade student with a learning disability to have mostly all of the state's high school graduation exam read aloud to him. However, the student was not permitted to use that accommodation for the reading subtest.

OCR upheld the same limitation in *Alabama Department of Education*, 29 IDELR 249 (OCR, Region IV 1998). In that LOF a student with dyslexia was permitted to use his Arkenstone scanner (a device to scan and read text to an individual) for all parts of his exit exam except the reading subtest.

> The allowable testing modifications on the Exit Exam excludes the use of an Arkenstone scanner on the Reading subtest of the Exit Exam. ...

> The basis for the exclusion of the scanner on the Reading subtest of the Exit Exam is because the Reading subtest assesses whether a student can read well enough to comprehend everyday material. The reading modification, if allowed, would not show the Student's ability to read and comprehend, only the Student's listening skills.

29 IDELR at 250.

But the Alaska Department of Education is one educational agency that appears to disagree. Stating (in connection with statewide assessments) that it defines a required test accommodation as one that "levels the playing field," it opined as follows:

> One example of an accommodation that gives an [unfair] advantage is when a teacher actively assists a disabled student in answering *test questions*, such as reading test questions to a student. It may be appropriate, however, to read *test directions* to a student.[5]

The Illinois State Board of Education takes the same position.[6]

6. When is extended test time a reasonable accommodation?

Typically, a test is mainly content-driven, with some "speededness" or completion-time concerns. In these typical instances, extended test time is generally considered a reasonable accommodation when a student's disability prevents demonstration of mastery of the tested material within the allotted time. Extended test time is a routinely granted accommodation for students with learning disabilities related to reading or writing when assessment of the student's mastery of content is the main purpose of the testing.

On the other hand, when a particular test is designed to measure a student's ability to think and answer questions within time constraints, extended time is probably not a reasonable accommodation. Rather, oral reading of the test questions or dictating the test answers might be alternative reasonable accommodations for particular students.

Analogous considerations came into play in *Ann Arbor (MI) Public School District*, 30 IDELR 405 (OCR, Region XII 1998), a LOF in which OCR supported the district's refusal to allow a disabled student extended test time to complete a particular test. The IEP of the high school student in *Ann Arbor* specified that the student receive extended time on tests and other assignments in her business education class (BEC). When the BEC teacher refused to allow extended time to complete tests of computer keyboarding skills, her parent lodged a complaint alleging discrimination. Questioned by OCR, the BEC teacher explained that proficiency on the computer keyboard necessarily involved testing for speed and accuracy. Had she (the teacher) allowed the student extended time to complete the tests, their stated purpose would have been defeated. OCR supported the district, finding there had been no discrimination in this instance.

That said, "speeded" tests are not the norm for in-school testing. In the ordinary course, a teacher merely sets what seems to be an adequate amount of time for the average student to answer the questions posed. In that sense, there may appear to be no good reason not to grant the request of a student with a disability for extended test time. Even so, school districts should allow extended test time only when the student demonstrates a disability-related need for the accommodation.

One school district that refused to take the path of least resistance won the support of the hearing officer in *Apple Valley Unified School District*, 25 IDELR 1128 (SEA Cal. 1997). Among the specific complaints made by the parents of a 13-year-old student with a learning disability was that the district should have granted the request for extended time to complete all assignments, including tests, quizzes, homework and classwork. At due process, however, the school district demonstrated why it had concluded that the requested accommodation was not necessary. One of the student's teachers testified that the student always completed tests in less than the time allotted. Whether the student performed well or poorly on a test (and, in fact, she earned mostly "As"), one thing was a constant: the student completed the test quickly. According to another teacher, the student had been advised to work more slowly to no avail; she continued to work at her own rapid pace.

7. Can dictation of test responses be a reasonable accommodation for a student with a learning disability?

Maybe. Oral dictation of a writing sample is not a reasonable accommodation under any circumstances. More generally, it would not be reasonable to allow a student to dictate answers when one purpose of the test or assessment is to gauge the student's ability to express himself in writing. But when a student's subject matter knowledge is what is being tested, dictation of test responses may be an appropriate accommodation when the student's disability results in limited ability to produce written responses.

The school district in *Board of Education of the City School District of the City of New York*, 25 IDELR 1154 (SEA N.Y. 1997), for example, provided various testing modifications for a student with a learning disability, including extended time limits and separate testing locations. In addition, because the child had difficulty expressing himself in writing, he was permitted to give oral, rather than written, responses to portions of tests.

This is not to say that all a school district has to do for a learning-disabled student who has trouble expressing himself in writing is provide an amanuensis. Special education services intended to help the student improve his ability to write may also be required. In *Evans v. Board of Education of Rhinebeck Central School District*, 24 IDELR 338 (S.D.N.Y. 1996), for example, the IEP for a high school student with dyslexia called for modified testing in all subject areas. He was given multiple choice questions, with short answers; often he dictated his answers. But the IEP also included annual goals and special education related to improvement of writing skills.

8. Who selects the particular in-school test accommodations a school district must provide to an individual student with a disability?

School district personnel charged with making individual decisions about the needs of students with disabilities decide who gets what. When the student is covered by the IDEA, then the IEP team has that responsibility. When the student is disabled only for purposes of Section 504, then the student's placement team decides.

Unlike the more specific Section 504 regulations governing testing accommodations for college students,[7] Section 504 regulations governing public elementary or secondary schools do not delineate the types of regular education classroom testing modifications that will be deemed reasonable on a categorical basis. Each student's need for test accommodations is treated as unique, subject to individual review. When a student is identified as disabled for purposes of Section 504 only, any required test modifications become part of the district's menu of aids, services, modifications, proposed and provided in accordance with Section 504 regulations.

Under controlling section 34 C.F.R. § 104.35(c) decisions about test modifications and testing accommodations must be made by a group of persons, including persons knowledgeable about the student, the meaning of the evaluation data and the placement options. Parental participation in the formulation of the agreed modifications is not essential. Instead, parental involvement can be after-the-fact, with the school district providing notice of what will be provided.

When the IDEA as well as Section 504 cover a student with a disability, testing modifications, agreed to by the IEP team, become part of the student's IEP. Section 300.347(a)(3) directs IEP teams to consider and identify in the written IEP all services, modifications and accommodations, among other things, the student needs to progress in the general curriculum and participate in the same academic programs with other students with disabilities and nondisabled students.

Whether the student's IEP team or another group of individuals makes the decision to modify testing procedures for a student with a disability, one thing remains the same: The decision must be the result of individual analysis, based on a consideration of both the test and the student. While one accommodation may be appropriate for one student in one test situation, the same accommodation may not be apt for another disabled student taking the same test — or even for the same student, when taking a different test.

9. Is there any regulatory guidance identifying appropriate test accommodations for students with learning disabilities?

No. Despite the fact that students with learning disabilities are far and away the majority of students requiring test accommodations, there are no special legal provisions governing selection of appropriate accommodations.

Whatever Congress might have originally anticipated when it first enacted the IDEA, it has turned out that over half of all students entitled to special education and related services under the IDEA establish eligibility on the basis of a specific learning disability (34 C.F.R.§ 300.7(c)(10).[8] No one knows precisely how many students with learning disabilities receive services under Section 504, but undoubtedly that number is also substantial.[9]

As OCR observed the following in *Georgia Department of Education*, EHLR 352:480 (OCR, Region IV 1987) with respect to accommodations for students with learning disabilities:

> Learning disabilities include a multiplicity of disorders which are manifested in a variety of ways and which to varying degrees affect an individual's ability to listen, think, speak, read, write, spell, or perform mathematical calculations. Therefore, the testing modifications which are appropriate to individual LD students are virtually limitless. The issue of appropriateness of test modifications, as it relates to the validity of test assessment, is more appropriately resolved on the basis of individual assessments.

EHLR 352 at 482.

SLDs are often referred to as "mild" disabilities. But that label should not allow an educator to discount the criticality of diligent review of each individual student's need for accommodations.

> Because a disability is mild, does not mean it is trivial or that it magically disappears at age 18 or 21. Students with SLD are seriously impaired in one of the most important developmental tasks in a technologically complex society: literacy skills and using them to master bodies of knowledge. Poor reading skills in particular constitute formidable barriers to academic progress and significantly limit adult career opportunities.[10]

Endnotes

[1] We discuss minimum competency tests, and high school exit examinations generally, in chapter 8.

[2] LORRAINE M. MCDONNELL, MARGARET J. MCLAUGHLIN, PATRICIA MORISON, EDS., EDUCATING ONE AND ALL: STUDENTS WITH DISABILITIES AND STANDARDS-BASED REFORMS 171-177 (National Academy Press 1997).

[3] The question is premised upon students not being permitted to use a spell check device in examinations, as a general rule.

[4] "Fast Facts" <http://www.educ.state.ak.us/tls/assessment/fastfactsaccommodations.html> Alaska Department of Education & Early Development (November 15, 1999).

[5] "Fast Facts," *supra*, note 4.

[6] "ISAT & PSAE" <http://www.isbe.state.il.us/isat/FAQnew.htm> Illinois State Board of Education (November 15, 1999).

[7] See Question 1 in chapter 3 in this regard.

[8] JAY P. HEUBERT, ROBERT M. HAUSER, EDS., HIGH STAKES: TESTING FOR TRACKING, PROMOTION, AND GRADUATION 190 (National Academy Press 1999).

[9] *Id.*, 191.

[10] LORRAINE M. MCDONNELL, MARGARET J. MCLAUGHLIN, PATRICIA MORISON, EDS., EDUCATING ONE AND ALL: STUDENTS WITH DISABILITIES AND STANDARDS BASED-REFORMS 76 (National Academy Press 1997).

Chapter 2

IDENTIFYING STUDENTS WITH DISABILITIES WHO REQUIRE TESTING ACCOMMODATIONS

1. Why do the IDEA regulations contain special evaluation procedures for specific learning disabilities?

No statutory directive compelled the promulgation of the regulations creating additional procedures for evaluating students with specific learning disabilities (at 34 C.F.R. §§ 300.540-300.543), under either the 1997 IDEA Amendments or the prior law. It appears to have been the "invisible nature" of the disability that motivated DOE establishment of supplemental regulatory provisions for the evaluation of specific learning disabilities (SLD).

Specific learning disabilities affect academic performance but do not impact a student's ability to perform activities of daily living. For this reason, SLDs are often referred to as "mild" disabilities.[1] Because an SLD presents as significant academic underachievement, specific learning disabilities are difficult to diagnose when students are young. But when the academic performance of an older student is poor, or becomes worse than it was, any number of factors other than having an SLD may account for the low level of achievement. These diagnostic challenges motivated DOE to regulate the evaluation process with more particularity than it did under the generally applicable regulations concerning procedures for evaluating and determining eligibility. 34 C.F.R. §§ 300.530-300.536.

DOE's particular reasoning was set out at its fullest in discussion accompanying the publication of IDEA regulations in 1977. That discussion included the following:

> Those with specific learning disabilities may demonstrate their handicap through a variety of symptoms such as hyperactivity, distractibility, attention problems, concept association problems, etc. The end result of the effects of these symptoms is a severe discrepancy between achievement and ability. If there is no severe discrepancy between how much should have been learned and what has been learned, there would not be a disability in learning. However, other handicapping and sociological conditions may result in a discrepancy between ability and achievement. There are those for whom these conditions are the primary factors affecting achievement. In such cases, the severe discrepancy may be primarily the result of these factors and not of a severe learning problem. For the purpose of these regulations, when a severe discrepancy between ability and achievement exist which cannot be explained by the presence of other known factors that lead to such a discrepancy, the cause is believed to be a specific learning disability. It was on this basic concept that these regulations were developed.[2]

A further explanation of what DOE was thinking more than 20 years ago does not seem likely to help you do your job today. So we will not pursue that line of analysis any further. This is particularly true because DOE is on record as questioning whether its chosen approach to evaluating for possible specific learning disabilities needs an overhaul. In the preamble to the 1997 Notice of proposed rulemaking, DOE announced:

> The Secretary intends to review carefully over the next several years the additional procedures for evaluating children suspected of having a specific learning disability contained

[in the regulations] in light of research, expert opinion and practical knowledge of identifying children with a specific learning disability with the purpose of considering whether legislative proposals should be advanced for revising these provisions.[3]

They're still working on it. That's what DOE advised in 1999 when it published the final regulations.[4]

2. How do the IDEA evaluation procedures for specific learning disabilities differ from those established for all other classifications of disabilities?

The general requirements and procedures for evaluating all students suspected of having a disability, contained in 34 C.F.R. §§ 300.530-300.536, also govern evaluation of students suspected of having a specific learning disability. The regulations governing evaluations of students for possible specific learning disabilities set out at 34 C.F.R. §§ 300.540-300.543 supplement the generally applicable regulations. We explain how below.

Members of evaluation team: Under 34 C.F.R. §300.533(a) the evaluation team must be the IEP team "and other qualified professionals, as appropriate." Section 300.540 states that the determination of whether a student has a qualifying SLD must be made by:

- the student's parents;

- a team of qualified professionals which must include the student's regular teacher or, if the student does not have a regular teacher, a regular classroom teacher qualified to teach a student of the same age; and

- at least one person qualified to conduct individual diagnostic examinations of children, such as a school psychologist, speech-language pathologist, or remedial reading teacher.

In the author's view, 34 C.F.R. § 300.540 adds little of substance to the 1999 IDEA regulations. The individuals it identifies would almost certainly be included even without this specific directive.

Determining Eligibility: Section 300.532 sets no specific guidelines for when an evaluation team should conclude that a particular student has an underlying medical or psychological condition identified as a basis for potential eligibility under 34 C.F.R. § 300.7. Section 300.541, on the other hand, establishes standard IDEA criteria for determining when a student has a specific learning disability, as well as "rule-out" criteria. Section 300.541 is thus analogous to 34 C.F.R. § 300.7(b)(4), establishing both eligibility and "rule-out" criteria for students with emotional disturbances. Another drafter might have chosen to include this requirement as part of 34 C.F.R. § 300.7(b)(10).

Tests and Other Evaluation Procedures: No directive to use particular tests or evaluation procedures is included in 34 C.F.R. § 300.532. Selection is a matter of state and local discretion, limited only by the general standards for suitability set out in regulations. Section 300.542 has DOE stepping in more forcefully where evaluation for an SLD is concerned, requiring that "at least one team member other than the child's regular teacher shall observe the child's academic performance in the regular classroom setting." In *Letter to Hartman*, EHLR 213:252 (OSERS 1989) OSEP opined that observation by someone other than the student's teacher will always be a necessary part of the evaluation, safeguarding the accuracy of the team's assessment of whether the student is, or is not, performing in accordance with his ability.

If one wonders why DOE believed school districts would not come to the same conclusion on its own merits, the 1998 administrative decision in *Long Beach Unified School District*, 29 IDELR 818 (SEA Cal. 1998) may clue you in. More than 20 years after the publication of the regulations a school district did not have the student's behavior in class observed by anyone other than her teachers when it assessed her for possible specific learning disabilities. Holding that teacher report forms could not substitute for firsthand observation by a person other than the teacher, the hearing officer ordered the school district to fund an IEE.

Evaluation Report: The IDEA regulations at 34 C.F.R. §§ 300.530-300.536 assume that a written evaluation report will be prepared and distributed, to serve as the basis for preparation of any resulting IEP and to substantiate the evaluation team's findings, in any event. Section 300.543(a) does not. It explicitly requires production of a written report and even describes in detail what that report's content should be. The requirements are statements of:

- whether the student has a specific learning disability;

- the basis for that determination;

- the relevant behavior noted during the observation of the student;

- the relationship of that behavior to the student's academic functioning;

- the educationally relevant medical findings, if any;

- whether there is a severe discrepancy between achievement and ability that is not correctable without special education and related services; and

- the determination of the team concerning the effects of environmental, cultural, or economic disadvantage.

The decision of the hearing officer in *Montgomery County Public Schools,* 24 IDELR 400 (SEA Md. 1996) illustrates why it may be necessary to have such a specific directive in the regulations. In *Montgomery County Public Schools* the evaluation team for a student with a suspected specific learning disability did not prepare a report that met the requirements of 34 C.F.R. § 300.543(a). The hearing officer found from the evidence that the team based its decision that the student was not learning disabled primarily on the discrepancy between his Broad reading, math, written language and knowledge test scores and his I.Q. score. The hearing officer concluded that, had the team complied with the written report requirement, it would have been compelled to thoroughly review all the student's subtest scores and his classroom performance. And had it done that, it might have reached a different conclusion about whether the student had a specific learning disability.

The directive contained in 34 C.F.R. § 300.543(b) clearly adds to the general evaluation requirements of 34 C.F.R. §§ 300.530-300.536 and may run counter to the approach states and local school districts would take, were this requirement not a part of the IDEA. Under this section, each team member must certify in writing whether the team's report reflects that member's conclusion or submit a separate statement presenting that member's independent views.

3. What is the severe discrepancy that must be established to demonstrate that a student has a specific learning disability?

Under the IDEA a student must have a severe discrepancy between intellectual ability and achievement in order to be eligible under the IDEA on the basis of a specific learning disability.[5]

IDEA regulations at 34 C.F.R. §300.541(a)(2) state:

(a) A team may determine that a child has a specific learning disability if ...

(2) The team finds that a child has a severe discrepancy between achievement and intellectual ability in one or more of the following areas:

(i) Oral expression.

(ii) Listening comprehension.

(iii) Written expression.

(iv) Basic reading skill.

(v) Reading comprehension.

(vi) Mathematics calculation

(vii) Mathematics reasoning

The review officer in *Conrad Weiser Area School District*, 27 IDELR 100 (SEA Pa. 1997) confirmed what most educators have long believed. The "discrepancy" has to exist between "ability" and "achievement" in one or more of the areas identified in subsections (a)(2)(i)-(a)(2)(vii), rather than between those areas themselves. The parents in that instance claimed that discrepancies between achievement in written expression and reading comprehension established that the student had a specific learning disability.

"With all due respect to parents and their counsel's admirable efforts to establish eligibility for what they sincerely believe [the student] needs, their analytical approach is fundamentally flawed," the panel diplomatically wrote.

> [C]urrent law defines specific learning disabilities solely in terms of ability versus achievement. ... As the parents suggest, children may be better served by shifting the definition's focus from causation to result oriented factors, and in the context of children who need special education services that may be more successfully argued before those empowered to alter it.

27 IDELR at 103.

As to the areas in which the discrepancy between ability and achievement should be assessed, OSEP made it clear in *Letter to Lillie/Felton*, 23 IDELR 714 (OSEP 1995) that, when it said seven areas, it meant seven areas. Responding to an allegation that a state had consolidated testing of basic reading skills [34 C.F.R. § 300.541(a)(2)(iv)] with reading comprehension [34 C.F.R. § 300.541(a)(2)(v)] and mathematics calculation [34 C.F.R. § 300.541(a)(2)(vi)] with mathematics comprehension [34 C.F.R. § 300.541(a)(2)(vi)], OSEP stated that none of the areas listed at 34 C.F.R. § 300.541(a)(2)(i)-(vii) can be categorically excluded — or merged out of existence. All seven areas must be separately assessed in deciding if a student has a specific learning disability.

Looking on the bright side, though, in *Philadelphia School District*, 27 IDELR 447 (SEA Pa. 1997) a review officer opined quite convincingly that a state does not have to test in an eighth area.

Philadelphia School District concerned a middle school student participating in a mentally gifted program at a magnet school who was having trouble with Spanish. The district agreed to conduct the evaluation requested by the parent and concluded that the student had a "mild language-based learning disability manifesting in foreign language difficulty." Interventions were proposed, implemented, and ultimately proven ineffective.

The parent then filed for due process, demanding that the district waive the course requirement altogether. The hearing officer overruled the district by concluding that the student's discrepancy between achievement and intellect in Spanish was enough to establish eligibility on the basis of an SLD. A new subsection 34 C.F.R. § 300.541(a)(2)(viii), if you will. The hearing officer refused to waive the course requirement, as requested by the parent, but did order the district to provide Spanish itinerant support, visual, auditory, kinesthetic and tactile approaches, and a reduction in the pace of instruction.

Because there was something for everyone to object to, both parties filed for administrative appeal. The review panel reversed the finding of eligibility in an opinion that combined legal reasoning with a *reductio ad absurdum* argument.

Although the legal definition of SLD is over 20 years old, no reported court decision has ever held that one or more of the seven enumerated areas in the definition may be based solely on a foreign language. Although the legislative history does not specifically address foreign languages or other such subjects, Congress did express concern requiring the U.S. Department of Education promulgate more specific standards, or criteria, for SLD 'to assure that no abuse takes place.' Similarly, the courts have taken a restrictive view of SLD; the overwhelming majority of their decisions have denied such eligibility. The administrative rulings have followed suit. Thus, such a major policy change would appear to be a matter for Congress or the Department of Education, not for a hearing officer.

The seven enumerated areas in the definition are obviously basic skills that are generic, not subject specific. Opening up any one or more of the five non-math areas to foreign language does not stop at Spanish; not only are there scores of foreign tongues, many of which present obvious difficulty for American students, but also other subjects, according to the parent's argument, such as music, are also included.

27 IDELR at 448 (footnotes omitted).

4. Can a state exclude from eligibility under the IDEA on the basis of a specific learning disability (SLD) a student who has been identified as intellectually gifted under state standards?

No. A categorical exclusion from eligibility on the basis of identification as gifted under state law violates the IDEA. On an individual student level, there may be students who are mentally gifted, but still meet the eligibility criteria set out in 34 C.F.R. § 300.541.

One's first thought might be that a student who is classified as mentally gifted could not possibly be learning disabled: obviously an either/or issue. But this is not the case, as a matter of educational psychology. A student can be both mentally gifted and have a learning disability. And OSEP has made in clear in policy guidance that a student classified as mentally gifted may nonetheless meet the eligibility criteria set out in 34 C.F.R. § 300.541(a)(1) and (2).

In fact, when you think about it, it is vastly more likely that students who are IDEA-eligible on the basis of an SLD will be highly intelligent. If a student's cognitive ability is within the average range, achievement scores in the high average to low average range probably will not establish a severe discrepancy. The National Research Council goes further, opining in 1997 that "it is virtually impossible for a student whose achievement level is average or near average to be diagnosed in a category like SLD."[6]

OSEP opined on the illegality of categorical exclusion of students who have a high level of intelligence in *Letter to Ulissi*, 18 IDELR 683 (OSEP 1992).

Neither Part B nor the Part B regulations provide for any exclusions based on intelligence level in determining eligibility for Part B services. The regulations, at 34 CFR § 300.541(b), do provide that: '[t]he team may not identify a child as having a specific learning disability if the severe discrepancy between ability and achievement is primarily the result of (1) A visual, hearing, or motor [disability]; (2) Mental retardation; (3) Emotional disturbance; or (4) Environmental, cultural, or economic disadvantages.' No mention is made in the regulations of any exclusions solely on the basis of intelligence. All children, except those specifically excluded in the regulations, regardless of I.Q., are eligible to be considered as having a specific learning disability, if they meet the eligibility requirements contained in the Part B regulations.

18 IDELR at 684.

In *Letter to Ulissi* OSEP also addressed a more subtle issue relating to whether a mentally gifted student could meet the eligibility criteria set out in 34 C.F.R. § 300.541(a)(1). That paragraph states that:

A team may determine that a child has a specific learning disability if —

(1) The child does not achieve commensurate with his or her age *and* ability levels in one or more of the areas listed in paragraph (a)(2) of this section, if provided with learning experiences appropriate for the child's age and ability levels.

In *Letter to Hartman*, EHLR 213:252 (OSEP 1989) OSEP appeared to substitute "or" for "and" when interpreting the regulation. If an intellectually gifted student was able to use his cognitive skills to compensate for a processing disorder and achieve on a level commensurate with his non-gifted age peers, he was not eligible under the IDEA on the basis of an SLD.

OSEP rethought this position, though, when questioned about it by Dr. Ulissi. In *Letter to Ulissi, supra*, OSEP opined that a gifted student's achievement should be measured against his own expected performance, not against a more general age peer standard.

OSEP affirmed this interpretation in *Letter to Lillie/Felton*, 23 IDELR 714 (OSEP 1995), stating that to the extent the earlier *Letter to Hartman* contradicted this interpretation of the regulations, it should be considered superceded.

5. How "severe" a discrepancy must a student have in order to establish eligibility?

The IDEA regulations do not define how much of a discrepancy will be deemed "severe." State law or regulation is the best source for a definitive answer.

Clearly, the use of the modifier "severe" in 34 C.F.R. § 300.541(a)(2) establishes that not all discrepancies between ability and achievement will establish eligibility on the basis of a specific learning disability. *See, e.g., San Antonio Indep. Sch. Dist.*, 29 IDELR 630 (SEA Tex. 1998) (student with processing disorder whose scores on standardized intelligence and achievement tests reflected a discrepancy between ability and achievement was not eligible on the basis of an SLD because scores were not significantly discrepant).

When a state uses standardized test scores to determine if there is the requisite discrepancy, it must develop a numeric formula to determine how much of a discrepancy is "severe." Different states may adopt different formulas. California, for example, used the following formula in 1997:

When standardized test scores are considered to be valid for a specific pupil, a severe discrepancy is demonstrated by: first, converting into common standard scores, using a mean of 100 and a standard deviation of 15, the achievement test score and the ability test score to be compared; second, computing the difference between these common standard scores; and third, comparing this computed difference to the standard criterion which is the product of 1.5 multiplied by the standard deviation of the distribution of computed differences of students taking these achievement and ability tests. A computed difference which equals or exceeds this standard criterion, adjusted by one standard error of measurement, the adjustment not to exceed 4 common standard score points, indicates a severe discrepancy when such a discrepancy is corroborated by other assessment data which may include other tests, scales, instruments, observations and work samples, as appropriate.[7]

In this regard, DOE has stated that a purely numeric formula may be used to determine severity only if an IEP team has the authority to override a mechanical application of the formula to deny eligibility to students who are entitled to special education and related services under the IDEA. *Letter to Murphy*, EHLR 213:216 (OSERS 1989).

In *Riley v. Ambach*, EHLR 552:410 (2d Cir.1980) the court held that strict adherence to the local numeric formula for determining a severe discrepancy could deny special education to students otherwise eligible under the IDEA severe discrepancy standard. The hearing officer in *Montgomery County Public Schools*, 24 IDELR 400 (SEA Md. 1996) harked back to that decades-old decision when it overturned a decision of ineligibility based on a mechanical application of a numeric formula for calculating a severe discrepancy. In that instance an evaluation team had determined that a student did not have a specific learning disability because the discrepancy between his achievement and ability test scores did not meet the state's two standard deviation formula. The hearing officer found that for this particular student the achievement test scores were misleading because the student had been permitted to take the tests on an untimed basis. The student's information processing *speed* was precisely what was material in evaluating whether the student had an SLD. As a result, the test scores did not adequately reflect the degree of academic difficulty the student was having. In this instance, a timed test should have been used to assess the student's achievement.

The hearing officer also went further, opining that as a general matter:

> For [an evaluation team] to base their conclusion of the existence of a learning disability on a formula for all children violates the fundamental requirement of IDEA that children be treated individually[.] ...The formula is intended as a guide not to be rigidly adhered to for all children, but flexibly applied taking into account how deficits are impacting on an individual child's academic functioning.

24 IDELR at 404.

6. Must a school district evaluate a highly intelligent student who is getting poor grades for a specific learning disability?

Unless a school district is absolutely convinced that the student's poor grades are the consequence of something other than a processing disorder, it should conduct an evaluation for a learning disability. Note that, for purposes of this question, we are assuming that the student is, indeed, highly intelligent. But there may be instances when testing is required to confirm the student's perceived high level of ability in the first instance.

IDEA regulations at 34 C.F.R. §§ 300.541(b) and 300.7(c)(10)(ii) confirm the requirement at 34 C.F.R. § 300.7(c)(10)(i) that a student must have a basic psychological processing disorder in order to be eligible on the basis of a specific learning disability. Both sections state that learning problems, or a discrepancy between ability and achievement, that are primarily the result of visual, hearing, or motor impairments, mental retardation, emotional disturbance, or of environmental, cultural, or economic disadvantages will not support a determination of eligibility.

Thus, when a school district knows that a bright student's poor grades are primarily the result of any of these factors set out in 34 C.F.R. § 300.541(b) (or 34 C.F.R. § 300.7(c)(10)(ii)) it does not have to determine if the student has an SLD. But how can a school district "know" that the student's grades are best explained as the result of an emotional disturbance, or environmental, cultural, or economic disadvantages? Don't look to DOE to answer that question. The inquirer in *Letter to Copenhaver*, 25 IDELR 640, 641 (OSEP 1996) hit the mark when he wrote the following:

> There is no guidance given and little is written about the word culture and what was meant by this word when the regulations were written. Each person assumes that others know what it is, and they rule it out as a reason for the disability routinely. In fact, in the form we now use from BIA Multidisciplinary Team Summary Report there is one check off for all three of these considerations — environmental, cultural, and economic disadvantage as if they were one concept.

2 : 7

OSEP refused to take the bait. "The determination of the effect that these factors have on the student's learning problems are within the discretion of the evaluation team." 25 IDELR at 642.

Unlike the federal law, state law or local policy may be a source of guidance. In *Ogden (UT) City School District*, 21 IDELR 387 (OCR, Region VIII 1994), for example, the school district's Special Education Policies and Procedures manual advised as follows:

> To determine whether the discrepancy is the result of such a 'disadvantage,' the multidisciplinary assessment team must collect information including educational history and family background. Once the information is collected, the team must determine the effect of the possible disadvantage on the student's achievement.

In its 1995 decision in *Capistrano Unified School District v. Wartenberg*, 22 IDELR 804 (9th Cir. 1995) the court noted that there were very few published judicial or administrative decisions concerning whether an emotional disturbance or environmental, cultural, or economic disadvantage was the primary cause of a student's learning problems. This continues to be the case. In one of the few published decisions in the LRP Publications' database, the hearing officer in *Petaluma Joint Unified School District*, 25 IDELR 262 (SEA Cal. 1996) suggested that grief over a death in the family may be the type of emotional disadvantage contemplated by the regulations.

In this regard, it should be noted that when the SLD regulations were originally promulgated, "serious emotional disturbance" was the term of art for a distinct disability classification. Emotional disturbance was not. In *Capistrano Unified School District v. Wartenberg, supra*, the court interpreted 34 C.F.R. § 300.541(b) as meaning "non-serious emotional disturbance." There is no reason to think the change in terminology in the 1997 IDEA Amendments from serious emotional disturbance to emotional disturbance changes the scope of the exclusion in 34 C.F.R. § 300.541(b).

7. Can a bright student whose poor grades reflect lack of motivation or effort be IDEA-eligible on the basis of a specific learning disability?

Not according to the Ninth Circuit Court of Appeals. A more detailed analysis by a New Hampshire hearing officer suggests otherwise. The author's opinion is a firm "it depends."

We start this response by endorsing the rueful conclusion of the National Research Council: "It is not clear how to distinguish between various degrees of below-average achievement and SLD [.]" As a matter of professional concern, the search for reliable psychometric criteria that distinguish students with learning disabilities from other students with records of low academic achievement has not been successful.[8] It is no surprise, then, that applying the legal criteria set out in the IDEA leads to inconsistent judicial results.

In *Kelby v. Morgan Hill Unified School District*, 18 IDELR 831 (9th Cir. 1992) the court opined that when poor grades are the result of a student's poor work habits, the student is not eligible for IDEA services on the basis of a specific learning disability, even if the student actually has a psychological processing disorder.

In that case the lower court ruled that a fifth grade student met the criteria for eligibility as SLD because: (1) he was not achieving commensurately with his age peers; (2) he was not achieving commensurately with his intellectual ability; and (3) he had a clinically diagnosed processing disorder.

The appeals court accepted those findings, but nonetheless reversed the finding of eligibility. It opined that the evidence established that the student's poor grades were the result of his poor work habits and disruptive behavior. The court opined that under these circumstances, a student does not need special education, he needs a good talking-to. "[A]n unsuccessful educational experience does not, in itself, qualify a student for special education. Not every student with a learning difficulty has a 'specific learning disability.'" 18 IDELR at 833.

The *Kelby* court did not perform the detailed analysis of 34 C.F.R. § 300.541 that the hearing officer in *Manchester School District*, 18 IDELR 425 (SEA N.H. 1990) did. The hearing officer started with the observation that 34 C.F.R. § 300.541(b) does not expressly include "lack of motivation" as an exclusionary circumstance. Unwilling to add an implied fifth exclusionary circumstance to the four set out at 34 C.F.R. § 300.541(b)(1)-(4), the hearing officer ruled that a school district could not exclude students from eligibility on the basis of "lack of motivation." Only if the school district could devise objective criteria for determining when "lack of motivation" is a manifestation of emotional disturbance could it exclude a student from eligibility as SLD on that basis. And the school district would also have to precisely define "lack of motivation" in behavioral terms. An impossible task, the hearing officer implied.

The following excerpt from the opinion sets out the hearing officer's reasoning in greater detail:

> The parents allege that the use of lack of motivation as excluding criteria is illegal. I tend to agree. [The district representative] testified that he had included this in the [school district's] Handbook because he found it in other handbooks[9] ... [.] He also gave his opinion that lack of motivation was really just another environmental factor, and was therefore acceptable. The problem with the district's inclusion of this factor is that 'lack of motivation' is a vague term, relating as much to psychological as to environmental factors. The purpose of the excluding factors in the federal regulations and state Standards is to insure that a student is not identified as learning disabled when his learning problems are due primarily to some other cause, such as an environmental, cultural or economic disadvantage, some other handicap, emotional disturbance, or mental retardation. Adding this factor to those outlined in existing law does nothing to further the law's aims, and may possibly confuse the situation.

18 IDELR at 435.

In the author's view, a school district should think twice before concluding that a bright student who is a classic "underachiever" (low grades being the deserved reward for lack of effort) cannot be IDEA-eligible on the basis of an SLD. Parents have been known to argue successfully that a student refused to work up to his potential because he was frustrated by his disability-related lack of progress and *your* failure to offer an appropriate remedial program. *See, e.g., Dale County Bd. of Educ.*, 28 IDELR 138 (SEA Ala. 1998); *In re Child with Disabilities*, 19 IDELR 448 (SEA Vt. 1992).

8. Is every student who has a processing disorder that is causing a severe discrepancy between intellectual ability and achievement eligible under the IDEA on the basis of a specific learning disability?

"Not every student with a learning disability has a 'specific learning disability.'" *Kelby v. Morgan Hill Unified School District*, 18 IDELR 831, 833 (9th Cir. 1992). Even a student who has the requisite severe discrepancy between ability and achievement may not qualify for special education services if his disability-related educational needs can be met through the school district's regular education program, modified as appropriate.

Remember that the one constant of IDEA eligibility is that the student must need special education as a result of his disability. Learning disabilities are not "curable" conditions. In some cases, modifications to a student's regular education may be all that is required for the student to receive a meaningful educational benefit.

The Ninth Circuit Court of Appeals explained it well in *Norton v. Orinda Union School District*, 29 IDELR 1068 (9th Cir. 1999).[10]

A learning disability, by itself, is insufficient to qualify a child for IDEA services under California's IDEA statutes and implementing regulations.[11] A student has a 'specific learning disability' only if he exhibits (1) a discrepancy between ability and achievement in one or more specified academic areas that is caused by a psychological processing disorder, and (2) that discrepancy cannot be corrected through 'other regular or categorical services offered within the regular instructional program.' [citations omitted] The [parents] insist that [the student] was eligible for IDEA protection in 1994[12] because his test scores showed a severe discrepancy between ability and achievement, the statutory requirement for IDEA eligibility. To prevail, however, [the parents] must also show that [the student] was not benefiting from his regular classroom environment, which, for [the student], included the special modifications implemented by the school district at the suggestion of doctors and others who had evaluated [the student].

24 IDELR at 1069.

Unlike the IDEA regulations at 34 C.F.R. § 300.541, the California state law referenced by the court clearly conditions SLD on the student's need for special education. As explained by the hearing officer in *Long Beach Unified School District*, 29 IDELR 818 (SEA Cal. 1998), California Education Code section 56337 provides that a student must meet the following three requirements to qualify for special education services as a student with a specific learning disability (SLD):

1. A severe discrepancy exists between the intellectual ability and achievement in one or more of the following academic areas: oral expression; listening comprehension; written expression; basic reading skills; reading comprehension; mathematics calculation; and mathematics reasoning.

2. The discrepancy is due to a disorder in one or more of the basic psychological processes and is not the result of environmental, cultural, or economic disadvantages.

3. The discrepancy cannot be corrected through other regular or categorical services offered within the regular instructional program.

9. Is attention deficit disorder (ADD) a psychological processing disorder for purposes of establishing eligibility on the basis of a specific learning disability?

It may be. A student diagnosed as having ADD may be eligible under the IDEA on the basis of a specific learning disability, provided the impact of the ADD on the student's academic performance meets the criteria set out in the IDEA regulations at 34 C.F.R. §§ 300.540-300.543.

IDEA regulations at 34 C.F.R.§ 300.7(c)(10)(i) define a specific learning disability as "a disorder in one or more of the basic psychological processes involved in understanding or in using language, spoken or written, that may manifest itself in an imperfect ability to listen, think, speak, read, write, spell, or to do mathematical calculations, including conditions such as perceptual disabilities, brain injury, *minimal brain dysfunction*, dyslexia, and developmental aphasia."

As you can see, nowhere in the regulation will you find the words "attention deficit disorder." But back in the day, educational psychologists used the archaic-sounding term "minimal brain dysfunction" to encompass ADD. Legislative history relating to the 1990 reauthorization of the IDEA reflects Congress' intent that the term 'minimal brain dysfunction,' appearing in the regulatory definition of 'specific learning disability,' be interpreted as including the condition of attention deficit disorder.[13]

Legislative history is not legislation, however. Responding to an extraordinarily detailed letter from the Directors of the National Center for Law and Learning Disabilities setting out the case for specifically identifying ADD and ADHD as processing disorders, OSEP opined as follows in *Letter to Latham*, 21 IDELR 1179 (OSEP 1994):

> We understand your position to be that, based on your analysis of research, the term 'minimal brain dysfunction,' a subcategory of the definition of the disability category 'specific learning disability' at [then-current] 34 CFR § 300.7(b)(10), is synonymous with the term 'ADD.' Thus, you conclude that 'children with attention deficit disorder' are children with 'specific learning disabilities' who are covered by the IDEA when 'by reason thereof' they 'need special education and related services.' As your letter indicates, the Department has previously concluded that children with ADD could be eligible for services under the specific learning disability category if they satisfy the criteria for that category.[14]

21 IDELR at 1183.

See also, Norton v. Orinda Union Sch. Dist., 29 IDELR 1068 (9th Cir. 1999) (a student with ADD will be eligible on the basis of an SLD if he has a processing disorder and a severe discrepancy between ability and achievement and needs special education as a result).

10. Is attention deficit hyperactivity disorder (ADHD) a psychological processing disorder for purposes of establishing eligibility on the basis of a specific learning disability?

It may be. While behavioral problems related to ADHD are sometimes the more prominent deficits, a student diagnosed as having this disorder may also be found eligible for services and programming on the basis of a specific learning disability.

The policy guidance discussed in Question 9 with respect to students who have ADD applies to students with ADHD as well. In addition, in *Letter to Williams*, 21 IDELR 73 (OSEP 1995) DOE explicitly recognized the possibility that a student with ADHD may have behavioral problems and needs, over and above, those relating to identification as a student with a specific learning disability. "A child with ADD or ADHD may be served under one of several disability categories such as SLD or serious emotional disturbance (SED) or OHI, if the child meets the eligibility criteria for the specific disability category." 21 IDELR at 75.

11. Must a school district use standardized tests to determine whether a student has a severe discrepancy between ability and achievement?

No, the IDEA does not compel use of specific measures of intellectual ability or achievement to measure discrepancy.

Responding to an inquirer who asked if standardized tests must be used to determine a severe discrepancy, OSEP opined to the contrary in *Letter to Copenhaver*, 25 IDELR 640 (OSEP 1996). Only those sections of the regulations governing all evaluations, e.g., 34 C.F.R. § 300.532, apply to selection of tests and other materials for purposes of testing under 34 C.F.R. § 300.541. Those requirements include the directive that tests be validated for the specific purpose for which they are being used.

A review of the testing procedures used throughout the country might reveal that standardized tests are used to assess both intelligence and achievement. But that does not have to be the case, insofar as the IDELR is concerned. *See, e.g., Independent Sch. Dist. 204 Kasson-Mantorville, MN*, 22 IDELR 380 (SEA Minn. 1994) (then-current state law providing that demonstration of a severe discrepancy could not be based solely on the use of standardized tests was consistent with federal law).

The administrative decision in *Los Alamitos Unified School District*, 26 IDELR 1053 (SEA Cal. 1997) explains how state standards are used by evaluation teams. Under then-current state law a severe discrepancy could be demonstrated through use of a formula using standardized test scores, unless the evaluation team determined that standardized tests should not be used for that particular student. In those instances, when comparison of standardized test scores does not reveal a severe discrepancy, the evaluation team may rely on other documentation to support a determination that a non-severe discrepancy is the result of a processing disorder.

12. Must a student with a learning disability meet the IDEA criteria for a specific learning disability in order to be learning-disabled under Section 504?

No. Any student who has a psychological processing disorder (termed a "learning disability" for purposes of this response) affecting his ability to learn is eligible for modifications, services and protections under Section 504. The student need not have a "severe discrepancy" between ability and achievement, as required under 34 C.F.R. § 300.541(a)(2). Nor must the student's level of achievement fall short, when compared to that of his age and ability peers, as required under 34 C.F.R. § 300.541(a)(1).

Section 504 is a wider net that, by design, catches many more fish. Unlike the IDEA, Section 504 does not have a limited number of discrete eligibility categories, such as mental retardation, blindness, orthopedic impairment, or, more to the point, specific learning disability. Instead, a student is covered under Section 504 if he has a "physical or mental impairment" that "substantially limits one or more major life activities." 29 U.S.C. § 706(8)(B).

Implementing regulations at 34 C.F.R. § 104.3(j)(1) lists specific disorders, including "specific learning disabilities," for purposes of illustration only. Clearly, a disorder in one or more of the basic psychological processes described in the IDEA definition of a specific learning disability at 34 C.F.R. § 300.7(c)(10)(i) is a qualifying physical or mental impairment.

Learning is a covered major life activity under 34 C.F.R. § 104.3(j)(2)(ii). But there is no regulatory support for equating a substantial limitation with a severe discrepancy. OCR has opined that school districts must make decisions about whether a particular impairment substantially limits a major life activity on an individual basis, but generally the term connotes an important and material limitation. *See, e.g., Pinellas County*, 20 IDELR 561 (OCR 1993).

Neither is there an explicit requirement that the student be performing below the level one would expect of someone with his raw intelligence.

Reinforcing the flexibility in the Section 504 definitional requirements, Section 504 regulations governing evaluations for eligibility at 34 C.F.R. § 104.35(b)(1)-(3) are substantially similar to those set out in IDEA regulations at 34 C.F.R. § 300.532. There are no requirements similar to those found in 34 C.F.R. §§ 300.540-300.543 ("Additional Procedures for Evaluating Children with Specific Learning Disabilities").

Because 34 C.F.R. § 104.35 requires evaluation of any student who needs or is believed to need special education or related services, a school district that evaluates students with learning disabilities only to see if there is a "severe discrepancy" between ability and achievement does so at its peril. For example, in *Baldwin County (AL) School District*, 17 EHLR 756 (OCR, Region IV 1991) OCR found that a school district discriminated against a student with a learning disability when it failed to evaluate his need for related services, as measured by criteria other than the IDEA discrepancy formula.

The issue of whether a student with a learning disability is eligible for services under Section 504 typically arises when the parents claim the student is IDEA-eligible, but the school district is only willing to provide accommodations under Section 504. (The less typical dispute will concern whether a student has a learning disability for purposes of coverage under Section 504 or is not disabled at all, that is, either does not have a processing disorder or has a processing order that does not substantially impact learning.) In the ordinary course, the parents believe that the student requires instruction in accordance with a specific methodology not offered by the school district, such as the Orton-Gillingham reading instruction approach.

The archetypal dispute, stripped of all particulars, can be summed up in the following way:

The Parents' Position: The student has a learning disability and is entitled to an Individual Education Plan (IEP) as a special education student. The 504 accommodation plan proposed by the school district is inappropriate because it does not provide the special programming and range of related services the student needs to address his educational needs.

The School District's Position: The school district does not dispute that the student has a processing disorder but does contend that the student nonetheless does not meet the eligibility criteria for special education services under both federal and consistent state special education law. The school district also acknowledges that the student's learning disability has a substantial impact on the student's learning in the area of his disability and has offered a Section 504 plan to providing reasonable accommodations to the student as part of his regular education. The school district contends, however, that the student does not need special education.

What a review of published administrative and judicial decisions illustrates is that sometimes the battling parents should count their blessings. If a school district's only options were IDEA eligibility or nothing, some students with acknowledged learning disabilities would receive no special help at all. It is only the more expansive eligibility criteria of Section 504 that requires schools to throw out a rope to certain classes of students with learning disabilities.

For example, a student with a learning disability can receive popular accommodations, such as extended test time, under Section 504 even if his good academic progress in regular education obviates the need for special education services. *See, e.g., Conrad Weiser Area Sch. Dist.*, 27 IDELR 100 (SEA Pa. 1997); *Mount Greylock Regional Schs.*, 26 IDELR 1238 (SEA Mass. 1997).

On the other end of the spectrum, a student with a learning disability whose poor level of academic achievement is commensurate with established low levels of ability will not be eligible under the IDEA as SLD; the discrepancy between achievement and ability is not "severe." He may, however, be entitled to Section 504 accommodations. *See, e.g., San Antonio Indep. Sch. Dist.*, 29 IDELR 630 (SEA Tex. 1998).

13. Are intelligence tests (IQ tests) racially or culturally discriminatory, for purposes of conducting IDEA evaluations?

Not as a matter of law and not in most instances as a matter of practice, assuming the evaluation is otherwise conducted in compliance with the IDEA.

IQ tests are norm-referenced tests[15] designed to measure learning ability or intellectual capacity by measuring cognitive behaviors associated with mental ability, such as discrimination, generalization, vocabulary, comprehension, abstract thinking or reasoning, memory or sequencing. The Wechsler Intelligence Scale for Children-III (WISC-III) is an individually administered instrument that produces what we typically think of as IQ scores. Other IQ tests include the Stanford-Binet Intelligence Scale - Fourth Edition and the Kaufman Assessment Battery for Children.

Charges of racial or cultural bias have been leveled against the publishers of these tests for two reasons. First, the standardization sample is not representative of students with diverse racial or cultural identities. Second, the content of the test is not representative of the life experiences or belief systems of many segments of a diverse student population.

It is likely that both Congress and DOE had these charges of bias in mind when they acted to bar selection of tests that discriminate on a racial or cultural basis for purposes of IDEA eligibility assessments. The regulations at 34 C.F.R. § 300.532(a)(1)(i) provide that "[e]ach public agency shall ensure,

2 : 13

at a minimum, that ... [t]ests and other evaluation materials used to assess a child under Part B of the Act ... [a]re selected and administered so as not to be discriminatory on a racial or cultural basis[.]"

However, IQ tests are not expressly identified in that section, or elsewhere in the regulations, as a racially or socially discriminatory test. IDEA regulations at 34 C.F.R. § 300.532(d) state that "[t]ests and other evaluation materials [must] include those tailored to assess specific areas of educational need and not merely those that are designed to provide a single general intelligence quotient." But there is no provision barring their use under all circumstances. In fact, under 34 C.F.R. § 300.541(a) school districts have little choice but to use IQ tests when evaluating students suspected of having a specific learning disability, with the IQ test being used to assess the student's intellectual ability.

All that being the case, the casual student of IDEA jurisprudence could understandably be under the misimpression that the IDEA bars use of IQ tests. That was, after all, the ruling of the Ninth Circuit Court of Appeals in its celebrated decisions in the "*Larry P.* series": *Larry P. v. Riles*, EHLR 555:304 (9th Cir. 1984); *Larry P. v. Riles*, EHLR 557:433 (9th Cir. 1986); and *Crawford v. Honig*, 21 IDELR 799 (9th Cir. 1994). In the 1984 *Larry P.* ruling, the court affirmed the granting of an injunction banning the use of standardized IQ tests to evaluate African-American students as eligible for placement in Educable Mentally Retarded (E.M.R.) [sic] classes.

The court in *Larry P.* found that use of standardized IQ tests discriminated against African-American students because they failed to consider the students' cultural background and home experiences, and, as a result, mistakenly identified and over-identified a disproportionately large number of students as mentally retarded. The misidentified students were then placed in self-contained classes. The injunction was enlarged two years later in the next (1986) *Larry P.* ruling to ban I.Q. testing for any type of special education evaluation conducted for African-American students. The court then reversed itself in the *Crawford* decision, vacating the broad 1986 injunction in response to a challenge by learning-disabled African-American students.

The court's opinion in *Crawford* made it clear that it does not interpret either the IDEA or Section 504 as per se prohibiting the use of IQ tests. Rather, the laws bar their use only when:

- It can be proven to be discriminatory to specific classes of students with disabilities on the basis of race or culture, with the burden of proof being placed upon the challenger [current 34 C.F.R. § 300.532(a)(1)(i)]; or

- Use of the IQ test has not been validated for the specific purpose for which it was or is being used [current 34 C.F.R. § 300.532(c)(1)(i)]; or

- The school district uses the IQ test as the sole criterion for determining whether a student is eligible under the IDEA [current 34 C.F.R. § 300.532(f)(1)(i)].

As explained by the *Crawford* court:

[T]he 1986 modification [to the ban on IQ testing for E.M.R. placement of African-American students] was not supported by the factual findings in the 1979 proceedings. This is not to say that the district court was not concerned in 1979 with the potentially racist nature of IQ testing. This concern is manifest in its extensive discussion of the racial and cultural biases of I.Q. tests and the lack of scientific validation of the 'tests for different culturally and racially different groups.' ... But the focus of the district court inquiry was the disproportionate enrollment of African-American children in dead-end E.M.R. classes, not the use of IQ tests generally. ... Indeed, the district court stated that its decision 'should not be construed as a final judgment on the scientific validity of intelligence tests' generally and held only that '[w]hatever the general scientific merits of the tests ... [the school districts] have failed to show a valid legal justification for their use for black E.M.R. placements.'

21 IDELR at 801.

DOE interprets the IDEA the same way. OSEP opined in *Letter to Warrington*, 20 IDELR 539 (OSEP 1993) that the use of intelligence tests is not discriminatory, per se. A state may require the use of an intelligence test in determining whether children have mental or learning disabilities, as long as:

- The test has been validated for the purpose for which it is used;

- Neither the test itself nor its administration is racially or culturally discriminatory; and

- The test does not constitute the sole criterion for determining an appropriate educational program for a particular student.

14. When will a test instrument be considered discriminatory on a cultural basis, for purposes of the IDEA?

Well, deferring to President Clinton, it depends on what the word "culture" is. IDEA regulations at 34 C.F.R. § 300.532(a)(1) bar use of tests and other evaluation materials that discriminate on a racial or cultural basis. But there is no legal definition of the concept of discrimination "on a cultural basis" or even of the word "culture" itself. DOE's most direct published guidance on this point seems to be that you'll know it when you see it.

In 1995 a noted educational advocate wrote to OSEP asking what should be made of the term "cultural", when used as a rule-out condition for a specific learning disability in 34 C.F.R. § 300.541(b)(4).[16] "There is no guidance given and little is written about the word culture and what was meant by this word when the regulations were written. Each person assumes that others know what it is," the inquirer observed in *Letter to Copenhaver*, 25 IDELR 640, 641(OSEP 1996). And, to add insult to injury, he noted that even professionals in the social sciences have not been able to arrive at a consensus about the meaning of the concept of "culture" and a working definition.

OSEP agreed that the IDEA regulations do not specifically address this issue and that DOE had provided no legal guidance. Nor was it going to do so now, it advised.

> Whether evaluations are to be accomplished by means of testing or other evaluation materials is a matter left to the discretion of the student's multidisciplinary team, provided that the particular test or evaluation material satisfies the requirements at [current 34 CFR § 300.532] and any other applicable State or local requirements.

25 IDELR at 642.

The same obscurity applies to assessing discrimination on a cultural basis for purposes of 34 CFR § 300.532(a)(1)(i). The IDEA itself is not a source for helpful guidance. State law may fill in some of the details. But more likely, states simply mandate participation of professionals who have whatever training is deemed necessary to recognize discrimination on the basis of culture when they see it. See Question 15 in this regard.

The few published administrative decisions addressing this issue shed light on one thing, though. The burden is on the parents to present "hard evidence" to prevail on a claim that an assessment test was culturally biased.

The parents in *Fontana Unified School District*, 27 IDELR 978 (SEA Cal. 1997), for example, contended that the evaluation conducted prior to making a decision to expel their teen-age son was racially and culturally biased. The basis of their claim was the identification of the student as a "gang member" in the written psychoeducational report. The parents presented no other evidence to support their allegation of bias and the evaluation was otherwise conducted in accordance with the procedural requirements set out in IDEA and state regulations. The hearing officer accordingly found that the parents had not carried their burden of proving that the materials and procedures used to test the student were racially or culturally biased.

2 : 15

15. Is an evaluation of an African-American student administered in a racially discriminatory manner if the evaluator is not also an African-American?

No. A gynecologist doesn't have to be a woman. Similarly, the IDEA does not establish a student's right to be evaluated by a person of the same race, ethnicity, sex, socioeconomic class, ad nauseum.

If an evaluation team does not take into account a student's particular circumstances, including any related to his race, it runs the risk of misidentifying a particular student, and, in the aggregate, over-identifying students who are African-American or Hispanic. *Letter to Allen*, 21 IDELR 1130 (OSEP 1994).

Because a student whose native language is not English runs a significant risk of being misidentified (either way) both the IDEA and Section 504 contain regulatory provisions addressing evaluation of these students. See Questions 16 to 18. In addition, IDEA regulations at 34 C.F.R. § 300.532(a)(1)(i) create by implication a student's right to not be evaluated by individuals who discriminate against the student on the basis of race or culture.

But do these directives translate into a right to be evaluated by an individual of the same race? That was, in fact, the assertion of the parent in *Chester-Upland School District*, 25 IDELR 907, 908 (SEA Pa. 1997). She claimed that under the IDEA her African-American son was entitled to an evaluation by "an African American, who identifies with African American culture, as it is reflected in a large urban community." The review panel considered whether the parent had stated a claim under the IDEA. They came to the same instinctively correct answer. There is no such right. Its exact words were:

> [T]he parent has not proffered, and we have not found, any legal basis for the purported right to an evaluator who is African American. The applicable regulations [34 C.F.R. § 300.532(a)(1)(i) and state education regulations] require that the evaluation materials and procedures be selected and administered "so as not to be racially or culturally discriminatory," which falls far short of the purported entitlement[.]

25 IDELR at 908 (footnote omitted).

Notwithstanding the above, state law may contain provisions designed to ensure that an individual whose professional background allows understanding of students of diverse racial and ethnic backgrounds participate in evaluation teams. California state regulations, for example, require that a credentialed school psychologist who is trained and prepared to assess cultural and ethnic factors appropriate to the student being assessed conduct the psychological assessment. *See, e.g., Old Adobe Union Elem. Sch. Dist.*, 27 IDELR 70 (SEA Cal. 1997) and *Hacienda La Puente Unified Sch. Dist.*, 26 IDELR 666 (SEA Cal. 1997). The Pennsylvania state regulations at issue in *Chester-Upland School District, supra*, require that, "when possible," members of the evaluation team be familiar with the student's cultural background.

16. How do the IDEA regulations concerning evaluation address over-identification of ethnic minorities in special education?[17]

As a general matter, school districts are not permitted to select or administer tests or other evaluation materials so as to discriminate against students on a racial or cultural basis. 34 C.F.R. § 300.532(a)(1)(i). In addition, when students are limited English proficient (LEP), the IDEA further governs the selection and administration of evaluations. 34 C.F.R.§ 300.532(a)(1)(ii), (a)(2).

The concern, of course, is that if a school district tests an LEP student in English, it may wind up assessing the student's competence in English, rather than whatever disability the district suspects the student may have. Then the school district risks making either of two possible bad decisions. On the one hand, if the school district erroneously considers a student's poor results to be related to limitations in his ability to speak or understand English, it might deny an eligible student needed services. On the other hand, if the school district attributes qualifying test results to a disability when the real problem for the student was limited English proficiency, the school district has both unjustifiably identified the student as disabled and lurched into the quagmire of the civil rights laws.[18]

In enacting the 1997 IDEA Amendments Congress identified over-identification of ethnically diverse students who are limited-English proficient as a major concern. For this reason it emphasized the importance of using tests and other evaluation materials that assess a student's skills and deficits, not his ability to speak and understand English, and incorporated pertinent parts of the IDEA regulations into the statute itself.

As they now stand, the regulations contain the following two provisions. Section 300.532(a)(1)(ii) states that school districts must ensure that all tests and other evaluation materials be selected and administered in the student's native language or other mode of communication, unless it is clearly not feasible to do so. Section 300.532(a)(2) forbids school districts from making limited English proficiency the "determinant factor" in determinations of eligibility for special education placement and services.

Recognize that the IDEA protections for limited-English proficient students benefits all students, not only those whose who are members of the ethnic minorities identified by Congress as having gained its particular concern, i.e., Hispanic, Asian-American, or American Indian.[19]

The school district in *Fairfax County Public School*, 17 EHLR 926 (SEA Va. 1991) had a big price to pay — reimbursement of parental expenses for the Lab School of Washington — because it refused to evaluate a student suspected of having an SLD in French, his native language. The student in that case, a 15-year-old, must have been considered a pretty fast learner by the school district. He spoke no English when he came to the United States from France in 1986. But three years later, the school district refused to conduct speech and language evaluations in French, despite strong recommendations to do so by the clinical psychologist who conducted the neuro-psychological evaluation. Defending its proposed placement in due process, the school district could offer no rationale to support its refusal to conduct the evaluations as recommended. Accordingly, the hearing officer ordered the school district to go back to the drawing board and reevaluate the student in French. In the meantime, until the student was appropriately evaluated and placed, he could continue his education at the Lab School at district expense.

17. What additional evaluation procedures, if any, govern evaluation for IDEA eligibility of students who are limited-English proficient (LEP)?

The school district must, as a threshold matter, assess the student's proficiency in both English and his native language in order to determine in which language the eligibility evaluation should be conducted. "Native language" is defined, for purposes of conducting an evaluation in accordance with 34 C.F.R. § 300.532 as "the language normally used by the child in the home or learning environment." 34 C.F.R. § 300.19(a)(2).

Title VI of the Civil Rights Act requires school districts to provide equal educational opportunity to national-origin minority students who are deficient in English language skills. In a 1970 policy memorandum entitled "Identification of Discrimination and Denial of Services on the Basis of National Origin"[20] OCR interpreted the civil rights law directive to include provision of equal educational opportunity to limited-English proficient (LEP) students with disabilities. School districts are required to provide services to enable the student to become proficient in English while also providing instruction in the general curriculum and any required special education or related services. The Memorandum was upheld as a valid interpretation of Title VI by the Supreme Court in *Lau v. Nichols*, 414 U.S. 564 (1974).

For possibly disabled LEP students equal educational opportunity includes an evaluation for IDEA eligibility that measures the student's disability-related deficits and needs, not his English-speaking ability. In discussion accompanying the publication of the 1999 IDEA final regulations, DOE explained the additional — in the sense of not explicitly stated in the regulations — procedural requirements for evaluations that result from the intersection of Title VI and the IDEA:

> [U]nder Title VI of the Civil Rights Act of 1964: (1) in order to properly evaluate a child who may be limited English proficient, a public agency should assess the child's proficiency in English as well as the child's native language to distinguish language proficiency form disability needs; and (2) an accurate assessment of the child's language proficiency should include objective assessment of reading, writing, speaking, and understanding.[21]

The school district in *Houston Independent School District*, 30 IDELR 564 (SEA Tex. 1999), for example, elected to evaluate in English a student whose native language was Spanish. When challenged by the parent, the school district defended the decision with the results of the language dominance testing that it had conducted prior to performing the comprehensive individual assessment. That initial testing had revealed that the student demonstrated higher levels of receptive and expressive proficiency in English than in Spanish. The hearing officer supported the school district's decision.

Another alternative, seemingly not contemplated by Title VI or the IDEA regulations, is for the school district to conduct a bilingual evaluation. In two recently published administrative decisions, the school district's decision to conduct the evaluation in two languages was found to be consistent with the IDEA. In *Bridgeport Board of Education*, 28 IDELR 1043 (SEA Conn. 1998) the student's language proficiency was described by experts as "mixed dominance." Put more bluntly, the student had mastered neither Spanish nor English. When the school district administered achievement testing in English, the student's scores were low. When it administered the tests in Spanish, her scores were even lower. Similarly, an evaluation conducted in both English and Hebrew was found to be appropriate in *Board of Education of the City School District of the City of New York*, 26 IDELR 215 (SEA N.Y. 1997). The student was addressed in both Hebrew, the dominant language in the student's home, and English. Although he easily understood instructions given in English, the use of Hebrew allowed him to be more spontaneous and self-confident.

18. What should a school district do if evaluation in a student's native language is necessary but not feasible?

Do the best you can, DOE advises.

Even if it is a small world after all, some school districts may indeed be faced with a situation when it cannot administer and interpret a particular test instrument in the student's native language. Language diversity varies among school districts, naturally, but one should not assume that the melting pot is a "big city" phenomenon only. Way back in 1991, for example, the *Irvine Unified School District* had among its population of students with disabilities students whose native languages included Chinese (Mandarin, Cantonese and Taiwanese), Japanese, Korean, Russian, Spanish, Vietnamese, Farsi and Portuguese, as well as more than 40 others characterized as "low incidence languages." *Irvine (CA) Unified Sch. Dist.*, 17 EHLR 1128 (OCR 1991).

Even if one assumes a school district will always be able to identify an individual qualified to translate an instrument into a student's native language, the reliability and validity of the translated test may be open to question.

Despite the difficulty, a school district must make its best efforts to evaluate a student in his native language in all instances. Nonetheless, the regulations acknowledge that a school district may be faced with a situation when even its best efforts will not be enough. Section 300.532(a)(1)(ii) thus requires school districts to provide and administer tests in the student's native language (or other mode of communication), "unless it is clearly not feasible to do so."

"Clearly not feasible" seems like it would be a very difficult standard to meet. The author is not aware of any published guidance elaborating on when it will be considered "clearly not feasible" or even "not feasible" to assess the student in his native language, for purposes of 34 C.F.R. § 300.532(a)(1)(ii). The one time a plaintiff asked for an interpretation of that language, a court said the issue was not ripe for review. "The parameters of the 'clearly not feasible' exemption and defendants' alleged abuse of this exemption will be reviewed by the courts when the merits of the case are properly before it. This issue has no bearing on class certification and will not be addressed herein." *Ray M. v. Board of Educ. of the City Sch. Dist. of the City of New York*, 22 IDELR 776 (E.D.N.Y. 1995).

In the author's opinion, two good arguments (there could be others) would be that the test cannot be validated for the specific purpose for which it is used or that it cannot be administered in accordance with the instructions provided by the publisher if given in the student's native language.

But assuming there will indeed be circumstances when the IDEA regulations excuse performance of an evaluation in the student's native language, here is what the school district should do instead, according to DOE:

> [P]aragraphs (a)(1)(i) and (2)(ii) when read together require that even in situations where it is clearly not feasible to provide and administer tests in the child's native language or mode of communication for a child with limited English proficiency, the public agency must still obtain and consider accurate and reliable information that will enable the agency to make an informed decision as to whether the child has a disability and the effects of the disability on the child's educational needs.[22]

Endnotes

[1]   LORRAINE M. MCDONNELL, MARGARET J. MCLAUGHLIN, PATRICIA MORRISON, EDS., EDUCATING ONE AND ALL: STUDENTS WITH DISABILITIES AND STANDARDS-BASED REFORM 76 (National Academy Press 1997).

[2]   42 *Fed. Reg.* 65085 (Dec. 29, 1977).

[3]   62 *Fed. Reg.* 55048 (1997).

[4]   64 *Fed. Reg.* 12637 (1999).

[5]   A severe discrepancy between intellectual ability and achievement is not the only requirement for eligibility. Question 8 sets out all the requirements.

[6]   LORRAINE M. MCDONNELL, MARGARET J. MCLAUGHLIN, PATRICIA MORISON, EDS., EDUCATING ONE AND ALL: STUDENTS WITH DISABILITIES AND STANDARDS-BASED REFORM 84 (National Research Council 1997).

[7]   5 C.C.R. § 3030(j)(4)(A).

[8]   MCDONNELL, MCLAUGLIN, & MORISON, *supra*, note 6.

[9]   This approach will surely get you in trouble, sooner or later.

[10]   This disposition is not appropriate for publication and may not be cited to or by the courts of this circuit except as may be provided by 9th Cir. R. 36-3.

[11]   The state's law and regulations are consistent with the IDEA. As discussed in Question 5, state standards for eligibility cannot operate to exclude students with disabilities who meet the federal criteria for eligibility.

[12]   1994! It took five years to finally resolve this dispute about whether the student, then a fifth-grader, was entitled to special education.

[13]   Senate Committee on Labor and Human Resources, S. REP. 204, 101 CONG. 1st SESS. at 9 (1989), cited in Letter to Bentsen, 16 EHLR 961 (OSERS 1990).

[14]   OSEP is referring to Joint Policy Memorandum, 18 IDELR 116 (OSERS 1991).

[15]   See Question 9 in chapter 6 for a brief explanation of norm-referenced and criterion-referenced tests.

[16]   See Question 6.

[17]   Of course, as Congress itself noted in its Findings, the term "minorities" is a misnomer even today when describing many "large-city school populations," with the growth in the Hispanic population, for example, expected to increase "rapidly" as we cross that bridge to the new millennium. 20 U.S.C. § 1401(b)(7).

[18]   See Question 17 concerning Title VI requirements concerning special education evaluations of students who are limited-English proficient.

[19]   20 U.S.C. § 1401(b)(7).

[20]   35 *Fed. Reg.* 11595 (1970).

[21]   64 *Fed. Reg.* 12633 (1999).

[22]   64 *Fed. Reg.* 12633 (1999).

Chapter 3

TESTING ACCOMMODATIONS AND SERVICES FOR COLLEGE-BOUND STUDENTS WITH DISABILITIES

1. Are colleges required to provide grading and testing modifications to students with learning disabilities?

Yes. Of course, the IDEA does not extend to colleges or other postsecondary educational institutions. But Section 504 does, in almost all instances. Virtually all colleges and universities are deemed recipients of federal financial assistance by virtue of enrolling students who have taken out federally guaranteed student loans.

Colleges are required to make "reasonable" modifications in academic requirements in order to meet their obligations under Section 504. Section 504 regulations at 34 C.F.R. § 104.44, entitled "Academic Adjustments," articulate the statutory requirement, as interpreted by the Supreme Court in *Alexander v. Choate*, EHLR 556:293 (1985). *Letter to Zirkel*, 20 IDELR 134 (OCR 1993).

The regulations read, in pertinent part:

(a) Academic requirements

A recipient to which this subpart applies shall make such modifications to its academic requirements as are necessary to ensure that such requirements do not discriminate or have the effect of discriminating, on the basis of handicap, against a qualified handicapped applicant or student. Academic requirements that the recipient can demonstrate are essential to the program of instruction being pursued by such student or to any directly related licensing requirement will not be regarded as discriminatory within the meaning of this section. Modifications may include changes in the length of time permitted for the completion of degree requirements, substitution of specific courses required for the completion of degree requirements, and adaptation of the manner in which specific courses are conducted. ...

(c) Course examinations

In its course examinations or other procedures for evaluating students' academic achievement in its program, a recipient to which this subpart applies shall provide such methods for evaluating the achievement of students who have a handicap that impairs sensory, manual, or speaking skills as will best ensure that the results of the evaluation represents the student's achievement in the course, rather than reflecting the student's impaired sensory, manual, or speaking skills (except where such skills are the factors that the test purports to measure).

Note that Subsection (c) refers explicitly to disabilities that impair "sensory, manual or speaking skills." There is no explicit reference made to requiring accommodations or modifications for students with learning disabilities. Nor does Appendix A to the Section 504 regulations address modifications for college students with learning disabilities. Truth to tell, there is more discussion about guide dogs and Braille readers than anything else.

3 : 1

But the times have changed. The overwhelming majority of students who request testing accommodations identify themselves as learning disabled.[1] While a stickler might make an argument that a learning disability impairs none of those skills, OCR has consistently interpreted the Section 504 regulations for postsecondary institutions as creating obligations toward students with learning disabilities.

2. How does a college's obligation to provide testing accommodations to students with learning disabilities impact school districts?

It is the limitations on a college's obligation to provide accommodations that lead to involvement of high schools. As first explained in OCR Policy *"Guidance on the Application of Section 504 Regulation Provisions Related to Academic Adjustments in Postsecondary Education Institutions,"* (May 13, 1986), Section 504 places the onus on students to notify the college of the disability, and to request any needed academic adjustments. Parents may want to shift that burden to school districts, looking to Section 504 or the IDEA to support their demands for required evaluation services.

Unlike school districts, colleges are not required to identify students with disabilities. The student himself must advise the college of the existence of a disability and the resulting need for academic adjustments. OCR has supported allocation of the burden of notification and demonstration of need to students in numerous LOFs. In *Lewis & Clark College (OR)*, 14 NDLR ¶ 102 (OCR, Region X 1998), for example, OCR held that disabled students who need academic adjustments must notify the college that they have a disability and must assist the college to identify necessary academic adjustments. Similarly, in *St. Thomas University (FL)*, 13 NDLR ¶ 259 (OCR, Region IV 1998) OCR opined that a postsecondary student with a disability was obligated to provide notification of the nature of the disabling condition to the college and give adequate notice of resulting needs for adjustments. Overall, as OCR explained in *Dartmouth College (NH)*, 11 NDLR ¶ 277 (OCR, Region I 1997), the responsibility is with the student to identify a disabling condition and to request academic adjustments.

Here is where school districts are brought into the picture. Parents will want to present an evaluation conducted during the student's senior year that supports the widest range of possible accommodations the student may want to request. And, frankly, they will be glad to have the school district pay for it. But is a school district obligated to comply with every parental request for a reevaluation under these circumstances? That is the issue we discuss in Question 4.

3. What documentation must a student with a disability present to a college to document his request for an academic adjustment for testing?

The student must present a "current" evaluation confirming the existence of a disability prepared by an appropriate professional.

Naturally enough, an incoming freshman with a disability cannot simply state his case. OCR permits colleges to require a student with a disability to establish his disability by presenting supporting medical, psychological, or educational diagnostic tests with professional prescriptions for academic adjustments. *E.g., Lewis & Clark College, supra. Accord, Texas Wesleyan University*, 13 NDLR ¶ 208 (OCR, Region VI 1998) (student must present relevant verifiable professional documentation or assessment reports confirming the existence of the disability and appropriate reasonable accommodations or academic adjustments).

As a matter of practice, colleges typically require that a student's request for testing modifications, or other academic adjustments under 34 C.F.R. § 104.44, be accompanied by submission of a "current" evaluation establishing the presence of the underlying disability. Guidelines promulgated by the Association for Higher Education and Disabilities ("AHEAD") provide standard criteria for colleges to adopt in verifying learning disabilities.[2]

With respect to student documentation of a disability, AHEAD takes the position that a complete set of aptitude and achievement test results, including actual test scores, are required to demonstrate discrepancies between achievement and ability. These test results must be the product of an evaluation conducted by a clinical or educational psychologist, neuropsychologist or other professional trained in evaluating learning disabilities.

Importantly, under AHEAD's guidelines students must present the results of "current" testing, with "current" meaning, in most cases, the results of testing conducted within the past three years. As explained in the guidelines: "Because the provision of all reasonable accommodations and services is based upon assessment of the current impact of the student's disabilities on his/her academic performance, it is in the student's best interest to provide recent and appropriate documentation."

In *Guckenberger v. Boston University*, 26 IDELR 573 (D. Mass. 1997) a class of BU students with learning disabilities challenged the university's documentation requirements with respect to its retesting requirement. BU took the position that a student with a learning disability had to be retested every three years. In the ordinary course, then, an undergraduate would have to undergo retesting at least once during the course of his enrollment. The students claimed the retesting requirement, called the "currency requirement" by the court, discriminated against students with learning disabilities in violation of Section 504 and the ADA. The court supported the students' interpretation of the law, ruling that the university had established an "eligibility criteria" that "screen[ed] out or tended to screen out students with specific learning disabilities" in violation of Section 504. 42 U.S.C. § 12182(b)(2)(I), 34 C.F.R. § 104.4(b)(4).

More pertinent for our purposes, the students conceded that the University's requirement for student submission of a "current" evaluation when first disclosing the need for accommodations was consistent with law. While the issue was thus not presented for decision, the court nonetheless endorsed that aspect of the AHEAD documentation guidelines.

OCR has also concluded that a college does not discriminate in violation of Section 504 (or the ADA) if it requires submission of a "current" evaluation in support of a learning disabled student's initial request for modifications. For example, in *Northwestern College (OH)*, 6 NDLR ¶ 261 (OCR 1995) the complainant alleged that the college discriminated against a student with a learning disability by denying his request for a testing modification. After investigation, OCR determined that the student had not provided sufficient evidence to justify his request. One evaluation he provided did not support his request at all. A second did, but it was not current. OCR opined that the college could require that students provide the results of current psychological or educational diagnostic tests.

The need for current professional documentation might not, in itself, present a difficulty for a student requesting accommodations. But the need to arrange and pay for it might. As a corollary of OCR's relieving colleges of child find responsibilities, it also relieves colleges of responsibility for providing individualized diagnostic or prescriptive services to students claiming disability-related needs. *Lewis & Clark College, supra. See also, North Seattle Community College (WA)*, 10 NDLR ¶ 42 (OCR, Region X 1996) (college did not have to provide specific request for an academic adjustment because the student did not provide the college with diagnostic documentation to support this request).

In *Axelrod v. Phillips Academy*, 30 IDELR 516 (D. Mass. 1999) the court went one better than OCR or other courts. Not only was a private school student with ADHD required to submit an evaluation documenting the existence of his disability, he was obliged to also submit a separate request for testing and academic coursework accommodations. The evaluation contained a number of recommended accommodations, but the court refused to buy into the parents' seemingly reasonable argument that the school should have understood the parents' submission of the report as an endorsement of, and request for, the accommodations recommended therein.

We provide the entirety of the court's reasoning below. No citation to controlling, or even persuasive authority has been excised; the court's reasoning is, to coin a phrase made famous (at least in very small circles) in a noted judicial decision concerning academic adjustments, *ipse dixit*. (According to Black's Law Dictionary (5th ed. 1979), "ipse dixit" means: "He himself said it; a bare assertion resting

3 : 3

on the authority of an individual." The decision is *Wynne v. Tufts University School of Medicine*, 3 NDLR ¶ 121 (1st Cir. 1992), discussed in Question 2 in chapter 1.)

> During trial, [parents] argued that [the evaluating psychologist's] report, which lists several changes that should be made to [the student's] learning environment, constitutes a request for an accommodation to which Phillips Academy was obligated to respond. The Court finds that [the psychologist's] report, which was sent to Phillips Academy, does not constitute a request for an accommodation. [The psychologist's]'s report would certainly document and support a request for an accommodation. By itself, however, it does not constitute such a request. First, the evidence indicates that students do not always request all of the accommodations that their doctors believe they might be entitled to, thus, the mere fact a doctor suggests an accommodation does not mean that the student or parent wants such an accommodation to be made. Rather, the student and parent are in the best position to determine what accommodations the student needs. Second, [the psychologist's] report does not differentiate between those accommodations that the school should make, those that the parent should make and those that [the student] should make. It would be unfair to hold Phillips Academy responsible for changing that which it has little control over.[3]

30 IDELR at 523.

4. Must a school district conduct an evaluation of a student for the sole purpose of presentation to a college in support of a request for academic adjustments?

No, the author does not interpret the federal disability laws as requiring school districts to conduct or pay for evaluations when requested by a college-bound student to support of his request for academic adjustments. Although graduation with a high school diploma is a change in placement, no reevaluation is required in that regard. 34 C.F.R. § 300.122.

On its face, the IDEA requires that the school district conduct a comprehensive reevaluation when parents so demand. 20 U.S.C. § 1414(a)(2)(A). That section states that a school district shall conduct a reevaluation if, among other things, the child's parents so request. The statute contains no explicit limitation on when a parent may make such a request or any requirement that the parent have a reasonable basis for making the request.

Under the prior law a parent also had the right to demand the school district conduct a reevaluation. However, a school district could file for due process to challenge the parental demand, claiming that there was no reason to believe the student's circumstances or needs had changed materially since the last evaluation. *Letter to Tinsley*, 16 EHLR 1076 (OSEP 1990).

As stated above, the 1997 IDEA Amendments continue the parental right to demand that the district conduct a reevaluation. However, the new statutory language does not give a school district the opportunity to demonstrate to the parent that such an undertaking is not required. Under Section 1414(c)(1)(A) and (B), substantially restated in 34 C.F.R. § 300.533, a school district may respond to a request for a reevaluation by reviewing existing evaluation data to identify if additional data is needed to determine whether the student meets eligibility criteria and continues to need special education and related services. If, after such review, the team determines that no additional data are needed to determine whether the student continues to be a child with a disability, the school district need not perform the reevaluation at that time. Instead it notifies the parents in writing of that determination and the reasons for it, also informing them of their right to request an assessment. If the parents then persist in their request, the school district is required to conduct the assessment. 20 U.S.C. § 1414(c)(1)(B)(2).

Commenters responded to the publication of the Notice of Proposed Rulemaking in 1997 by asking, in essence, whether a district *really* had to conduct a reevaluation upon parental request. Here is DOE's response:

> Under both prior law and the current regulations, if a parent requests a reevaluation, the public agency must either: (1) provide the parents with written notice of the agency's proposal to conduct the reevaluation; or (2) provide the parents with written notice of the agency's refusal to conduct a reevaluation. The parent may challenge such a proposal or refusal by requesting a hearing. If the agency conducts a reevaluation and the evaluation group concludes that under § 300.533(a) no additional data are needed to determine whether the child continues to be a child with a disability, the public agency must provide parents with the notice provided in § 300.533(c)(1), and must provide such assessment upon parental request.[4]

All this being the case, the author does not believe the IDEA should be interpreted to obligate school districts to conduct reevaluations for reasons that are not related to the provision of FAPE to the student during the course of his public school career, even when a parent so requests. The IDEA only concerns the provision of services to preschool, elementary or secondary school students, not college students. See, 34 C.F.R. §§ 300.13, 300.122(a)(3)(i). Further, by definition, there are only two purposes for which a school district must conduct an evaluation: to determine if a student has a disability and "the nature and extent of the special education and related services" that the student needs as a result. 34 C.F.R. § 300.530(b)(3).

There would seem to be only one way in which a parent could connect a demand for a reevaluation (that the student could submit to a college) to his entitlement to FAPE: his right to transition services. However, it would be a stretch to extend the definition of transition services set out at 34 C.F.R. § 300.29 to encompass performance of an evaluation in support of the student's need for academic adjustments in postsecondary education. That definition, set out in full in the endnotes,[5] defines transition services as "activities for a student with a disability," not activities for the school district relating to that student. There was no suggestion in the DOE comments accompanying the publication of IDEA final regulations that such an obligation is within the range of the statutory requirement.

But you don't have to take the author's word for it. The review panel in *Lower Moreland Township School District*, 25 IDELR 351 (SEA Pa. 1996) came to the same conclusion on the basis of its interpretation of similar state education law. That decision rejected, albeit without explanation, the claim of the parent of a high school senior with a "mild" learning disability for reimbursement of an independent educational evaluation. The student's chosen college, the University of Pittsburgh, had accepted the student and requested submission of an independent evaluation in support of the student's request for a range of instructional and testing accommodations. The parents had contended that funding of the evaluation was a required component of the student's transition plan, which identified matriculation at that college as the student's postsecondary objective.

5. Is a school district required to include in the IEP or Section 504 Plan of a college-bound student with a disability a statement of needed postsecondary education academic adjustments?

No, there is no provision in the IDEA or Section 504 that requires such a statement. With regard to the IDEA, such a requirement, if it existed, would be set out in the IDEA regulations at 34 C.F.R. § 300.347. The Section 504 regulations contain no written documentation requirement at all.

Rest assured, though, some parents will not leave it at that. *Lower Moreland Township School District*, 25 IDELR 351 (SEA Pa. 1996) is, to the best knowledge of the author, the first published decision that addresses this issue, one surely capable of repetition, yet apparently evading review so far. We provide a detailed summary below.

The student at issue had been identified as having a "mild" learning disability and was receiving resource room services under an agreed IEP. The IEP his parents approved also provided that the student would receive "nontraditional test taking methods (such as additional time, adapted length and format of tests) consistent with the requirements of specific subject matter." Entering his senior year of high school, the student had a history of success in his academic work and was on schedule to receive a regular high school diploma. He had been accepted for admission to the college of choice, the University of Pittsburgh.

In January of the student's senior year, the parents requested an IEP team meeting to propose a revision to the IEP to include more specific descriptions of the testing modifications being used by the student's teachers. According to the review officer, "in essence, his parents were seeking an IEP that would include a very detailed, optimal statement of how testing would be done." 25 IDELR at 352.

The school district was willing to make some modifications to the IEP, but not enough to satisfy the parents. After meeting at various times over the next three months, the parents continued to reject the district's proposed revisions, claiming they were too vague and, probably around Prom time, filed for due process to demand incorporation of the proposed IEP revisions. The hearing was held in October of the next year, after the student had graduated.

So the first question you might ask is: Why did the parents persist in pursuing their claim? The answer, it turns out, appears to have had more to do with the student's needed (or desired) college-level academic adjustments than the adequacy of his high school IEP. This being the case, the review panel affirmed the hearing officer's rejection of the parents' claims. As explained in the opinion:

> [T]he district was providing a free appropriate public education, including an IEP for [the student's] individual needs. Although the parents' request for more specific services is understandable from their point of view, more specific strategies about testing than those delineated in the proposed IEP is not required in this case.
>
> In this case, the parents sought an optimal special education IEP, which is not required by law. The testing strategies described by District Officials in the IEP is appropriate, though perhaps not the best possible way of planning for a student's needs. It has long been the law that a program of special education and related services merely be free and appropriate — that which allows a special needs student to participate and make progress in school. The parents, who understandably want the best possible program for their child, are not entitled to more than what is legally appropriate.
>
> Moreover, we see no authority in the regulatory language relating to transition plans that would require a statement of optimal testing such as the one sought by [the student's] parents.

25 IDELR at 352.

The *Lower Moreland* decision seems to illustrate a concern that its author, review officer Perry Zirkel, raised in a more general way in a 1997 article in THE SPECIAL EDUCATOR®. In his view, an increasing number of "upper-SES" socio-economic status parents are using the disability laws to gain a competitive edge for their college-bound children.[6]

6. Is a college required to provide a testing modification that a student with a disability did not receive in high school?

If a student with a disability can present an evaluation documenting to the satisfaction of the college the existence of the underlying disability and the resulting need for the requested accommodation, the college must provide it, even if the student has gotten this far without it. Section 104.44 of the Section 504 regulations does not foreclose in any way such a possibility. Nor does it relieve the college of its obligation under those circumstances.

But one published OCR LOF suggests that a disabled student who did not receive a particular test modification in high school will have a tough row to hoe if he claims he needs that modification to compete on a level playing field in college. The learning disabled student in *Northwestern College (OH)*, 6 NDLR ¶ 261 (OCR 1995) alleged that the college discriminated against him by denying his request that course performance be evaluated by means of oral testing. OCR determined that the college's denial was not discrimination. The college did not dispute that the student had a learning disability. But the current evaluation submitted by the student did not support his request for that particular modification. Putting the icing on the cake, oral testing was not an academic adjustment that had ever been used by the student in academic settings prior to his enrollment at the college. In closing the complaint, OCR concluded that it was not unreasonable under these circumstances to require the student to obtain a current psychological evaluation specifically addressing his need for oral testing.

7. Is a college required to provide all the testing modifications that a student with a disability received in high school?

No, a college has the right to make an independent determination of whether a student is entitled to receive academic adjustments. Each college has discretion to establish procedures to verify a student's disability and evaluate and approve the student's request for academic adjustments. See 34 C.F.R. §§ 104.41-104.47.

OCR's support of the college in *Lewis & Clark College (OR)*, 14 NDLR ¶ 102 (OCR, Region X 1998) illustrates this point. Prior to enrolling in the college as a first-year student, the complainant advised the college that he had attention deficit disorder (ADD) and had been identified by his high school as eligible for services under Section 504 on that basis. The student submitted a copy of his high school Section 504 Plan dated April 4, 1996, requesting provision of the five accommodations (written assignments, major assignments broken down into manageable parts, extended time, the opportunity to meet with instructors at the beginning of each course, and regular feedback on progress) identified in the document.

The college provisionally denied the student's request, directing the student to submit an evaluation relating to the nature of his diagnosis and the resulting adjustments that he required. The student complained to OCR about the college's failure to provide him with necessary academic adjustments. OCR rejected the allegation because it found the college's demand for additional documentation of the student's needs consistent with Section 504 and reasonable under the circumstances.

To similar effect, OCR found in *State University of New York*, 4 NDLR ¶ 432 (OCR, Region II 1993) that a college did not violate Section 504 when it refused to grant the disabled student's request for an academic adjustment, no multiple choice tests. Upon investigation, OCR learned that the college had provided a number of other adjustments and aids, including an alternate test location, extended time on examinations, information broken down into sequential form, and use of a tape recorder for lectures. But the student had never been exempted from testing in the multiple-choice format. Further, the documentation did not establish that the student required only essay-type examinations as an accommodation.

In this regard, note that when the parties disagree about whether a particular accommodation must be provided, a college student with a disability is, arguably, in a weaker position than is a high school student with a disability. In *Zukle v. Regents of the University of California*, 14 NDLR ¶ 188 (9th Cir. 1999) the Ninth Circuit affirmed OCR's consistently-taken position that a college student bears the initial burden of producing evidence of whether he has a disability and is requesting a necessary, reasonable accommodation.

8. Must colleges provide academic adjustments to students who have been diagnosed as having Attention Deficit Disorder (ADD) or Attention Deficit Hyperactivity Disorder (ADHD)?

Yes. Academic adjustments must be provided to students with either ADD or ADHD, to the extent such adjustments are required under 34 C.F.R. § 104.44. *See, e.g., Guckenberger v. Boston University*, 26 IDELR 573 (D. Mass. 1997); *Lewis & Clark College (OR)*, 14 NDLR ¶ 102 (OCR, Region X 1998); *San Jose State University (CA)*, 4 NDLR ¶ 358 (OCR, Region IX 1993).

No matter what one might think as a matter of philosophy, as a matter of law both Section 504 and the ADA protect individuals with such disabilities in matters relating to enrollment in two-year and four-year colleges, graduate and professional education, and employment. *See, e.g., Menkowitz v. Pottstown Memorial Medical Ctr.*, 13 NDLR ¶ 123 (3d Cir. 1998) (orthopedic surgeon with attention deficit disorder alleging that a hospital suspended his staff privileges and interfered with his patient relationships solely because of his disability stated a claim under Section 504 and Title III of the ADA). *See also, Kaltenberger v. Ohio College of Podiatric Medicine*, 14 NDLR ¶ 71(6th Cir. 1998) (defendant college stipulated that ADHD was a covered disability, triggering obligation for provision of academic adjustments). *But see, Price v. The National Bd. of Med. Examiners*, 10 NDLR ¶ 76 (S.D. W. Va. 1997) (medical students were not entitled to accommodations because ADHD was not a disability within the meaning of the ADA; that is, it did not limit their ability to learn as compared with most people).

That said, a college student with ADD or ADHD may not always be entitled to receive the same accommodations as academic adjustments that he received under his high school IEP or Section 504 Plan. For example in *University of Massachusetts*, 12 NDLR ¶ 315 (OCR, Region I 1998) OCR concluded that the university was not required to permit a student with ADHD to complete exams on a take-home basis or to be a "group of one" for a group project. In both instances OCR found the university had reasonably established why granting the requests would fundamentally alter course requirements.

It is interesting to note that in *University of Massachusetts* what was at stake was not simply whether the student had mastered the course content. The student was studying to be a school psychologist; the course concerned school psychology. The university found, quite rationally, in the author's opinion, that the student had to demonstrate her ability to work with others to achieve a common goal or reach a joint decision after engaging in cooperative fact-finding, analysis and problem solving. Similarly, if permitted to take her exams home, the student would not be tested on her ability to think on her feet, an imperative in practice.

9. What kinds of academic accommodations do colleges typically approve for students with learning disabilities?

At this point there is a fairly well established menu of academic adjustments that colleges offer to all learning disabled students who request them (assuming adequate supporting documentation). The battle is over; the students have won. These standard modifications were termed "vanilla accommodations" in *Guckenberger v. Boston University*, 26 IDELR 573 (D. Mass. 1997) because they do not involve course substitutions or similar substantive changes in course curricula. Instead they include extended time (time-and-a-half or double time) for exams, notetaking services, textbooks on audiocassettes, and permission to retake exams. *See, e.g., Zukle v. Regents of the Univ. of Cal.*, 14 NDLR ¶ 188 (9th Cir. 1999). (Please note that student requests for substantive changes raise the more complex issue of whether a requested academic adjustment fundamentally alters the college's academic standards or program requirements. 34 C.F.R. § 104.44(a). Because the issue has little bearing on the issue of testing accommodations for elementary and secondary school students, we do not address it in this publication.)

Sometimes, though, students may not clearly understand the difference between the special education and related services they were entitled to receive in high school and the more limited academic adjustments they are entitled to receive in college. For example, a student's high school IEP may have called for tutoring. But, according to OCR, tutoring is not an academic adjustment required under 34 C.F.R. § 104.44. OCR explained its reasoning in *Oregon State University*, 5 NDLR ¶ 19 (OCR, Region X 1993), opining that because tutoring is associated more closely with individual study aid, Section 504 does not require the provision of tutoring as a necessary academic adjustment. *See also, Hood College (MD)*, 12 NDLR ¶ 127 (OCR, Region III 1997) (college has no obligation under the Section 504 regulations to provide a disabled student with tutors, except to the extent that it provided tutors for students without disabilities); *Monmouth University (NJ)*, 8 NDLR ¶ 213 (OCR, Region II 1996) (because tutoring for students with learning disabilities is not required to be provided under Section 504 college can impose additional fees upon students who opt to be tutored).

10. Must testing accommodations be provided to students with learning disabilities taking standardized college entrance tests?

You bet. Accommodations must be provided for all standardized tests used as part of the admissions process to help assess a student's preparedness to attend college and successfully complete the first year of college work.

According to the Department of Education, the SAT (Scholastic Aptitude Test of the College Board) is one of two most commonly used entrance tests.[7] The SAT is designed and administered by Educational Testing Service ("ETS"), a nonprofit corporation that administers standardized tests for entrance to accredited colleges, universities and graduate schools.

ETS, as a recipient of Federal financial assistance from the Department, is subject to both Section 504 and Title II of the ADA. In *Educational Testing Service (NJ)*, 2 NDLR ¶ 227 (OCR, Region II 1991) OCR determined that any student with a disability who pays a fee and indicates a willingness to follow the rules when taking the test is a "qualified" individual entitled to the protection of the law. 34 C.F.R. § 104.3(k)(4). As a result, ETS has an obligation to make testing modifications available for disabled students in order to minimize any adverse effect of the student's disability.

OCR identified 34 C.F.R. § 104.4(a) as the particular regulatory source of the obligation. "[N]o handicapped person shall, on the basis of handicap, be excluded from participation in, be denied the benefits of, or otherwise be subjected to discrimination under any program or activity which receives or benefits from Federal financial assistance."

ETS concedes that it is also required to provide accommodations under Title III of the ADA.[8]

Discrimination under Section 12182(a)(2)(A)(I) of Title III of the ADA includes:

[t]he imposition or application of eligibility criteria that screen out or tend to screen out an individual with a disability or any class of individuals with disabilities from fully and equally enjoying any goods, services, facilities, privileges, advantages, or accommodations, unless such criteria can be shown to be necessary for the provision of the goods, services, facilities, privileges, advantages, or accommodations being offered [...]

Section 12189 (42 U.S.C. § 12189) contains a more specific prohibition relating to ETS:

Any person that offers examinations or courses related to applications, licensing, certification, or credentialing for secondary or postsecondary education, professional, or trade purposes shall offer such examinations or courses in a place and manner accessible to persons with disabilities or offer alternative accessible arrangements for such individuals.

Even if ETS were not directly regulated under any of these laws, its indirect obligation — not to mention, economic self-interest — would compel it to offer testing modifications to students with disabilities. Colleges are themselves obliged to accommodate such students.

Section 104.42(a) of the Section 504 regulations governing colleges bars admission policies under which qualified applicants with disabilities are denied admission on the basis of disability. That general prohibition translates into the following two regulatory limitations, both of which restrict a college's right to use the SAT (or any other publisher's standardized test) as part of the admissions process, if the publisher does not offer modifications to test-takers with disabilities.

(b) Admissions

In administering its admission policies, a recipient to which this subpart applies:

...

(2) May not make use of any test or criterion for admission that has a disproportionate, adverse effect on handicapped persons or any class of handicapped persons unless (i) the test or criterion, as used by the recipient, has been validated as a predictor of success in the education program or activity in question and (ii) alternate tests or criteria that have a less disproportionate, adverse effect are not shown by the Assistant Secretary to be available.

(3) Shall assure itself that (i) admissions tests are selected and administered so as best to ensure that, when a test is administered to an applicant who has a handicap that impairs sensory, manual, or speaking skills, the test results accurately reflect the applicant's aptitude or achievement level or whatever other factor the test purports to measure, rather than reflecting the applicant's impaired sensory, manual, or speaking skills (except where those skills are the factors that the test purports to measure); (ii) admissions tests that are designed for persons with impaired sensory, manual, or speaking skills are offered as often and in as timely a manner as are other admissions tests; and (iii) admissions tests are administered in facilities that, on the whole, are accessible to handicapped persons ...

11. What types of test modifications must be provided to students with learning disabilities taking the SAT?

In the words of the ETS, any accommodation "customarily used" will be provided "if documented by a qualified professional and approved in accordance with program policies and procedures."[9] We discuss documentation procedures in Question 13.

ADA Title III regulations at 28 C.F.R. § 36.309(b)(2), covering test administrators such as ETS, state that "required modifications to an examination may include changes in the length of time permitted for completion of the examination and adaptation of the manner in which the examination is given."

ETS' policies are consistent with the regulations. It identifies among the accommodations it may approve extended testing time, additional breaks, a test reader, a writer to record answers and a reader to dictate test questions.[10]

Note that "extended time" does not mean "unlimited time." The essential nature of the SAT is that it is a timed test. While ETS will, in appropriate instances, allow a student with a disability to take the test with a specific amount of extended time (e.g., time-and-a-half), it will not convert the SAT into an untimed test.[11]

12. Can a student who has not been identified as having a disability by his high school receive accommodations when taking the SAT?

Well, wouldn't that be the dream of many a parent? A student who has never been identified as disabled gets extra time to complete the SAT. Perhaps recognizing the potential for abuse, ETS policies and procedures safeguard against that possibility. And, hence, lay the groundwork for the over-identification of college-bound students with disabilities under Section 504.[12]

Under ETS policy only students with "documented" disabilities are eligible to take the SAT with testing accommodations. Specifically, a student is eligible for accommodations only if *all* of the following are true:

1. The student has a disability that necessitates testing accommodations.

2. There is documentation on file at school that supports the need for requested accommodations and otherwise meet the ETS Guidelines for Documentation (as set out in Question 13).

3. The student receives the same accommodations he is requesting for school-based tests.[13]

As we discuss in Question 5, OCR gives colleges discretion to establish policies and procedures to determine whether a student is entitled to testing accommodations. Presumably, the same leeway is extended to commercial test administrators under Section 504 and both Titles II and III of the ADA.

Nonetheless, the author questions whether the requirement for concurrent receipt of the requested accommodations could withstand a vigorous challenge by a student arguing that all the law requires is documentation of a disability that necessitates testing accommodations. The State of Massachusetts, for one, takes the position, with respect to providing accommodations for statewide or districtwide assessments, that a student does not have to be identified as disabled for purposes of the IDEA or Section 504 in order to be entitled to assessment accommodations. The request for accommodations is treated as a request for an evaluation.

> While the vast majority of students eligible for accommodations are those with an IEP or served by a 504 Plan, Title II of the ADA allows disabled students who do not fit this profile to request that accommodations be considered. Requests for accommodation, with supporting evidence of disability, must be provided to a senior level district staff member responsible for special education programs for determination of eligibility.[14]

Similarly, a college freshman who was not identified as a student with a disability in high school is entitled to academic adjustments in college, assuming the student submits an independent evaluation by a qualified professional in support of the request. See Question 6 in this regard.

13. Is a disabled student's IEP or Section 504 Plan sufficient documentation of eligibility for SAT testing accommodations?

No. In the ordinary course the student's IEP or Section 504 Plan will not include all the information ETS claims it requires in evaluating a student's request for accommodations. Submission of the IDEA or Section 504 eligibility evaluation itself, or the pertinent components thereof, is required.

ETS takes the position that "a school plan such as an individualized education program (IEP) or a Section 504 plan is insufficient documentation in and of itself, but can be included as part of a more comprehensive assessment battery[.]"[15]

ETS establishes the following general SAT Documentation Guidelines. Documentation to support the need for requested accommodations for an SAT Program test must:

- State the specific disability, as diagnosed;

- Be current (in most cases, the evaluation should be completed within three years of the SAT date);[16]

- Provide relevant educational, developmental, and medical history;

- Describe the comprehensive testing and techniques used to arrive at the diagnosis (including evaluation date[s] and test results with subtest scores from measures of cognitive ability, current academic achievement, and information processing);

- Describe the functional limitations supported by the test results;

- Describe the specific accommodations requested, and state why the disability qualifies the student for such accommodations for an SAT Program test; and

- Establish the professional credentials of the evaluator, including information about license or certification and area of specialization.[17]

ETS has also promulgated lengthy specific documentation requirements for students requesting accommodations on account of learning disabilities and attentional disorders.[18]

14. How does ETS determine the amount of extra time given to a student with a disability who is entitled to take the SAT on an extended time basis?

It punts. SAT Program Guidelines state that "a student's IEP or Section 504 team, along with teachers' in-class observations, determine how much extended time is appropriate."[19] ETS also notes therein that the determination of the appropriate amount of extra time should not be based upon how much time would guarantee that the student complete the test. (Only about 80 percent of nondisabled students do so.)[20] From the perspective of administrative convenience, particularly when the test is administered in a computer-based testing format, rounded allotments of extended time, such as time-and-a-half or double time, will be the norm.

Naturally, public school officials want to do what they can to assist students with disabilities obtain needed SAT accommodations and provide the information required to support their requests. In addition, Section 504 imposes a legal obligation to do so, as explained in Question 16.

15. What are a school district's legal obligations under the IDEA in connection with students with disabilities taking the SATs or other college entrance examinations?

The transition services requirement of the IDEA establishes school district obligations when college-bound students with disabilities prepare to take college entrance examinations.

Under the IDEA, school districts must provide appropriate transition services to students with disabilities starting no later than age 16. 34 C.F.R. § 300.347(b). Transition services include instruction to prepare students about to leave high school for independent living, postsecondary education, and community participation. 34 C.F.R. § 300.29. As observed by the Eighth Circuit Court of Appeals, "preparing disabled students for postsecondary education is one of the reasons for transition services under the IDEA." *Yankton Sch. Dist. v. Schramm*, 24 IDELR 704, 708 footnote 6 (8th Cir. 1996).

A particular aspect of that obligation involves support during the admissions process. *See, e.g., Cinnaminson Township Bd. of Educ.*, 26 IDELR 1378 (SEA N.J. 1997) (career exploration and transitioning services provided by the school district were appropriate; the district assisted the student in getting admitted to the college of her choice). As the hearing officer in *San Francisco Unified School District*, 29 IDELR 153 (SEA Cal. 1998) made clear, school districts should not assume that a disabled student who intends to attend college possesses all the skills and competencies necessary to navigate the application process unaided. In this instance the IEP for a student with an emotional disturbance stated that the student was to pursue information to select a college program by investigating catalogs and writing for information. Otherwise the IEP did not reflect any active transition planning on the part of the school district or identify any needed transition services related to the objective of postsecondary education. With respect to the student moving on to college, the hearing officer found the student's transition services inadequate. "Simply stating that a student with significant learning disabilities will look into colleges herself is not providing needed transition services." 29 IDELR at 164.

Certainly taking the SATs is a critical part of the process of moving on to college. So it stands to reason that assistance to help a student with a disability prepare to take the test may be a discrete item of required transition services. In practice, however, it is less than clear what particular assistance related to preparing a student with a disability to take the SAT must be provided and the extent to which SAT-readiness needs must be particularly addressed in the student's transition plan.

Consider, for example, the finding of the hearing officer in *Lancaster Independent School District*, 29 IDELR 281 (SEA Tex. 1998) that the school district had not provided appropriate transition services to a disabled student whose stated post-high school graduation goal was attending college. The student at issue was eligible for special education placement, programs and services on the basis of having ADHD and specific learning disabilities in the areas of spelling and written expression. The student identified three possible postsecondary goals that were then included in his Individual Transition Plan: attendance at a four year university, as a starting point for a career in architecture; military service; or starting a career as an aircraft mechanic. The school district claimed that it fulfilled its obligation to provide transition services by offering the student a number of opportunities for career counseling and academic support for post high school graduation goals during the final semester of the student's senior year. The student (through his parents) filed due process, claiming the services were too little and too late, with respect to preparation for college.

The hearing officer agreed with the parents. The district had not provided services to assist the student make the transition from high school to adult life. With respect to college preparation, the hearing officer was particularly harsh in his assessment of the adequacy of the school district's efforts. "It was unreasonable to expect a student operating on a sixth grade level, in his strongest subjects, who had never taken a TAAS[21] test, to make preparations to take the SAT or ACT." 29 IDELR at 284.

16. Must a school district assist students with disabilities in requesting SAT test accommodations?

Yes. Assuming a school district provides information or guidance about applying to colleges as a general matter, it must also provide information about any special aspects of the application process that are of particular concern to students with disabilities. To do otherwise is to discriminate in the provision of a service of counseling and information services on the basis of disability in violation of Section 504. For that reason OCR agreed with the complainant in *Cambridge (MA) Public School*, 17 EHLR 996 (OCR, Region I 1991) that the school district had violated Section 504 (34 C.F.R. §§104.4(b)(1)(iii), (vii) and 104.37(a)) by failing to adequately and effectively inform students with disabilities of ETS' special provisions for students with disabilities.

17. Is it illegal for the test administrator (ETS) to mark or "flag" SAT test scores to reflect that the test-taker was granted extended time as a disability-related accommodation?

The issue is both troubling and unresolved. Surprisingly, it is only this past summer (1999) that judicial challenges to the practice of "flagging" standardized test scores to show that the test-taker, or examinee, has received a disability-related accommodation were brought before the courts.

As an initial matter, we need to appreciate the relationship between a student having a disability and having his test score flagged because he has taken it on an extended time basis:

1. Extended test time is considered nonstandard administration by ETS.

2. The grant of extended time as an accommodation is at the discretion of ETS.

3. When a student takes a test with nonstandard administration his score report is marked, or flagged, "Nonstandard Administration."

4. Not all students who request this accommodation will receive it. One thing is for sure, though. Only students with disabilities are granted time-related accommodations.

5. All nondisabled students must take the test without accommodations, i.e., in accordance with standard administration. No nondisabled student is entitled to take the test on an extended-time basis.

6. No nondisabled student will have his test score report "flagged."[22]

Therefore, as sure as night follows day, the ineluctable result of these ETS policies and practices is: *A "flagged" score shows that the student is disabled.*

These are precisely the circumstances that OCR opined to be problematic under Section 504 and Title II of the ADA in *Letter to Runkel*, 25 IDELR 387, 388 (OCR, Region VIII 1996) in connection with public school transcripts.[23] As we prepare this book for publication, there are no published final judicial opinions or OCR guidance addressing this particular issue.

Waiting in the wings, though, is resolution of the class-action complaint against ETS brought by, among others, the International Dyslexia Association.[24] The plaintiffs charged that ETS' "flagging policy communicates a stigmatizing message that people with disabilities obtain an unfair advantage when they receive accommodations, and that their scores should therefore be viewed with skepticism." As a result, they claim ETS violates Section 504 and Title III of the ADA.

A similar challenge to flagging test scores was mounted by a student with a disability against the National Board of Medical Examiners (NBME), the administrator of the United States Medical Licensing Examination, an exam required for admission to medical residency programs. In this instance the plaintiff, a medical student with multiple sclerosis who received extended time to accommodate his physical needs, based his claims on Title III of the ADA only. The Memorandum and Order of the United States District Court for the Eastern District of Pennsylvania in *Doe v. National Board of Medical Examiners*, 16 NDLR ¶ 132 (E.D. Pa. 1999) supported the student's motion for a preliminary injunction. The judge opined that NBME's policy of flagging scores for which time-related accommodations are granted is, in and of itself, discrimination against examinees with disabilities in violation of Title III.

The opinion itself has little value as a statement of controlling law. Its decision was simply an order granting preliminary relief that is, at press time, stayed pending review by the Third Circuit Court of Appeals. Nevertheless, the judge provided a comprehensive recitation of the legal defense ETS might raise in connection with flagging SAT test scores, which we summarize for your better understanding of the issues involved.

First, ETS might argue that its policy of flagging test scores is not subject to review under Title III. While there is no dispute about the ETS' obligation to provide accommodations under the ADA, there is as yet no authoritative decision about whether that obligation also bars the test administrator's decision to flag test scores.

NBME could argue that the decision of the Third Circuit Court of Appeals in *Ford v. Schering-Plough Corporation*, 12 NDLR ¶ 291 (3d Cir. 1998) clearly limits a test administrator's responsibility under Title III to providing physical access to locations where its tests are administered. That decision concerned an insurer's provision of benefits in which the Court of Appeals for the Third Circuit interpreted Title III as limited to claims relating to physical access to a "place of public accommodation." According to the court:

> [T]he 'goods, services, facilities, privileges, advantages, or accommodations' concerning which a disabled person cannot suffer discrimination [under Title III] are not free-standing concepts but rather all refer to the statutory term 'public accommodation' and thus to what these places of public accommodation provide. [The plaintiff] cannot point to these terms as providing protection from discrimination unrelated to places.

The court supported its decision to confine Title III to discrimination connected to use of physical facilities by citing decisions to that effect by the Courts of Appeals for the Seventh and Ninth Circuits as well as Department of Justice regulations (at 28 C.F.R. pt. 36, app. B, at 640 (1997)).

The federal district court judge ruling against NMBE discounted the relevance of the *Ford* decision. "I believe [NMBE] reads the *Ford* decision too broadly and the scope of Title III too narrowly. ... I believe that [the student] has shown the required nexus between a physical place of public accommodation and the NMBE's annotation policy to state a cause of action under Title III."

Well, this is all pretty heady legal stuff, none of which is precisely on point with respect to coverage of test administrators under Title III as regards policies and procedures for test accommodations. So three more arguments ETS might raise concede coverage under Title III, but raise affirmative defenses to claims of discrimination on the basis of disability.

ETS might claim it has an absolute privilege to provide truthful information to third parties in response to examinees' request for reporting of test scores. It might rely, as did NBME, on the decision in *Rothman v. Emory University*, 10 NDLR ¶ 271 (7th Cir. 1997), in which the court dismissed a disabled student's claim of discrimination. The defendant in that case was the law school the student had attended. It's alleged act of discrimination was reporting to a state licensing board that the student had epilepsy.

ETS will also likely take the position that its flagging of scores is necessary to protect the integrity of the testing program. In this regard, NBME made the argument that, as a matter of psychometric science, the test administrator can only certify the meaning of scores that are obtained under standard administration conditions or comparable conditions.

As a related matter, ETS may assert as a defense that a failure to flag when test-takers have received extended test time substantially alters the nature of the test.

The opinion summarizes what appears to have been an extraordinary amount of expert testimony on these latter two points, which are also a matter of substantial uncertainty in connection with statewide and districtwide assessments. We discuss aspects of the experts' testimony in Question 12 in chapter 6 in that regard.

For purposes of this response, though, we simply note at this point that the court found that the test administrator did not meet the "likelihood of success" element of a challenge to the granting of a preliminary injunction. Making that finding, the judge almost audibly let out a sign of relief as she concluded that "fortunately, the larger issue of whether, in fact, standardized scores and scores obtained by disabled individuals for whom time-related accommodations were granted are comparable in psychometric terms ... need not be answered by me."

Like the judge, the National Research Council finds the "larger" issue of determining when test accommodations compromise validity "vexing," legally and ethically.[25] Parting company with the court, though, in the face of this uncertainty it guardedly supports flagging.

When testing technology is able to ensure that accommodations do not confound the measurement of underlying constructs, score notations will be unnecessary. Until then, however, flagging should be used only with the understanding that the need to protect the public and policymakers from misleading information must be weighed against the equally important need to protect student confidentiality and prevent discriminatory uses of testing information.[26]

18. Can a school district be ordered to provide compensatory education to students with disabilities attending college?

Apparently, yes. At least one federal district court agreed with a disabled student's contention that there could be situations when a student might be eligible for compensatory education services while attending a postsecondary school. *Straube v. Florida Union Free School District*, 19 IDELR 493 (S.D.N.Y. 1992).

As we discussed in Question 17 in chapter 9, the fact that a disabled student earns a bona fide high school diploma suggests that the school district has discharged its obligation to provide a meaningful educational benefit, as required under *Board of Education v. Rowley*, EHLR 553:656 (1982). When the student not only graduates, but also meets the admission criteria of an accredited postsecondary institution, any argument that the student has not received FAPE seems destined to fail. In fact, that was precisely the fate of the complaint of the learning disabled student in *Lower Moreland Township School District*, 25 IDELR 351 (SEA Pa. 1996). Because the student had received As and Bs and had been admitted to a well-regarded college, he had clearly received an educational benefit.

But there is an opposing point of view. A disabled student who has graduated and entered college may yet be able to establish that he was denied FAPE and is entitled to receive compensatory education. *E.g., Megan C. v. Independent Sch. Dist. No. 625*, 30 IDELR 132 (D. Minn. 1999); *Straube v. Florida Union Free School District*, 19 IDELR 131 (S.D.N.Y. 1992); *Puffer v. Raynolds*, 17 EHLR 618 (D. Mass. 1988).

The court's opinion in *Straube* contains a good exploration of the issue. In that case reading tests conducted when the student, who had dyslexia, was in the tenth grade revealed that he read on a third grade level. Frustrated, the parents unilaterally placed the student at a school exclusively for students with learning disabilities. Once enrolled, the student flourished. The parents then filed for due process. There was no real issue of whether the district had provided FAPE: without much difficulty, both the administrative decision-makers and the court appeared to come to the same conclusion that it had not.

Awarding appropriate relief was another matter. The court agreed with the parents that the school district was not able to provide appropriate programming to the student. The student would finish his secondary education at the private school and then go on to attend college. However, for reasons that are no longer controlling law, tuition reimbursement was not available.[27] Unless the student had an entitlement to relief after he completed his secondary education at the private school, the district's denial of FAPE would be a wrong without a remedy. Starting with the controlling ruling in the Second Circuit that a student with a disability can receive compensatory education beyond his twenty-first birthday, *Burr by Burr v. Ambach*, EHLR 441:314 (2d Cir. 1988), the court went on to hold that compensatory education may be available to students who are attending college. The court thus ordered the school district to provide one year of remedial educational services after graduation from high school.

19. Can a school district be ordered to pay for a student's college tuition as a remedy for failing to provide FAPE?

No. Tuition reimbursement extends only to tuition for preschool, elementary school, or secondary schools.

As discussed in Question 18, some courts have held that an award of compensatory education to a student with a disability who has graduated from high school and entered college may be appropriate. But all published decisions in LRP Publications' database show a unanimity of opinion on a school district's obligation to fund college: There is none. All decision-makers have refused to award college tuition payment or reimbursement.

In *Straube v. Florida Union Free School District*, 19 IDELR 131 (S.D.N.Y. 1992), for instance, the court ordered the school district to provide a year's worth of compensatory education to a student with dyslexia who had been denied FAPE. The parents requested that the relief take the form of payment of a year's tuition at a college that specialized in the education of dyslexic students. But the court refused to accede to their request. "The IDEA directs funds into special education at elementary and secondary schools and there is no provision in the Act for the payment of funds for postsecondary education." 19 IDELR at 138.

Other judicial and administrative decision-makers that have come to the same conclusion include: *Megan C. v. Independent Sch. Dist. No. 625*, 30 IDELR 132 (D. Minn. 1999); *In Re: Student with a Disability*, 27 IDELR 774 (SEA Conn. 1998); and *Ashland Sch. Dist.*, 28 IDELR 630 (SEA Or. 1998).

20. What compensatory education services have been found appropriate for students with disabilities who are attending college?

Two principles seem to guide the identification of the particular compensatory services that a student with a disability who is attending college should receive. Both flow from the "prime directive," so to speak, of the IDEA: FAPE involves preschool, elementary and secondary education services designed with the unique needs of the student with a disability in mind.

First, as a general matter, compensatory services should be of the same type as the services that should have been provided in the first instance. *E.g., Ashland Sch. Dist.*, 28 IDELR 630 (SEA Or. 1998).

Second, an award of compensatory education to a student who has graduated from high school and entered college must take into account the student's current (i.e. college) educational needs. *Novato Unified Sch. Dist.*, 22 IDELR 1056 (SEA Cal. 1995).

The opinion of the court in *Megan C. v. Independent School District No. 625*, 30 IDELR 132 (D. Minn. 1999) is illuminating. That decision concerned an attorney's fees petition submitted by the parents of a student with a disability after prevailing in a state complaint proceeding. The parents successfully claimed that the district failed to provide an appropriate IEP for the student while she was in high school.

The parents proposed as relief that the school district provide sufficient funds for the student to complete the equivalent of 4 years postsecondary education. That was not all. The parent's successor attorney submitted a memorandum in support of the parents' request, also requesting a smorgasbord of additional services or funding for services. The total request put before the state DOE was the following:

- Funding of tuition for two years at community college ($4,649.28).

- Funding of tuition for two years at a four-year public college ($7,182.00).

- Books and materials ($4,500.00).

- Transportation ($2,922.40).

- Purchase of a laptop computer and printer with the loan Windows '95 and Windows '95 upgrade.

- Tutoring for ten to fifteen hours per week for one to two years.

- Provision of a note taker during four years of college.

- Remedial books and classes, as needed ($1,220.00).

- Counseling one to two times per week for two years.

- Ten sessions of speech and language therapy.

The state DOE rejected the demand for funding of tuition and transportation. It also refused to order the district to fund the purchase of books, remedial or otherwise. However, it did order provision of a range of services that would keep the district involved in the student's educational program for another two years. Specifically, it found that the following were appropriate services for the student in light of her disability and status as a college-student:

(1) Counseling services provided one time a week for two years;

(2) Tutoring services for 10 hours per week for two years;

(3) Provision of a note taker for the student's college courses for two years; and

(4) Continued use of a district-loaned computer and software for two years.

Endnotes

[1]   TESTING ACCOMMODATIONS IN HIGHER EDUCATION: COMPLYING WITH THE ADA AND SECTION 504 (LRP Publications, 1998).

[2]   "Documentation of a Specific Learning Disability," summarized in Judge Saris' thorough opinion in Guckenberger v. Boston University, 26 IDELR 573 (D. Mass. 1997), included as Appendix A.

[3]   In the author's humble opinion, the court's two reasons seem to be made of whole cloth.

[4]   64 *Fed. Reg.* 12636 (1999).

[5]   As used in this part, transition services means a coordinated set of activities for a student with a disability that-

Is designed within an outcome-oriented process, that promotes movement from school to post-school activities, including postsecondary education, vocational training, integrated employment (including Transition services are defined in section 300.29 of the IDEA regulations as follows:)

supported employment, continuing and adult education, adult services, independent living, or community participation;

(2) Is based on the individual student's needs, taking into account the student's preferences and interests; and

(3) Includes—

(i) Instruction;

(ii) Related services;

(iii) Community experiences;

(iv) The development of employment and other post-school adult living objectives; and

(v) If appropriate, acquisition of daily living skills and functional vocational evaluation.

(b) Transition services for students with disabilities may be special education, if provided as specially designed instruction, or related services, if required to assist a student with a disability to benefit from special education.

[6] Perry Zirkel, J.D., Ph.D., *'Forming' a Plan for Sec. 504/ADA Eligibility and Accommodation,* THE SPECIAL EDUCATOR®, vol. 13, iss. 3 (Aug. 8, 1997). The author specifically referred to arguably abusive attempts to demand extended time for SATs as a disability-related accommodation. We discuss accommodations for students with disabilities taking SATs in Question 11.

[7] The ACT (American College Testing Program Assessment) is the other. Presentation by the ERIC Clearinghouse on Urban Education for the National Parent Information Network, <http://eric-web.tc.columbia.edu/families/nul/nultesting.html> (October 14, 1999).

[8] "Information About Testing Accommodations" <http://www.ets.org/distest/info.html> Educational Testing Service (October 14, 1999).

[9] *Id.*

[10] *Id.*

[11] "SAT Program Guidelines" <http://collegboard.org/sat/html/students/disable002.html> College Board Online (October 8, 1999).

[12] Perry Zirkel, J.D., Ph.D., *'Forming' a Plan for Sec. 504/ADA Eligibility and Accommodation, supra,* note 6.

[13] "SAT Program Guidelines" <http://collegboard.org/sat/html/students/disable001.html> College Board Online (October 8, 1999).

[14] "MCAS: Requests for Participation of Students with Disabilities" <http://www.doe.mass.edu/mcas/guides/spedmcas.htm> Massachusetts Department of Education (September 1, 1999).

[15] "Policy Statement for Documentation of a Learning Disability in Adolescents and Adults," January 1998 <http://www.ets.org.distest/ldpolicy.html> Educational Testing Service (October 8, 1999).

[16] This is the same currency requirement customarily adopted by colleges in connection with evaluating student requests for academic adjustments. See Question 3.

[17] "SAT Program Guidelines" <http://collegboard.org/sat/html/students/disable002.html> College Board Online (October 8, 1999).

[18] See "Policy Statement for Documentation of a Learning Disability in Adolescents and Adults," January 1998 <http://www.ets.org/distest/ldpolicy.html> Educational Testing Service (October 8, 1999); "Policy Statement for Documentation of Attention-Deficit/Hyperactivity Disorder in Adolescents and Adults" June 1999 (Revised) <http://www.ets.org/distest/adhdpolicy.html> Educational Testing Service (October 8, 1999).

[19] "SAT Program Guidelines," *supra,* note 17.

[20] *Id.*

[21] Texas Assessment of Academic Skills, a standardized test the passing of which is a state law requirement for graduating with a regular high school diploma. See Question 8 in chapter 8.

[22] "SAT Services for Students with Disabilities" <http://collegboard.org/sat/html/students/reg003.html> College Board Online (November 8, 1999).

[23] See Question 9 in chapter 5.

[24] Breimhorst v. Educational Testing Services, described in *California Suit Challenges Test Administrator's Policy of 'Flagging' Scores*, DISABILITY COMPLIANCE BULLETIN®, vol. 16, iss. 1 (September 23, 1999).

[25] JAY P. HEUBERT, ROBERT M. HAUSER, EDS., HIGH STAKES: TESTING FOR TRACKING, PROMOTION, AND GRADUATION 200-201 (National Academy Press 1999).

[26] *Id.*

[27] The parents were not entitled to tuition reimbursement because they chose a school that was not certified or approved by the state. Florence County Sch. Dist. Four v. Carter, 20 IDELR 532 (1993), eliminating the need for state approval, was not decided until one year later.

Chapter 4

MEASURING PROGRESS AND ASSIGNING GRADES FOR STUDENTS WITH DISABILITIES

Grades

1. May a school district use a different grading system for students with disabilities participating in the general curriculum?

Generally speaking, a district may use a different grading system for a student with a disability participating in the general curriculum only if the student's IEP team adopts an alternate system in response to the student's individual disability-related needs.

The Section 504 regulations do not specifically address how a student's progress is to be documented. *See Orcas Island (WA) Sch. Dist. No. 137*, 31 IDELR 12 (OCR, Region X 1999). However, Section 504 regulations at 34 CFR §104.4(a), (b)(1)(iv) contain a more general prohibition on provision of aids, benefits, or services to students with disabilities that are different from those provided to nondisabled students. Differences are only permitted when necessary to provide students with disabilities with aids, benefits, or services that are as effective as those provided to nondisabled students.

In the ordinary course, then, a student with a disability participating in the general curriculum in the regular education classroom is graded consistently with school district policies governing the grading of his classmates. OCR's findings in *Ottawa Township (IL) High School District*, 27 IDELR 373 (OCR, Region V 1997) illustrate the general rule. The school district did not discriminate when it held a student with a learning disability to the same standards of course performance as his Algebra II classmates in the absence of an IEP team decision to the contrary.

OCR's findings in *North Hunterdon/Voorhees Regional (NJ) High School District*, 25 IDELR 165 (OCR, Region II 1996) illustrate the exception. That LOF concerned a student with cerebral palsy and a seizure disorder who was subject to a different grading system than the one used for nondisabled students. OCR concluded that the student's IEP team had selected a grading system for the student — letter grades for her special education classes, pass/fail grades for electives and physical education and an audit grade for her regular education English class — based on a determination of her individual educational needs. Thus no violation of Section 504 occurred.

The parents in *Harrison County (WV) School District*, EHLR 353:120 (OCR, Region III 1988) complained to OCR precisely because a disabled student was not being graded differently. In this instance OCR found that the school district violated Section 504 rights of a student with a severe communication disorder when it insisted she be graded exactly like peers in language and writing skills, despite physical limitations that precluded the possibility of performance at a similar level.

The student's IEP team or Section 504 placement team specifically addresses how the student's academic progress will be evaluated, documented, and reported. *See Orcas Island (WA) Sch. Dist. No. 137, supra*. It is up to the IEP (or Section 504 placement) team to decide if the student should be graded on an alternate basis. *Letter to Runkel*, 25 IDELR 387, 388 (OCR, Region VIII 1996).

While it is not within OCR's purview to evaluate an individual teacher's grading policies (e.g., 50 percent of grade on test scores, 50 percent on homework assignments),[1] OCR will step in when a teacher unilaterally decides to use a different grading system for a student with a disability. For example, OCR held in *Ann Arbor (MI) Public School District*, 30 IDELR 405 (OCR, Region XII 1998) that a teacher should not have taken it upon herself to decide that a student with a disability in her Business Education Class should take the course pass/fail. The teacher contended that she did not offer the student the option to take the course for a letter grade because the student would not have been able to master the minimal keyboarding skills required to pass the course. OCR held, however, that the issue of which grading system to use should have been referred to the student's IEP team for resolution. The failure to do so denied the parent the attendant Section 504 procedural safeguards.

2. Does grading a student who has disability-related absences on the basis of attendance violate Section 504?

Not necessarily. A school district may adopt a policy that takes attendance into account for both disabled and nondisabled students without implicating Section 504, assuming accommodations are made for students with disability-related absenteeism.

Typically, a school district policy penalizing (or rewarding) students on the basis of their attendance are neutral on its face with respect to students with disabilities. When the absences of a student with a disability are disability-related, however, a school district must make reasonable accommodations to a facially neutral attendance policy.

That does not necessarily mean immunizing the student, even when the student is a sympathetic figure and the sanction for noncompliance is harsh. In this regard, the situation of the student in *Walpole Public School*, 22 IDELR 1075 (SEA Mass. 1995) was a school district's worst nightmare come true. The student in that case was a 19-year-old young man who required the use of a wheelchair as a result of spinal cord injuries received in an accident. Due to the student having excessive absences, as defined in the district's attendance policy, he was denied credit for coursework and did not graduate with his class. Not surprisingly, the parent filed for due process.

The hearing officer concluded, however, that the school district had made reasonable accommodations for the student. Because the student was having difficulty arriving on time for his first class, the district redesigned his schedule so he could come in at a later hour without requiring the student to provide a medical excuse to support those modifications. In fact, it was not until the student and his parent were notified that the student would not be graduating that they offered what were found to be flimsy medical excuses for his tardiness. Moreover, there was no evidence linking the student's attendance problem to his physical disabilities.

3. Can a school district modify the grade of a student with a disability receiving special education accommodations in a regular education class?

Yes, as long as the decision to give a modified grade is made by the student's IEP team based on his individual needs. School districts may not modify grades on the basis of a student's special education status alone, however, for that would raise "a strong inference that children with disabilities are being treated differently on the basis of their disabilities." *Letter to Runkel*, 25 IDELR 387, 389 (OCR, Region VIII 1996).

Based on that reasoning, a teacher should not reduce a student's grade merely because he received accommodations that are not related to course content. That was what the parent of an elementary school student with learning disabilities complained about to OCR in *Torrance (CA) Unified School District*, 24 IDELR 391 (OCR, Region IX 1995). In examining the grading methodology for the student's class, however, OCR found no convincing evidence that the teacher considered the accommodations made for the student, which included extended test time, fewer test questions, and a test reader, in the grading process. Had OCR found to the contrary, the district would have been faced with a finding of disability discrimination.

OCR explored the issue of modifying grades for students receiving special education accommodations in the course of setting out its findings in *Metropolitan (TN) Public School District*, 18 IDELR 971 (OCR, Region IV 1991). The district had a fairly complicated grading policy based upon coding regular education course numbers to indicate that the coursework had been modified for a student with a disability in accordance with the student's special education program.

Under the policy each regular education course was assigned a unique four-digit number to be used in recording students' grades on the students' cumulative records. All special education courses were assigned the same course number: 9-525. So far, clear enough. But when a student with a disability enrolled in a regular education course, things got complicated.

- If the student performed within the normal requirements of the course, the regular course number was used.

- If the student required course modifications, such as large print, oral tests or tape recorders, that "merely diminished the impact of the handicap" without "lowering course objectives" the regular course number was also used.

- If the student was graded on his individual level of performance or was otherwise not held to the same course objectives as the rest of the class, then the course number was identified as 9-525 (the special education course number) in the student's records.

The parents of a high school student with a learning disability taking regular education courses on a modified basis objected to the district's coding the student's regular education courses and grades with the same course number used for special education classrooms. The parents' desire to camouflage the information that ultimately appeared on the student's transcripts was understandable.

But OCR upheld the district's system, finding no violation of 34 C.F.R. § 104.4(a) or (b)(1)(ii)-(iv). OCR found that the district was authorized to establish course and grade requirements and that this authority was not abused in the present situation. In particular, the decision to code coursework as "special education" was made on an individualized basis. The IEP team recommended the modifications, but had given the student the option of earning a regular grade by foregoing recommended modifications of substantive course mastery requirements.

4. Can a district use a weighted grading system that arbitrarily assigns lower grade weights to all special education courses?

No, of course not. That would be discrimination on the basis of disability according to OCR, which responded to this question in *Letter to Runkel*, 25 IDELR 387, 389 (OCR, Region VIII 1996).[2]

The give-away in the question is the word "arbitrarily." But if you take that word out, the answer is not so clear-cut. As further explained by OCR in *Runkel*:

> If a weighting system is used, each subject or course must be analyzed separately and assigned a degree of difficulty factor based on its individual contents. In most situations, the faculty or administrative decision should be accorded great deference if any challenge develops, particularly if the school district can produce a record explaining the process and criteria used to assign various weights to each course or subject.

25 IDELR at 390.

4 : 3

OCR evaluated the nuances of just such a system for weighting grades in *North East (TX) Independent School District*, 24 IDELR 298 (OCR 1995). The school district in question used weighted grades to reflect different academic levels in coursework. Even though the district awarded students in "basic" and "special education" classes less academic credit than students who took "regular" courses in the same subject, OCR found no violation of Section 504. OCR articulated three factors that contributed to its conclusion that the weighting system was non-discriminatory:

- The district's practice of not awarding academic credit for the "basic" and "special education" classes equivalent to the academic credit it awarded for "regular" classes on the same subject was a legitimate educational decision.

- The differences in the method of instruction and in the quantity of the material covered between the classes were significant.

- Each disabled student's placement in "special," "basic," "regular," or "honors" classes was based on the IEP team's consideration of individual needs.

- Although only students with disabilities were placed in "basic" and "special education" classes, not all students with disabilities were placed in those classes; some students with disabilities were placed in "regular" or "honors" classes.

5. Who bears the burden of proof when a parent claims use of a weighted grading system violates Section 504?

Assuming a school district can present a coherent methodology that is consistent with guidance set out in Question 4, OCR will support the district's assignment of weights to courses. That is the reassurance OCR provided to school districts in *Letter to Runkel*, 25 IDELR 387, 390 (OCR Region VIII 1996). "In most situations, the faculty or administrative decisions should be accorded great deference if any challenge develops, particularly if the school district can produce a record explaining the process and criteria used to assign various weights to each course and subject."

6. May a school district use an alternative grading system for students being educated in special education classes?

Because deviations from customary grading must be based upon individual needs, across-the-board grading systems used solely for disabled students are suspect, at best.

OCR stated in *Letter to Runkel*, 25 IDELR 387, 388 (OCR, Region VIII 1996) that "alternate grading systems may be appropriate ... if they are available to all students, not just students with disabilities." A school district should not have anything identified as a districtwide grading policy regarding students with disabilities. *See, e.g., Ann Arbor (MI) Pub. Sch. Dist.*, 30 IDELR 405 (OCR, Region XII 1998) (compliant school district had a letter grade system and also provided both disabled and nondisabled students the option of taking courses pass/fail). *See also Marion County (WV) Pub. Schs.*, EHLR 352:112 (OCR, Region III 1985) (policy allowing students in LD, EMI and "basic" classes to elect pass/fail or number grades did not discriminate in violation of Section 504 because both disabled students and non-disabled slow-learning students were in "basic classes").

7. Can a parent of a student with a disability file for due process to challenge a grade?

No, in the ordinary course special education hearing officers have no basis on which to assert jurisdiction over a dispute about a grade.

As a general matter, a parent who claims a student should have received a higher grade has only limited avenues for appeal under state law. The concern, of course, is to avoid legal involvement in matters related to the exercise of professional judgment by educators.

There is no constitutional right to administrative or judicial review of promotion or retention decisions. The weight of judicial authority has held that students do not have the requisite liberty or property interest in promotion to trigger the right to procedural due process. *E.g., Killion v. Burl*, 860 F.2d 306 (8th Cir. 1988) (student has no due process liberty or property interest in promotion to next grade level). *Accord Hartfield v. East Grand Rapids Pub. Schs.*, 26 IDELR 1 (W.D. Mich. 1997). *See Gallagher v. Pontiac Sch. Dist.*, EHLR 558:191 (6th Cir. 1986) (Section 1983 relief not available to challenge exercise of school district discretionary actions that do not impact students' constitutional rights).

Federal statutory law limits the scope of grade disputes subject to federal review even further. The Family Educational Rights and Privacy Act (FERPA) allows parents to request administrative review to correct improperly recorded grades, i.e., grades misstated on the official records as a result of ministerial or computational errors. 20 U.S.C. § 1232g(a)(2); 34 C.F.R. §§ 99.20-99.22. FERPA is not available, however, when a parent's claim boils down to a belief that the teacher should have given the student a higher grade. Joint Statement in Explanation of the Buckley/Pell Amendment, 120 Cong. Rec. 39,862 (Dec. 13, 1974); *Tarka v. Cunningham*, 917 F. 2d 890 (5th Cir. 1990).

The IDEA regulations concerning amendment of education records at 34 C.F.R. §§ 300.567-300.570 are substantially similar to FERPA in all material ways.

A due process hearing under 34 C.F.R. § 300.507(a) will generally not be an option, unless the parent can cast the dispute in terms of an alleged denial of FAPE. Possibly, a claim that a student was graded inconsistently with the grading system or agreed modifications specified in his IEP could be brought before a hearing officer. But it seems more likely that the parent filing for due process to challenge a grade will, like the parent in *Hacienda La Puente Unified School District*, 27 IDELR 885 (SEA Cal. 1997), have his complaint dismissed for lack of jurisdiction. The hearing officer in that case concluded that he lacked jurisdiction under state special education law identical to 34 C.F.R. § 300.507. *Accord San Francisco Unified Sch. Dist.*, 29 IDELR 153 (SEA Cal. 1998) (state education code sets forth specific procedures regarding grade changes for both disabled and nondisabled students, with those procedures being entirely separate from special education due process hearings); *Los Angeles Unified Sch. Dist.*, 26 IDELR 373 (SEA Cal. 1997).

8. Is a special education due process hearing officer empowered to order the promotion of a student with a disability?

It appears not, although there is no discussion of this issue in the IDEA and only limited interpretive case law.

For a parent to be able to bring a claim concerning a district's wrongful retention of a student with a disability, he must be able to frame his complaint as a dispute about programming, placement, or denial of FAPE. 34 C.F.R. § 300.507(a)(2).

A decision to promote or not to promote might seem related to placement, but published decisions generally reflect the rejection of parental characterization of the proposed retention as a change in placement, for purposes of due process. The court in *Houston Independent School District v. Caius R.*, 30 IDELR 578 (S.D. Tex. 1998), for example, opined that promotion to a higher grade turns on achievement of the mainstream educational requirements of a student's grade level; advancement to the next level is distinct from placement. Administrative decisions coming to the same conclusion include the following:

4 : 5

- *In Re: D.G.*, 29 IDELR 501 (SEA Vt. 1998). Neither a "change of schools or classrooms" nor "grade promotion" are considered significant changes in placement under state education regulations.

- *Boston Pub. School*, 24 IDELR 985 (SEA Mass. 1996). Decisions about promotion are not related to special education. They are, instead, regular education decisions within the purview of the school district.

- *Greensburg Salem Sch. Dist.*, 21 IDELR 1144 (SEA Pa. 1994). Reasonable modifications to accommodate normal progression or grade promotion are permissible during pendency despite stay-put.

Assuming, for the sake of argument, that decisions about retention are subject to due process, it remains unclear if hearing officers are empowered to order promotion. The IDEA does not specifically address the types of relief that hearing officers may order. 34 C.F.R. § 300.510. State law may provide more detailed directions. In general, hearing officers have authority to award the types of relief commonly recognized as available remedies under special education law, such as an order to design and implement an appropriate IEP, placement in the student's LRE, compensatory education or tuition reimbursement. Grade promotion is not, in the author's opinion, a substantially similar remedy.

IEP Progress

9. Can an IEP team identify achievement of a passing grade in a regular education class as an IEP goal?

Achieving a passing grade may be a legitimate goal to include in the IEP of a student with a disability when the student's disability is adversely affecting his ability to make progress in the general curriculum.

Prior to enactment of the 1997 IDEA Amendments a student's IEP team took a narrow approach to establishing goals and objectives. IEP teams appeared to concentrate on establishing goals related to the special education to be provided. Sometimes the student's IEP progress was not considered in the context of the student's regular education program. The disconnect was most troubling when the special education called for in the student's IEP was limited to pull-out services to support the student's regular education classroom placement.

The 1999 IDEA regulations drag success in the general curriculum into the light with its newly emphasized focus on educational results for all students with disabilities. Section 300.347(a)(2)(i) states that an IEP must include, when appropriate, measurable annual goals related to "[m]eeting the child's needs that result from the child's disability to enable the child to be involved in and progress in the general curriculum (i.e., the same curriculum as for nondisabled children)[.]"

As a general matter, the term "standards-based IEP" is becoming part of the jargon as educators in states that have adopted standards use the IEP as the mechanism to ensure access to the general curriculum's standards, which are for all students. The "I" in IEP comes into play when a student's IEP team identifies and prioritizes the standards that are most affected by the student's disability. Specifically, IEP teams must use the relevance-reasonableness-time, or RRT method, to determine if a certain standard is appropriate for the student, whether it is reasonable to teach it to him, and whether there's enough time.[3]

The author expects that IEPs will more frequently embody goals similar to those upheld by OCR in *Mt. Pleasant Township (IN) Community School Corporation*, 20 IDELR 1256 (OCR, Region V

1993). In that instance the long-range goal for a student with a disability was maintaining a passing grade average in 8th grade classes with resource support.

But as the administrative decision in *Gaston School District*, 24 IDELR 1052 (SEA Or. 1996) illustrates, some parents may not appreciate the change in perspective. In that case an IEP goal for a student with a learning disability was passing his general education language arts course with a score of not less than 70 percent. The parent filed for due process, contending that the IEP should have contained an annual goal specifically addressing the student's deficits in written expression. But the hearing officer disagreed.

> [I]t is not clear that attaining a passing grade in a general education class is not a specific statement of what [the student] can be expected to reasonably accomplish during the twelve month period in the coming school year. In his case the goal is adequate because it was anticipated that [the student] graduate with a regular diploma. Passing regular education classes is an integral part of attaining that regular diploma.

24 IDELR at 1057.

The measure of FAPE is not always whether a student passes from grade to grade. *Board of Educ. v. Rowley*, EHLR 553:656 (1982); 34 C.F.R. § 300.121(e). Similarly, achieving passing grades may not always be an appropriate goal for a student with a disability participating in the general curriculum. In *Nineveh-Hensley-Jackson United School Corporation*, 28 IDELR 579 (SEA Ind. 1998), for instance, the review panel agreed that the IEP of a 13-year-old middle school student with dyslexia and dysgraphia did not contain adequate and appropriate annual goals commensurate with the student's level of performance and ability.

> The evidence was clear that the student did (and could in the future) easily surpass the school's stated goal of 'maintaining passing grades.' The IHO is in no way applying a 'maximization of potential' standard in this case, but the IEP goal is so unambitious for this unique individual student that it is inappropriate.

28 IDELR at 583.

The *Nineveh-Hensley* decision raises interesting issues that, to the best knowledge of the author, are not yet addressed in the published legal literature: Can achievement of a higher letter grade be an appropriate IEP goal when the student is clearly capable of passing a course, even if unassisted? In that case, how does the IEP team draw the line between agreeing to goals and services that offer FAPE and those that maximize the student's potential?

We note, as a related matter, that a passing score of a statewide or districtwide assessment seems a less apt indicator of educational progress and the provision of FAPE. According to the National Research Council, "[l]arge-scale assessments have not often been used [to monitor a student's IEP progress], because of their emphasis on broad content domains rather than on the specific skills that are usually represented in IEP goals."[4]

10. Are good grades[5] on the report cards of a student with a disability participating in the general curriculum conclusive proof that the school district has provided FAPE?

Good grades may be powerful evidence of compliance with the IDEA. But they do not, as a matter of law, end an inquiry into whether a school district provided FAPE.

Under IDEA regulations at 34 C.F.R. § 300.347(a)(2)(i) IEP teams must establish annual goals related to "[m]eeting the child's needs that result from the child's disability to enable the child to be involved in and progress in the general curriculum (i.e., the same curriculum as for nondisabled children)...[.]" It stands to reason, then, that when a student with a disability is participating in the general curriculum, good report card grades suggest that the student has made progress. And such progress, in turn, strongly suggests that the student has received FAPE.

In *Board of Education v. Rowley*, EHLR 553:656 (1982) the Supreme Court suggested that in some instances a student's receipt of merely "passing marks" may demonstrate that the school district has provided the required quantum of educational benefit.

> When that 'mainstreaming' preference of the [IDEA] has been met and a child is being educated in the regular classrooms of a public school system, the system itself monitors the educational progress of the child. Regular examinations are administered, grades are awarded, and yearly advancement to higher grade levels is permitted for those children who attain an adequate knowledge of the course material. The grading and advancement system thus constitutes an important factor in determining educational benefit.

EHLR at 553:668.

The *Rowley* Court thus proclaimed that grades are not the only factor that needs to be considered when assessing whether a student participating in the general curriculum received FAPE. Subsequent judicial rulings and administrative decisions have fleshed out what other indicia of a disabled student's degree of mastery of the general curriculum should be reviewed. In the author's opinion, one of the best expressed articulations of the range of evidence to be considered when the student's progress in regular education, i.e., academic growth, is at issue can be found in *Mount Greylock Regional Schools*, 26 IDELR 1238 (SEA Mass. 1997). The factors identified therein included: placement and achievement in appropriate chronological age-level and advanced courses; teacher assessments of depth of understanding of course content; results of in-school tests; grades; and results of standardized tests.

> A student will be found to be making effective progress where there is documented growth in the acquisition of knowledge and skills, including social/emotional development, within regular education, according to the chronological age and individual educational potential of the child. (603 C.M.R. 28.104.0b(ii)). Indices of inability to make effective progress would include not performing up to expected levels on standardized, criterion-referenced, or curriculum based assessments, or failing to earn promotion to the next grade level at the end of the school year. (Massachusetts Department of Education, Eligibility Guidelines for Special Education, 1994.)

26 IDELR at 1245.

Published judicial decisions reflect a number of instances when a student's passing grades were discounted and other evidence demonstrating less-than-adequate academic progress was found to be more probative. The most noteworthy decision is *Hall v. Vance City Board of Education*, EHLR 557:155 (4th Cir.1985). The student in that case was "bright," severely dyslexic, and, at the end of his fifth-grade year, "functionally illiterate." The court found that the student's standardized test scores and independent evaluations established that he had not received an educational benefit, despite passing grades and promotions from grade to grade. The court in *Chris D. v. Montgomery County Board of Education*, 17 EHLR 267 (M.D. Ala. 1990) similarly held that the grades of a student with a behavioral disorder did not accurately reflect what he had learned, which was virtually nothing. His standardized test scores were a more reliable indicator of the extent of his educational progress, characterized by the court as "trivial."

The issue in both cases was the degree of deference that should be paid to passing grades and resulting advancement from grade to grade when the school district has applied a policy of social promotion, a pedagogic approach that President Clinton, among others, have gone on record as strongly opposing in all instances.[6]

In other instances, good grades not awarded in furtherance of social promotion have also been discounted as a reliable indicator of FAPE.

The hearing officer in *Fayetteville-Perry Local School District*, 20 IDELR 1289 (SEA Ohio 1994), for example, found that the student with a disability received good report card grades in order to encourage her to continue her efforts, rather than to provide meaningful information about the extent of her progress.

Similarly, the hearing officer in *Tucson Unified School District*, 30 IDELR 478 (SEA Ariz. 1999) found that the progress reports and report cards issued for the student with a disability were not useful measurements of actual progress. The student had received grades of "Excellent," "Good," or "Satisfactory" for both performance and effort in an attempt to reward and encourage the student's continued effort. After considering the progress notes in the student's IEP and the results of her standardized tests the hearing officer concluded that the progress reports and report cards did not accurately report the student's lack of educational progress.

To like effect, in *Craven County Board of Education*, 27 IDELR 255 (SEA N.C. 1997) the review officer affirmed the hearing officers' determination that grades were not the sole indicator of the educational progress made by a bright student with specific learning disabilities in written expression and reading. Promotion from grade to grade and achieving As and Bs was not the full measure of an appropriate education in this instance. More probative, and indicative of the district's failure to provide FAPE, was the discouraging fact that standardized testing conducted over three years showed an eight point increase in discrepancy between ability and achievement (from 25 percent to 33 percent) in written expression and a similar increase (from 21 percent to 29 percent) in reading.

Just as passing grades do not always establish the provision of FAPE, failing grades do not always indict a school district. The amount of appropriate regular education progress, in terms of passing grades and grade-to-grade advancement, necessarily depends upon the abilities of each individual student with a disability. *Carter v. Florence County Sch. Dist. Four*, 18 IDELR 350 (4th Cir. 1991), *aff'd* 20 IDELR 532 (1993).

> [S]ome children, due to the extent of their handicaps, will never be able to perform at grade level and will require several years to achieve what would be to a non-handicapped child a year's worth of progress. ... [P]assing marks and annual grade promotion are important to the [IDEA], but a child's ability or inability to achieve such marks and progress does not automatically resolve the inquiry where the 'free appropriate public education' requirement is concerned, and to the extent that the district court, in dicta, invested passing marks and annual grade advancement with more significance than the *Rowley* Court, those dicta must yield to the language and logic of the *Rowley* opinion.

Conklin ex rel. Conklin v. Anne Arundel County Bd. of Educ., 18 IDELR 197, 202 (4th Cir. 1991).

11. What are "measurable" annual goals?

When an annual goal is measurable, there exist objective criteria under which one can determine if a student with a disability has achieved the goal. Conversely, when there are only subjective criteria available to assess achievement, an annual goal is not measurable. Neither are goals that are broad, generic or vague.

The IDEA compels recitation of "measurable" annual goals in the IEP of a student with a disability. Under 34 C.F.R. § 300.347(a)(2)(i) of the IDEA regulations the IEP of a student with a disability must include "[a] statement of *measurable* annual goals, including benchmarks or short-term

4 : 9

objectives[.]" The regulations do not define what particular gloss the word "measurable" adds to the requirement. Nor does Appendix A.

Nor did the prior regulations (or the related Appendix C), come to think of it. The explicit requirement that IEP annual goals be measurable was, in fact, added to the statute and regulations by the 1997 IDEA Amendments. Under the prior law (at 34 C.F.R. § 300.346(a)(5) and Appendix C, Questions 37, 38 and 39) only short-term instructional objectives — the component parts of annual goals — had to be "measurable."

Even so, prior to enactment of the 1997 IDEA Amendments the issue of how to determine whether a student's IEP contained appropriate goals involved in many instances assessing the amount of progress the student had made toward the goals contained in the IEP. For this reason, some published decisions under the prior law turned on whether the goals included in the student's IEP were measurable, by some objective criteria. The clearly written opinion issued by the District Court for the Southern District of New York in *Evans v. Board of Education of Rhinebeck Central School District*, 24 IDELR 338 (S.D.N.Y. 1996) in connection with the goals set out in several years' IEPs for a student with a learning disability is a good example.

That said, a post-1997 IDEA Amendments administrative decision illustrates when annual goals are "measurable" under the current law. The hearing officer in *Windsor C-1 School District*, 29 IDELR 170 (SEA Mo. 1998) held that the school district had formulated the student's IEP goals on the basis of evaluation by objective criteria. As a result, they were measurable.

The student in *Windsor C-1 School District*, was a 6-year-old boy diagnosed as having Asperger's Syndrome and classified as Other Health-Impaired for purposes of eligibility under the IDEA. The seven goals in his IEP addressed a variety of behavioral and emotional issues.[7] The district managed in almost each instance to formulate the goal in terms of an objective standard to evaluate progress. We set out the goals below, italicizing the language that makes each goal "measurable," for purposes of compliance with 34 C.F.R. § 300.347(a)(2)(i).

- Student will develop appropriate school-related behaviors *by at least one standard score when measured on the BES behavior Rating Scale by three teachers working with Student.*

- Student will develop and use appropriate interaction skills.

- Student will develop solutions options *by at least one standard score when measured in the area of interpersonal difficulties on the BES Behavior Rating Scale by three teachers working with Student.*

- Student will use language for a variety of pragmatic functions in spontaneous language *to be evaluated through the use of tape recorders and video taping. Pre and post evaluations will occur in order to measure improvement.*

- Student will develop visual motor skills *by increasing his ability level from 5 years, 7 months to 6 years, 7 months on the test of visual motor skills.*

- Student will improve his motor skills *by raising his basal level by 10 months when measured on the Peabody Developmental Motor Scale.*

- Student will develop behaviors that enhance self-concept by increasing the areas of physical symptoms/fears and unhappiness/depression *by at least one standard score to be measured on the BES Behavior Rating Scale by at least three teachers working with Student.*

Another 1998 administrative decision, *Blacklick Valley School District*, 28 IDELR 896 (SEA Pa. 1998), shows exactly what *not* to do. The annual goal for reading in the IEP for a 9-year-old student with a learning disability was "increase reading skill." Vague, generic, and "woefully short" of legal standards, the review panel opined in a finding that the school district has denied the student FAPE.

12. Must the IEP of a student with a disability who participates in the general curriculum include goals other than making progress therein?

Not in all cases. To the extent a student with a disability has additional disability-related educational needs, the student's IEP must identify goals and offer special education and related services to address them.

IDEA regulations at 34 C.F.R. § 300.347(a)(2) provide that a statement of measurable annual goals, including benchmarks or short-term objectives, must be included in the IEP of a student with a disability. To comply with federal requirements the goals in each student's IEP must include goals addressing two distinct types of educational needs. Specifically, goals must be related to both:

- Meeting the student's needs that result from the student's disability to enable the student to be involved in and progress in the general curriculum (34 C.F.R. § 300.347(a)(2)(i)); and

- Meeting each of the [student's] "other educational needs" that result from the [student's] disability (34 C.F.R. § 300.347(a)(2)(ii)).

DOE has not addressed with any specificity what bona fide educational needs not related to progress in the general curriculum should be considered disability-related "other educational needs" for a student with a disability participating in the general curriculum.

Under the prior law educators were often called upon to decide whether a particular student's need for services or programming not related to progress in the general curriculum were educational, as opposed to familial, social or medical. There is no reason to conclude that legislators intended to change the law governing analysis of students' needs in this regard. Consider, just for purposes of illustration, the decision of the hearing officer in *Houston Independent School District*, 30 IDELR 321 (SEA Tex. 1999). All concerned parties therein agreed that the primary educational need of an 11-year-old student with Asperger's syndrome was the promotion of more appropriate, less distressing social interaction.

13. If the IEP of a student with a disability does not contain measurable annual goals has the school district denied the student FAPE?

Not always. It depends upon the extent to which the defect in the IEP's statement of goals directly relates to a failure to provide needed special education and related services to the student with a disability.

Measurable annual goals are a required component of IEPs for students with disabilities. 34 C.F.R. § 300.347(a)(2). Ergo, failure to include them violates the IDEA. *See, e.g., In re Sara P.*, EHLR 401:260 (SEA Wash. 1988) (IEP that contained neither specific annual goals nor instructional objectives was legally inadequate and fatally defective).

When a school district fails to include a statement of measurable annual goals in a student's IEP, there is reason to suspect it also may have failed to provide the special education and related services required by a disabled student to meaningfully benefit from his education. In addition, the district has not created a standard by which to measure the student's educational progress to see if he has, indeed, received a benefit.

In the real world, though, some school district failures to articulate measurable annual goals in a student's IEP should be interpreted as a technical defect in draftsmanship rather than a violation of the law. The school district does not get an "A" in IEP writing. Nonetheless, it has not fallen woefully short in meeting its obligations to the student to provide FAPE, either. As the hearing officer in *Salem-Keizer School District #24J*, 23 IDELR 922 (SEA Or. 1996) perceptively observed:

Perfection is not the standard for reviewing an IEP's statements of current performance, goals and objectives. There are frequently some ambiguities in or omissions from those elements. They do not necessarily result in a failure to provide a FAPE to the child.

23 IDELR at 928.

The following are among the decisions in LRP Publications' database in which a school district's failure to include annual goals (in accordance with either the 1997 IDEA Amendments or the prior law's IEP requirements at 34 C.F.R. § 300.346(a)(2)) was not a denial of FAPE:

- *Pomona Unified Sch. Dist.*, 30 IDELR 158 (SEA Cal. 1998): The hearing officer held that even accepting as true the parents' allegations that the student's IEP failed to include statements of present levels of performance and measurable annual goals related to preacademic/academic skills, that was not enough to prevail. The parents failed to offer evidence demonstrating that the alleged procedural violations resulted in a loss of educational opportunity to the student. The parents' claims were accordingly rejected.

- *Board of Educ. of the Jericho Union Free Sch. Dist.*, 29 IDELR 135 (SEA N.Y. 1998): The proposed IEP did not include objectives for achieving the student's science goals. Nonetheless, the review officer concluded that the proposed IEP offered FAPE to the student. The short-term objectives reflected the annual goals and were adequately stated. In addition, the academic support and counseling services called for in the IEP were appropriate.

- *Board of Educ. of the City Sch. Dist. of the City of Ithaca*, 28 IDELR 71 (SEA Pa. 1998): Although the IEP lacked a means for measuring the student's progress, this omission was not significant enough to invalidate the IEP. The annual goals were designed to improve the student's weaknesses in reading, writing and study skills and the related objectives. The services offered under the IEP were designed to address the student's special education needs, and the placement was the student's LRE. Overall, the IEP was designed to provide the student with educational benefit.

Endnotes

[1]   *See, e.g.*, Torrance (CA) Unified Sch. Dist., 24 IDELR 391 (OCR, Region IX 1995).

[2]   Interestingly, ten years earlier a special education due process hearing officer was more tentative. The hearing officer in Plymouth-Carver Public Schools, EHLR 508:284 (SEA Mass. 1986) opined that a grade weighting system which relegated all special needs courses to the lowest weight assignable (to wit: number 1 on a scale of 1 to 6) "may well discriminate against handicapped students, and as such, contravenes the dictates of Section 504."

[3]   See *Access the General Curriculum with a Standards-Referenced IEP*, THE SPECIAL EDUCATOR®, vol. 15, iss. 11 (Dec. 13, 1999).

[4]   JAY P. HEUBERT, ROBERT M. HAUSER, EDS., HIGH STAKES: TESTING FOR TRACKING, PROMOTION, AND GRADUATION 193 (National Academy Press 1999).

[5]   The author uses the term "good grades" loosely to mean a report card with mostly As and Bs. (Harking back to the author's own high school humiliations, a poor grade in gym doesn't count.)

[6]   "Students are often passed from grade to grade regardless of whether they have mastered required material and are academically prepared to do the work at the next level. This practice is called social promotion. ... This situation is unacceptable for students, teachers, employers, and taxpayers." Presidential Directive dated February 23, 1998, included in "Taking Responsibility for Ending Social Promotion: A Guide for Educators and State and Local Leaders," DOE May 1999 (page 1).

[7]   In this regard, it is important to emphasize that the regulations do not limit the requirement that goals be measurable to goals relating to academic success or participation in the general curriculum.

Chapter 5

REGULAR EDUCATION REPORT CARDS AND IEP REPORT CARDS FOR STUDENTS WITH DISABILITIES

Report Cards

1. Is there such a thing as an IEP report card?

Yes, although there is no specific kind of document identified as "an IEP report card" in either the statute or the regulations. The 1997 IDEA Amendments enacted a new requirement for provision of written information to parents about students' progress toward IEP goals and objectives. The term "IEP Report Card" was used with reference to that requirement in congressional committee reports accompanying the bills that ultimately became the new legislation.

IDEA regulations at 34 C.F.R. § 300.347(a)(7)(ii), a verbatim recapitulation of new statutory requirement 20 U.S.C. § 1414(d)(1)(A)(viii), establish the parental right to receive regular reports about the progress their child is making in special education. The regulations provide that a student's IEP must include among the required disclosures a statement concerning:

(ii) How the child's parents will be regularly informed (through such means as periodic report cards), at least as often as parents are informed of their nondisabled children's progress, of —

(A) Their child's progress toward the annual goals; and

(B) The extent to which that progress is sufficient to enable the child to achieve the goals by the end of the year.

The legislative committee report explained why Congress brought the issue of how to report progress to the IEP table. In so doing it coined the term "IEP report card."

The Committee believes that informing parents of children with disabilities as often as other parents will, in fact, reduce the cost of informing parents of children with disabilities and will facilitate more useful feedback on their child's performance. One method recommended by the committee would be providing an IEP report card with the general education report card, if the latter is appropriate and provided for the child.[1]

Note that production of a unique document called an IEP report card is not a regulatory requirement. It is merely one possible way that a school district may provide parents the documentation of progress toward IEP goals required by 34 C.F.R. § 300.347(a)(7)(ii).[2]

In the unlikely event a school district elected to conduct regular in-person IEP team meetings in order to comply with 34 C.F.R. § 300.347(a)(7)(ii), it could do so. But thankfully, multiple IEP meetings each year are not required.

The statute and regulations make clear that a written report is sufficient, although in some instances, an agency may decide that a meeting with the parents (which does not have to be an IEP meeting) would be a more effective means of communication.[3]

If a school district violates the law, though, it may not have a choice. Issued prior to the regulations, the decision of the federal district court in *Corey H. v. Board of Education of the City of Chicago*, 27 IDELR 688 (N.D. Ill. 1998) ordered both production of IEP report cards *and* meetings with parents in all cases. The court specifically directed the large urban school district to distribute "IEP Report Cards" at the same time as general report cards and to discuss them with the parents twice each year on report card pick-up days. In addition, whenever a teacher believed changes in the student's IEP should be considered, a notice to the parents calling for a future IEP conference date had to be included with the IEP Report Card.

2. What specific information about a student's progress toward IEP goals must be provided in order to meet the IDEA's progress reporting requirement?

Federal law dictates neither the form nor the precise content of the documentation of progress toward IEP goals. Those decisions rest within the discretion of states, local school districts, and educators, based upon the individual circumstances of each particular student with a disability.

As a threshold matter, a student's IEP team decides how progress toward the annual goals identified in a student's IEP will be measured. 34 C.F.R. § 300.347(a)(7)(i). By extension, it is the student's IEP team that must decide what type of reporting will adequately inform the parents of the student's progress toward his individual goals.

Nonetheless, Congress proposed some possible alternatives for reporting progress in committee reports accompanying the legislation. "An IEP report card could also be made more useful by including checkboxes or equivalent options that enable the parents and the special educator to review and judge the performance of the child." Congress made it clear, however, that any example posited was just that: an example, "not intended to indicate the committee's preference for a single means of compliance with this requirement."[4]

Responding to concerns that the new IDEA reporting requirements necessarily entailed turning school district officials into full-time report-writers, DOE provided reassurance that "detailed written narratives" are not required so long as district reports provide parents "sufficient information" to apprise them of the two items set out in 34 C.F.R. § 300.347(a)(7)(ii)(A) and (B)(as shown in Question 1).[5]

In *Corey H. v. Board of Education of the City of Chicago*, 27 IDELR 688 (N.D. Ill. 1998) the court propounded detailed directives about actions the school district and the state (as the entity ultimately responsible for the school district) were required to take to comply with the IDEA. Finding systemic violations, the court ordered the state to submit a compliance plan addressing the progress reporting requirement of 34 C.F.R. § 300.347(a)(7)(ii). Adopting the terminology of the IDEA legislative history, the court ordered the school district to develop "IEP report cards." The court expanded the content requirement for progress reports beyond that of the statute and the regulations by requiring reporting of the student's progress in meeting his or her IEP annual goals, and the extent to which the special education and supports identified on the IEP are being provided.

3. How often must a school district provide progress reports on IEP goals to parents?

The IDEA sets a floor, tied to the standards established by each school district for progress reporting about nondisabled students.

Under the IDEA parents of students with disabilities must be "regularly informed" of whether a student's progress toward his annual goals is proceeding at a pace that will enable the student to achieve those goals by the end of the school year. The IDEA regulations at 34 C.F.R. § 300.347(a)(7)(ii) appear to establish a safe harbor for determining when a district has "regularly informed" parents. That section states that a student's IEP must include a statement of "[h]ow the child's parents will be regularly informed (through such means as periodic report cards), at least as often as parents are informed of their nondisabled children's progress ..."

DOE comments accompanying the publication of IDEA final regulations also seem to state that providing progress reports no less frequently than general education report cards will always satisfy the IDEA regulatory requirement. "With respect to the frequency of reporting, the statute and regulations are both clear that the parents of a child with a disability must be regularly informed of their child's progress at least as often as parents are informed of their nondisabled children's progress."[6]

But such an interpretation is inconsistent with the "individual needs" mantra of the IDEA. A school district should not feel comfortable relying on that small snippet of regulatory language to relieve itself of the need to determine on an individual basis how frequently progress reports must be provided to the parents of a disabled student. More frequent reporting may be appropriate for some students with disabilities. *See, e.g., Kankakee Sch. Dist. 111*, 30 IDELR 497 (SEA Ill. 1999) (school district provided weekly progress reports to the parents of an 11-year-old student with a learning disability, with each report showing work done by the student during the week); *Harford County (MD) Pub. Schs.*, 28 IDELR 488 (OCR, Region III 1997) (IEP for a high school student with an unspecified disability required provision of a progress report to the student's parents every two weeks); and *Spring-Ford Area Sch. Dist.*, 27 IDELR 1083 (SEA Pa. 1997) (IEP team for a 16-year-old student with pervasive developmental disorder met monthly to review student's progress).

4. Must a school district's IEP report card address a disabled student's performance in regular education classes for which he needs only modifications or accommodations to participate in the general curriculum?

It would appear not. According to DOE, the IDEA parental progress reporting requirements do not encompass everything about the participation of students with disabilities in the general curriculum. Only those aspects of the student's performance relating to his need for special education or related services are reportable. The reasoning supporting that conclusion is the following.

First, school districts must regularly inform parents of the progress toward the annual goals set out in the IEPs of students with disabilities in accordance with 34 C.F.R. § 300.347(a)(2). 34 C.F.R. § 300.347(a)(7)(ii).

Second, the annual goals in a student's IEP do not have to address all areas of the general curriculum, only those areas in which the child's involvement and progress are affected by the student's disability. As explained by DOE in Question 4 of Appendix A:

A public agency is not required to include in an IEP annual goals that relate to areas of the general curriculum in which the child's disability does not affect the child's ability to be involved in and progress in the general curriculum. If a child with a disability needs only modifications or accommodations in order to progress in an area of the general curriculum, the IEP does not need to include a goal for that area [.]

As a result, Section 300.347(a)(2)(ii) does not compel school districts to regularly inform parents of the progress students with disabilities are making in the general curriculum when the student is participating without special education or related services.

Q.E.D.

Despite this flawless logic, do not be surprised if some parents assert that a student's IEP must include goals related to all aspects of a student's participation in the general curriculum. They will likely argue that the position taken by DOE in Appendix A is an overly restrictive interpretation of the statutory and regulatory provisions concerning IEP goals.

The decision of the hearing officer in *Daleville City Board of Education*, 28 IDELR 144 (SEA Ala. 1998) illustrates the potential for confusion about what kind of goals related to progress in the general curriculum must be included in the IEP of a student with a disability. The student in this instance was a fourth-grader with an emotional disturbance and ADD. She was placed in a resource room for 10 hours a week with instruction in English and reading; otherwise she was educated in the regular education class-room. The student's instruction was based upon use of regular fourth-grade reading, English and spelling materials. All math instruction took place in the regular education classroom.

The student received various classroom modifications to accommodate her disabilities. But she did not receive any special education or related services related to progressing in the general curriculum.

Under these circumstances should the school district have included mastery of the state's entire fourth-grade Course of Study as an IEP goal for this student? The school district thought so, but the hearing officer did not. She concluded that the goal totally failed to be individualized, as required in an "individualized educational program." Because the IEP team had determined that the student did not need "specially designed instruction" to meet her unique needs in this respect, the goal was in no way individualized for the student, as required by the IDEA.

5. May a school district use regular education letter grades to report to parents the progress a student with a disability is making toward annual goals?

Although the IDEA requires regular reporting of progress toward IEP goals, the specifics of implementation are left to states and school districts. 34 C.F.R. § 300.347(a)(7)(ii). Nevertheless, in discussion accompanying the publication of IDEA final regulations DOE indicated that it is less than enthralled with the idea of using letter grades as short-hand for a coherent statement of a student's special education progress.

> Requiring a 'detailed written narrative' of how a child is progressing toward meeting IEP objectives, as suggested by a commenter, could add an unnecessary burden. However, the commenter's concern about using a grade to designate a child' progress in meeting the IEP objectives in some cases may be valid because a grade does not always lend itself to sufficiently describing progress toward the annual goals.[7]

Congressional committee reports suggested, however, that an alternative grade-like system clearly passes muster.

> An example [of a compliant progress report] would be to state a goal or benchmark on the IEP report card and rank it on a multipoint continuum. The goal might be, 'Ted will demonstrate effective literal comprehension.' The ranking system would then state the following, as indicated by a checkbox: No progress; some progress; good progress; almost complete; completed.[8]

6. Can a school district provide information about progress toward IEP goals as part of the regular education report card issued to the parents of a student with a disability?

Yes. The IDEA does not prohibit including the information required by 34 C.F.R. § 300.347(a)(7) in regular education report cards.

In comments accompanying the publication of IDEA final regulations, DOE indicated that a school district could use report cards to provide information to parents about a student's IEP goal progress. Responding to commenters who complained that it would be burdensome to require school districts to design, produce and distribute new "progress reports," DOE opined as follows:

> Under the statute and regulations, the manner in which that requirement [to provide information about the student's progress in meeting annual goals] is implemented is left to the discretion of each State. Therefore a State could elect to ensure that report cards used for children with disabilities contain information about each child's progress toward meeting the child's IEP goals, as suggested by commenters, but would not be required to do so.[9]

The author wonders, however, if Section 504 is implicated if a school district chooses to append an IEP progress report to the regular education report cards of students with disabilities.

The basis for that concern is the discussion of disability discrimination in connection with the issuance of report cards contained in *Tennessee Department of Education*, 24 IDELR 1046 (OCR, Region IV 1996). In that LOF the parent objected to the state Department of Education's use of student management software programs that produced report cards for local school districts which identified the grade level for nondisabled students, but identified all students with disabilities as "non-graded."

This distinction was differential treatment that discriminated on the basis of disability in violation of Section 504, the parent alleged. Overcoming the jurisdictional objection interposed by the state, OCR opined as an initial matter that the production and distribution of report cards was a covered activity for purposes of triggering the prohibition on the basis of disability in programs and activities of state agencies receiving Federal financial assistance.

In this particular instance, though, that was as far as OCR had to go in its official legal analysis. The parties entered into a resolution agreement under which the state department of education agreed that the code "non-graded" would no longer be used to identify grade level for students with disabilities. Nonetheless, the lesson to be taken away from the LOF is that school districts need to proceed carefully in creating different report cards for disabled and nondisabled students.

As further support of the author's reservations about including an IEP report card in the regular education report card, OCR's interpretation of Section 504 with respect to coding high school transcripts to indicate modified curriculum set out in *Letter to Runkel*, 25 IDELR 387 (OCR, Region VIII 1996), is pertinent.

> The [state] bulletin [submitted for review by OCR] response indicating that modifications or exceptions to the grading scale may be identified on the academic transcript as long as grades and courses of all students, and not just students with disabilities, are similarly treated is generally correct. For example, if the modification code system covers enhanced or greater difficulty course-work completed by gifted and talented program students as well as students taking remedial courses, it may not necessarily violate Section 504 or Title II to also include special education courses. The key will be to determine if the modification identification tends to focus on students with disabilities as a category. If it does, it strongly suggests that it may be prohibited under Section 504 or Title II.

25 IDELR at 389.

7. What remedies are available to parents if a school district does not regularly inform them of the student's progress toward IEP goals?

There is no specific statutory or regulatory remedy. Presumably, a judicial or administrative decision-maker is empowered to select an appropriate remedy, consistent with the IDEA and tailored to the specific circumstances.

Under IDEA regulations at 34 C.F.R. § 300.347(a)(7)(ii), a school district's commitment to provide regular updates to parents about the progress their child is making toward achieving yearly IEP goals is a part of the student's IEP. Applying long-standing IDEA principles one may conclude that a failure to inform is a failure to provide services promised in the IEP and is, for that reason, a denial of FAPE. But periodic updates to parents are not services (or special education or modifications) provided to the student or on his behalf, so that approach seems to be a stretch.

An alternative approach would be to treat the requirement as akin to the procedural safeguards afforded parents under 34 C.F.R. § 300.345 and Subpart E (34 C.F.R. §§ 300.500-300.517). This was the approach taken by the state department of education in *Beaverton School District*, 30 IDELR 740 (SEA Or. 1999), discussed in greater detail below.

Procedural safeguards are required under the IDEA to ensure that parents are knowledgeable about important decisions that school districts make. There is no doubt that a school district's failure to afford procedural protections may be a denial of FAPE. *See, e.g., Gadsby by Gadsby v. Grasmick*, 25 IDELR 621 (4th Cir. 1997); *Tennessee Dep't of Health & Mental Retardation v. Paul B.*, 24 IDELR 452 (6th Cir.1996).

Whether one views the notice requirement of 34 C.F.R. § 300.347(a)(7)(ii) as a substantive or a procedural right, the appropriate remedy for failure to provide notice as agreed in the IEP is a decision left to the individual decision-maker. Following the judicial guidelines promulgated by the Supreme Court in *Burlington School Commission v. Massachusetts Department of Education*, 1984-85 EHLR 556:389 (1985),[10] that decision-maker surely will consider the degree to which the district's failure to provide progress reports resulted in a denial of FAPE.

In resolving a complaint filed and processed in accordance with the procedures set out in 34 C.F.R. §§ 300.660-300.662 a state department of education weighed the equities and found their proper balance supported the school district. The resulting written decision, published as *Beaverton School District*, 30 IDELR 740 (SEA Or. 1999), appears to be the first published decision of any stripe concerning the appropriate remedy for a school district's failure to regularly inform parents of their child's progress toward the goals established in his IEP. In this instance, the school district had not provided to the parent of a 7-year-old student with autism written progress reports on IEP goals as frequently as it issued report cards.

The state reviewer found from the evidence, however, that the district "appeared" to have otherwise kept the parent apprised of the student's progress toward meeting the goals set forth in his IEP. In addition, the reviewer amassed and evaluated evidence that led him to conclude the district had otherwise met its obligations under the IDEA.[11] Taking both these evidentiary findings into account, the reviewer concluded that the district's failure to provide periodic reports did not interfere with the provision of appropriate services to the student. No compensatory education was required; the only relief which was due was the implementation of a corrective action plan by the district to ensure that parents would be informed of their child's IEP progress in a timely manner.

8. Does the use of different report cards for students in special education classes or facilities violate Section 504?

Only in the most limited of circumstances may a school district use a different report card for students in self-contained programs. Otherwise, the school district must use the same report card form as it would use if the student were not disabled.

In *Saddleback Valley (CA) Unified School District*, 17 EHLR 251 (OCR, Region IX 1990) OCR opined that 34 C.F.R. § 104.4(b)(1)(iii) governed the use of different report cards for students with disabilities and required that school districts provide disabled students and their parents/guardians with a reporting/evaluation system that is as effective in conveying information as that provided to nondisabled students and their parents. The alternate reporting must also be provided as frequently as the district issues report cards for regular education students.

The *Saddleback Valley* LOF itself concerned allegations by parents of students placed at a special education school that the district failed to provide regular report cards or progress evaluations. While the complaint was resolved by a settlement, OCR acknowledged that severely disabled children could have unique needs that make the use of report cards and progress reports used in other schools ineffective or irrelevant. In such an instance, a school district's use of an alternate reporting system to provide evaluative information to a parent that is at least equivalent to the information in a report card or progress report, and provided with at least the same frequency, is consistent with Section 504.

9. May a transcript identify a student as having taken special education classes?

No. Students with disabilities can't be identified on a categorical basis. That is discrimination. Identification of special education coursework completed by a student with a disability is another issue. "Where ... a designation for a special education course is shown to be based on a difference in course content, rather than the manner in which the course is taught, such designations do not rise to the level of a violation of Section 504 and the ADA." *Ann Arbor (MI) Pub. Sch. Dist*, 30 IDELR 405 (OCR, Region XII 1998). OCR expects that will be the case only in "limited circumstances."

The issue of disclosure of a student's status as disabled is at its most sensitive when a disabled student who has participated in regular education classes with an individually designed modified curriculum intends to continue his education. It may not always be in the best interest of a college-bound disabled student to minimize the impact of his disability or his disability-related needs. Specifically, students with disabilities may want to establish previous receipt of requested college-level accommodations. See chapter 3 in this regard. But when a disabled student is applying to colleges, the more discreet the transcript, the better. Or at least that is the position taken by many parents.

OCR's extended discussion in *Letter to Runkel*, 25 IDELR 387, 388 (OCR, Region VIII 1996) of what should — and should not — be revealed on the high school transcript of a student who has had a modified curriculum in a regular education class is explained in detail below. Cautioning that there was at that time no "definitive standards enunciated in any court or OCR decision," OCR made several suggestions, all with the qualification that state and local law and usage need to be taken into account.

With regard to course names or labels:

- It is better to use terms that can be applied to remedial courses taken by both disabled and nondisabled students, such as "basic," "level I" or "practical," rather than identify a course as "special education."

- Terms that are also used in connection with "at risk" students, who need not be students with disabilities, should be acceptable by virtue of the same reasoning. Nevertheless, OCR advises districts "carefully review" their use of terms such as "L.C. [learning center]," "H.B. [homebound instruction]," "resource room," or "S.O.S. [special opportunity school]."

- Going in the other direction, terms that are used for the gifted and talented program, such as "independent study" or "modified curriculum," could also be used to identify modified programming provided for special education students.

With regard to grades:

- Asterisks or other symbols or codes may be used to indicate a modification or exception to the generally applicable grading scale, provided the symbols or codes are also used for nondisabled students who are also exceptions to the scale on another basis. A best bet for use of such a system might be if it is used for both special education and enhanced or greater difficulty course work.

Overall, in *Letter to Runkel*, OCR appeared to suggest that a course label or designation that is used only for special education programs may not pass muster. "The key will be to determine if the modification identification tends to focus on students with disabilities as a category. If it does, it strongly suggests that it may be prohibited under Section 504 or Title II." 25 IDELR at 389.

But not always! Two years later, in *Ann Arbor (MI) Public School District*, 30 IDELR 405 (OCR, Region XII 1998) OCR approved a school district's use of the unique terminology to identify courses with modified curriculum offered to students with disabilities.

The school district adopted the term "ILC" to identify classes taken by special education students only and also used different terms (AC) for accelerated course and (AP) for advanced placement to indicate courses with enhanced or advanced curriculum requirements. Even though the term ILC focused exclusively on students with disabilities, OCR found its use was legitimate and nondiscriminatory because it reflected the markedly reduced mastery requirements of the ILC English and math courses. The ILC English course covered only about half of the textbook and students were required to read less than half the number of books read by the regular education students. The ILC math course covered only about 30 percent of the material contained in the textbook used by the regular math class. In addition, simpler math concepts covered in ILC math, such as making change for a dollar, were not addressed in the regular education math course.

10. Must a school district provide prior notice of the disability-related information it displays on students' academic transcripts?

Yes. While the decision to include disability-related information in students' transcripts is within the sole discretion of the school district, parents and students have the right to disclosure of just what that information is.

The Family Educational Rights and Privacy Act (FERPA) governs the disclosure of the education records of both disabled and nondisabled students. Generally speaking, a school district must obtain the permission of the student (or his parent) prior to disclosing the student's transcript to a third party, such as a prospective employer. 34 C.F.R. § 99.30. There is no explicit "informed consent" requirement in FERPA; the records to be released must be identified, but the content of the records need not be itemized.

In some instances prior consent to disclosure is not required. FERPA regulations at 34 C.F.R. § 99.31(a)(2) allow release of a student's academic transcript to "officials of another school, school system, or institution of postsecondary education where the student seeks or intends to enroll" without prior consent when the district takes the actions set out in 34 C.F.R. § 99.34. That section, in turns, requires that the district give parents prior notice of the intent to release, a copy of the transcript and an opportunity to challenge the transcript. Again, there is no requirement for an explanation of any symbols or legends that identify the student as having received special education programming.

In *Letter to Runkel*, 25 IDELR 387 (OCR, Region VIII 1996) OCR goes one step further, stating that parents or students "must know what is on the transcript and give written consent 'specific to the information sent.'"

Awards

11. Can a school district exclude students with disabilities from recognition on the honor roll?

Across-the-board exclusion of students with disabilities is discrimination on the basis of disability in violation of Section 504 and the ADA. However, a school district may under some circumstances establish an honor roll policy that forecloses recognition of students with disabilities.

Exclusion from the honor roll on a categorical basis violates Section 504 and its implementing regulations at 34 C.F.R. §§ 104.4(a) and 104.37(a). "Grades earned by students with disabilities cannot categorically be disregarded or excluded, even if earned with the support of special education standards services." *Letter to Runkel*, 25 IDELR 387, 389 (OCR, Region VIII 1996). *See also Letter to Ickes*, EHLR 305:50 (OCR 1989) (categorization of courses based solely on the status or classification of the students enrolled could violate Section 504).

Notwithstanding the above, a school district may establish eligibility standards that will recognize levels of academic excellence that some students with disabilities will never be able to achieve. "OCR will not find a violation of Section 504 when academic distinctions are made on a nondiscriminatory basis, i.e., when objective criteria, closely related to the purpose of the program, are applied to all students equally, without regard to handicap." *Letter to Ickes*, EHLR 305:50 (OCR 1989). Or, as expressed by OCR in *Letter to Runkel*, 25 IDELR 387, 389 (OCR, Region VIII 1996), an honor roll policy that is neutral on its face and based on valid educational standards is not discriminatory.

OCR's resolution of a parental complaint about a student's failure to be included on the honor roll in *Prince William County (VA) School District*, 25 IDELR 538 (OCR Region III 1996) illustrates the general principles set out above. The honor roll policy at the student's elementary school required grade-level performance and achievement of specified letter grades. The parent alleged that this policy discriminated against her son, who she claimed was prevented from meeting the standards because of his disability. In response to the parent's complaint, OCR examined the elementary school's written honor roll policy and concluded it was not discriminatory on its face. Since the student was not performing at grade level in one of his classes, he failed to meet the eligibility requirements for honor roll.

12. Can a school district's honor roll policy exclude grades earned by students with disabilities taking special education or modified general curriculum courses?

No. "Grades earned by students with disabilities cannot categorically be disregarded or excluded, even if earned with the support of special education services." *Letter to Runkel*, 25 IDELR 387, 389 (OCR, Region VIII 1996). Other options to accomplish the same objective have been endorsed by OCR, however.

Alternative award systems that parallel alternative grading systems may be acceptable, according to OCR in *Fort Smith (AR) Public School*, 20 IDELR 97 (OCR, Region VI 1993).

The school district in *Fort Smith* had a two-track grading system. All nondisabled students were graded based on mastery of the general curriculum and in competition with each other ("competitive grades"). On the other hand, the grading method used for a student with a disability was determined by the student's IEP team and delineated in the student's individualized education plan. Specifically, the IEP team decided among three possibilities when determining the grading system to be used for a disabled student. If the student participated in the general curriculum without any modification he received a competitive grade. Similarly, if the student required "mechanical modifications" (e.g., a reader, extended time for exams) he also earned a competitive grade. But if the student required major content modifications on account of his disability, he received an "ability/effort grade."

When the Fort Smith school district established its honor roll system for high schools and junior high schools its objective was to recognize academic achievement. For this reason, students were required to achieve a 3.0 or better GPA to be placed on the honor roll. Competitive grades were considered; ability/effort grades were not. Further, a student with a disability who was graded in even one course on the basis of ability/effort could not be considered for the honor roll, even if he had earned a 3.0 or better GPA in his competitively graded courses.

In finding that the school district had violated Section 504, OCR started its reasoning by acknowledging that sure and certain exclusion of some students with disabilities from the honor roll may serve the educationally sound purpose of recognizing high academic achievement. But then it went on as follows:

> [E]xcluding a group of enrolled students only because of their classification can violate Section 504. In this case, only students with disabilities are graded according to ability/effort. The 66 students with disabilities who were graded according to ability/effort achieved a GPA of 3.0 or higher, but were not eligible for the district's honor roll. Consequently, the 66 students' opportunity to be placed on the honor roll was restricted by their not being on a competitive grading system. The [school district] provided no alternative opportunity to earn honors or awards reflecting their efforts and achievements. Therefore, these 66 students with disabilities were not given an opportunity to earn honors and awards reflecting their efforts and achievements because ability/effort grading precluded them from eligibility.

20 IDELR at 98.

Although OCR thus concluded that the honor roll policy adopted by the school district denied students with disabilities an equal opportunity to participate in an awards program in violation of 34 C.F.R. § 104.4(a), (b)(1)(i), (ii), OCR did not order the school district to consider ability/effort grades or even the competitive grades of students with disabilities earning ability/effort grades when selecting students for the honor roll. Instead, OCR approved a voluntary settlement under which the school district was permitted to continue its honor roll program, provided it also establish an alternate program under which students with disabilities whose opportunity for honor roll placement was restricted by ability/effort grading could earn honors and awards on the basis of their efforts and achievement.

In *Letter to Runkel*, 25 IDELR 387 (OCR Region VIII 1996) OCR suggested two other ways a district can elect to honor high academic achievement without discriminating against students with disabilities. One of the possibilities, using a system of weighted grades, is discussed in Question 13. The other involves a school district establishing a list of "core courses" which must be completed in order to be eligible for honor roll recognition.

13. Can a district use a system of weighted grades in an honor roll program?

In *Letter to Runkel*, 25 IDELR 387 (OCR Region VIII 1996) OCR gave a qualified "yes," endorsing and giving an example of what it termed an "uncomplicated system of weighted grades." In essence, weighted grades convert course grades to numeric points based upon the difficulty of the subject matter and the grade received. OCR posited this example: An "A" earned in advanced algebra may be rated worth 5 points in a student's over-all honors competition compared with another "A" in basic arithmetic given a weight of only one point. One obvious advantage of this system is that it should not discourage brighter students from taking more challenging courses. A "B" or even a "C" earned in a tougher course can still be worth more points for purposes of academic comparisons than an "A" in a less challenging subject.

According to OCR such a system will pass muster under Section 504 and Title II of the ADA under the following circumstances:

- The weighting system is based on objective rating criteria.

- Each subject or course is individually analyzed and assigned a "degree of difficulty factor based upon its individual contents." OCR will look askance at a system in which all special education courses have lower grade weights. Such a result has the odor of arbitrariness. *See, e.g., Plymouth-Carver (MA) Regional School District*, EHLR 353:134 (OCR, Region I

1988) (weighted grading system which assigned lowest weight (number 1 on a scale of 1 to 6) to all special education courses discriminates on the basis of disability).

• The system is fair and simple to understand.

14. Must a school district include letter grades earned by students in special education or modified general curriculum courses in schoolwide or districtwide GPA standings?

Generally yes, letter grades earned by students with disabilities that do not reflect performance in the general curriculum have to be included in GPA standings nonetheless. OCR will consider categorical exclusion as discrimination on the basis of disability. However, school districts have the same options to exclude or discount such grades in connection with honor roll recognition. OCR makes no legal distinction between ranking students by GPA (used, for example, to determine eligibility for college scholarships) and determining which students will be identified on a school's honor roll. *Letter to Runkel*, 25 IDELR 387 (OCR Region VIII 1996).

Endnotes

[1]   S. Rep. No. 105-17, 105th Cong., 1st Sess. 22 (1997); H.R. Rep. No. 105-95, 105th Cong., 1st Sess. 102 (1997).

[2]   But see Question 6 with regard to including information about progress toward IEP goals on the regular education reports issued to both students with disabilities and non-disabled students.

[3]   64 *Fed. Reg.* 12535, 12594 (1999).

[4]   S. Rep. No. 105-17, H.R. Rep. 105-95.

[5]   64 *Fed. Reg.* 12535, 12594 (1999).

[6]   *Id.*

[7]   *Id.*

[8]   S. Rep. No. 105-17, H.R. Rep. 105-95.

[9]   64 *Fed. Reg.* 12535, 12594 (1999).

[10]   [W]e note that once a court holds that the public placement violated IDEA, it is authorized to 'grant such relief as the court determines is appropriate.' . . . Under this provision 'equitable considerations are relevant in fashioning relief,' . . . and the court enjoys 'broad discretion' in doing so. . . . Courts fashioning discretionary equitable relief under IDEA must consider all relevant factors, including the appropriate and reasonable level of reimbursement that should be required. EHLR at 556:396.

[11]   The parent also raised for resolution the following substantive claims: (1) the district failed to provide an instructional assistant (IA) for sufficient periods of time; (2) the district failed to provide adequate training for the instructional assistants; (3) the district failed to implement math, speech, language and reading services as required by the student's program (IEP); and (4) the district failed to implement the supplementary aids and services (specifically, the visual cues and sensory program) described in the student's IEP.

Chapter 6

PARTICIPATION OF STUDENTS WITH DISABILITIES IN GENERAL STATEWIDE ASSESSMENTS

1. Did the 1997 IDEA Amendments direct states and school districts to conduct statewide or districtwide assessment programs?

No, the IDEA does not compel performance of statewide or districtwide assessments. The law merely concerns participation by students with disabilities in those assessments that are conducted, as a matter of state law or school district policy.

Generally speaking, states still have discretion to decide the frequency and educational purposes for general assessments of students and, in the first instance, whether to have a statewide or district-wide assessment program at all. Federal law directs states to conduct assessments in only limited circumstances related to grants to states and local school districts under various titles of the Elementary and Secondary Education Act. Participation in the federally sponsored National Assessment of Educational Progress (NAEP) is voluntary. See Questions 19 to 22 regarding these federal programs.

One purpose of the changes made to the IDEA by the 1997 IDEA Amendments was to stress the need to improve educational results for students with disabilities. To that end, a new statutory provision was enacted to require inclusion of most students with disabilities in all general state or local assessment programs that are conducted by those entities. 20 U.S.C. § 1412(a)(17)(A).

Relating to the same objective, another new provision added to the law in 1997 compelled states to establish performance goals for students with disabilities participating in such assessments. 20 U.S.C. § 1412(a)(16)(B).

This being the federal government, the new law also created new reporting requirements. States must disclose to DOE and the public the extent to which students with disabilities are participating in general assessments and how well those students do on the tests. 20 U.S.C. § 1412(a)(16)(C), 20 U.S.C. § 1412(a)(17)(B).

That said, a state would certainly be swimming against the tide these days if it chose not to conduct general assessments of core competencies at multiple times in the course of a student's K-12 education. A 1998 survey disclosed that only three states do not have a statewide assessment program. States are using the assessment results for a variety of purposes. Student accountability is one.[1] Assessments also may be able to monitor the performance of school districts and school buildings and to modify curriculum.[2]

2. Is the IDEA the source of the federal directive to include students with disabilities in statewide and districtwide assessments?

Actually, no. OCR has always interpreted Section 504 and the ADA as mandating inclusion of all students with disabilities, not just those who are IDEA-eligible, in statewide and districtwide assessments. During the early years of the 1990's Congress enacted legislation (i.e., Goals 2000: Educate America Act, Improving America's Schools Act, and the School-to-Work Opportunities Act) that provided funding opportunities to states to encourage including students with disabilities in statewide and districtwide assessments.[3] But provisions added to the IDEA by the 1997 IDEA Amendments shone klieg lights on this long-standing requirement.

As explained by OSERS and OCR in *Joint Policy Memorandum on Assessments*, 27 IDELR 138 (OSEP 1997), a causal connection can be established between exclusion of students with disabilities from participation in student assessments and provision of inferior educational services to this student population. For this reason, DOE takes the following position:

> [E]xclusion from assessments based on disability generally would not only undermine the value of the assessment but also violate Section 504 of the Rehabilitation Act of 1973 (Section 504), which prohibits exclusion from participation of, denial of benefits to, or discrimination against, individuals with disabilities on the basis of their disability in Federally-assisted programs or activities. 29 U.S.C. § 794. Similarly Title II of the Americans with Disabilities Act (ADA) of 1990 provides that no qualified individual with a disability shall, by reason of such disability, be excluded from participation in or be denied the benefits of the services, programs, or activities of a public entity, or be subjected to discrimination by such entity. 42 U.S.C. § 12132.

27 IDELR at 138.

Accord Letter to Muhlenkamp, 30 IDELR 603 (OSEP 1998) (inclusion of students with disabilities in statewide and districtwide assessments, with appropriate accommodations where necessary, is a requirement of Section 504 of the Rehabilitation Act of 1973 and Title II of the Americans with Disabilities Act of 1990).

Historically, about fifty percent of IDEA-eligible students with disabilities were excluded from participation in these large-scale assessments.[4] Some states categorically excluded all students being educated in accordance with IEPs.[5] Apparently, many educational agencies thought the relationship between inclusion of students with disabilities in statewide or districtwide assessments and federal discrimination law attenuated.

In the 1997 IDEA Amendments Congress, in effect, chided states for skirting existing law in this regard by incorporating the inclusion requirement in a new provision that will prove far harder to ignore. New requirement 1412(a)(17) (20 U.S.C. § 1412(a)(17)) conditions state eligibility for receipt of Part B funding upon having in place policies and procedures to ensure that students with disabilities are included in general statewide and districtwide assessments. Accommodations must be provided whenever appropriate to allow participation.

Recognizing that some disabled students may not be able to participate, the statute also directs states to develop guidelines for the participation of students with disabilities in "alternate assessments" and to actually conduct such assessments beginning not later than July 1, 2000. Chapter 7 concerns the IDEA's alternate assessment requirement.

As a related matter, note that nothing contained in the IDEA or Section 504 prohibits states from also specifically mandating inclusion of students with disabilities in statewide or districtwide assessments.

3. Must states comply with the IDEA provisions governing evaluations when students with disabilities participate in statewide or districtwide assessments?

No. The detailed IDEA requirements governing assessments apply only to "tests and other evaluation materials" used to determine Part B eligibility and special education needs. 34 C.F.R. § 300.532(a)(1).

"[T]he highly individualized testing, conducted for the purpose of diagnosis or instructional planning, differs considerably from large-scale group assessments of achievement."[6] For that reason, some of the IDEA procedural requirements for the conduct of evaluations, for example 34 C.F.R. §§ 300.532(f), (g) and (h), are irrelevant or counter-productive in the context of inclusion of students with disabilities in statewide or districtwide assessments.

This is not to say that there is no common ground. Principles of fairness and nondiscrimination are the foundation for all educational testing. Some procedural rules set out in the IDEA reflect sound professional practice and federal nondiscrimination laws. As a result, they govern the participation of both disabled and nondisabled students in large-scale assessments, even if the regulations themselves do not apply.

4. Who decides which students with disabilities should be provided with accommodations when taking general statewide or districtwide assessments?

School districts should avoid blanket, across-the-board policies on testing accommodations. Like the development of an IEP, consideration of an accommodation should be done by those familiar with the child and his educational program, with those individuals taking into account the student's unique disability-related needs.

When a student is eligible under the IDEA, the IEP team decides which students require accommodations for assessments. The team's decisions must be documented in the student's IEP. IDEA regulations at 34 C.F.R. § 300.347(a)(5)(i) state that a student's IEP must include "a statement of any individual modifications in the administration of State or districtwide assessments of student achievement that are needed in order for the child to participate in the assessment."

The answer is less clear as a matter of federal law when a student is considered disabled under Section 504 only and the assessment is not "high stakes," from the student's point of view. But all signs point to having the group of individuals who decide placement issues (the Section 504 team) generally also make determinations about assessment accommodations.[7]

The language of implementing regulations at 34 C.F.R. § 104.35(c) does not, in all fairness, seem to have been written with participation in general assessments in mind. In *Joint Policy Memorandum on Assessments*, 27 IDELR 138 (OSEP 1997), however, DOE seems to direct that a student's 504 team make accommodation decisions consistent with the procedures set out in Section 104.35.

> The individualized determinations of whether a student will participate in a particular assessment, and what accommodations, if any, are appropriate should be addressed through the individualized education program process or other evaluation and placement process and included in either the student's IEP or Section 504 plan.

27 IDELR at 139.

Under both the IDEA and Section 504 the state is the ultimate arbiter of when an accommodation will be appropriate for use with a particular assessment instrument. While the decision to provide accommodations — and which accommodations to provide — rests with each student's IEP or placement team, the menu of accommodations from which to choose is limited in order to ensure the reliability and validity of the test results. We discuss this issue in greater detail in Question 5.

5. What are "appropriate" accommodations for students with disabilities participating in general statewide or districtwide assessments?

Appropriate accommodations are like snowflakes. They seem pretty much alike to the naked eye, but are, in reality, unique. Whether a particular accommodation is appropriate is a function of the identity of the particular student and the particular test. State law or policy has an essential role to play, as well.

6 : 3

Clearly, then, generalizations are not going to be sufficient when taking action to comply with the new IDEA requirements at 20 U.S.C. § 1412(a)(17). Each reader needs to become familiar with the specific guidelines for defining appropriate accommodations established in his or her own state and school district. With this caveat, we offer the following response.

Like "reasonable accommodations" under Section 504 or the ADA, "appropriate accommodations" under the IDEA are test modifications that allow a student with a disability to demonstrate mastery of the skills or knowledge being tested without altering the test in a substantive way, in terms of either its content or standards. There is no reason to believe that the 1997 IDEA Amendments intended to alter or replace established Section 504 jurisprudence limning the concept of reasonable accommodations in connection with "high stakes testing."[8]

Section 1412(a)(17)(A) mandates inclusion of children with disabilities in general statewide and districtwide assessments, "with appropriate accommodations, where necessary." IDEA regulations at 34 C.F.R. § 300.138(a) direct provision of "appropriate accommodations and modifications in administration, if necessary" in connection with inclusion of students with disabilities in general statewide and districtwide assessment programs.

Neither the IDEA statute nor regulations explain, however, when an accommodation will be "appropriate." This is purposeful. DOE opted to include only minimum requirements in the regulations in order to allow states and school districts "flexibility."[9]

Due to the recent enactment of 20 U.S.C. § 1412(a)(17)(A) there is an enormous amount of published theorizing about what types of accommodations will be deemed appropriate under the IDEA. But, to the best knowledge of the author, there are as yet no published administrative or judicial decisions putting a particular state or school district's interpretation of the law's requirements to the test.

As a general matter, published guidance articulates the consensus view that an appropriate accommodation for a student with a disability is one that the student needs in order to demonstrate what he knows. Without the accommodation, the student would be placed at a disadvantage solely on account of his disability. On the other hand, the accommodation should not change the substantive character of the test. The difference is essentially one of how the test is administered, not what it contains.

In that regard, one possible way to interpret the statutory term "appropriate accommodations" is to relate it to terminology commonly used to describe test administration.[10]

- Standard Administration. Use of exactly the same procedures used during test development, typically defined by the test publisher.

- Accommodated Administration. Changes in test setting, scheduling, timing, presentation format, or response format that do not change the content mastery being tested or the meaning of the scores.

- Modified Administration. Changes in the content mastery being measured or modified scoring of test results.

Based upon authoritative judicial and administrative interpretation of reasonable accommodations under Section 504,[11] the author agrees with those educators who are interpreting the term "appropriate accommodations" as equivalent to "accommodated administration." Based on the same reasoning, changes in test administration meeting the definition of modified administration are, in effect, content modifications or "inappropriate accommodations."[12]

Appropriate accommodations will typically be those changing the following aspects of an assessment: (1) presentation of questions; (2) required response mode; (3) timing or scheduling; or (4) setting. We identify examples of accommodations for each category in Question 14.

On the more specific level of an appropriate accommodation for a particular individual student with a disability, the guidance promulgated by the State of Montana (Montana Guidelines) states the following:

There should be a close link between instruction and assessment. Therefore, it is generally held that accommodations should be similar to those used for instruction and should be designed so that the assessment instrument accurately measures the student's knowledge and skill related to the particular area being assessed.[13]

In this regard, IEP or Section 504 teams have to gauge the impact that a particular accommodation will have on the validity of the assessment. The Montana Guidelines emphasize the importance of coordination with each test's publishers, but lament that in some instances the teams will be venturing into uncharted territory. In those instances, the Montana Guidelines give district personnel the green light to use common sense, suggesting that, for example, reading test items to a student may not be an appropriate accommodation for a test purporting to measure silent reading comprehension.

6. Who decides which particular accommodations should be provided to students with disabilities when taking general statewide or districtwide assessments?

IEP teams and Section 504 teams make those decisions, subject to overall state and school district guidance. In most states the IEP team decides which accommodations listed on a statewide list of "approved accommodations" should be provided to a student."[14]

Each student's IEP must include "a statement of any individual modifications in the administration of State or districtwide assessments of student achievement that are needed in order for the child to participate in such assessment." 34 C.F.R. § 300.347(a)(5)(i). For students without IEPs, the student's Section 504 team selects what those accommodations should be. *Joint Policy Memorandum on Assessments*, 27 IDELR 138 (OSEP 1997).

One might infer from the literal language of the regulation that a student's IEP team has sole discretion to decide the particular accommodations that will be provided. That is what DOE interpretive guidance also seems to suggest. "Section 300.347(a)(5) requires that the IEP team have the responsibility and the authority to determine what, if any, individual modifications, in the administration of State or districtwide assessments are needed in order for a particular child with a disability to participate in the assessment."[15]

But it is clear to the author that the regulatory language cannot be read in a vacuum. In order to aggregate students' assessment scores in a meaningful manner, states will have to consider on a global level the impact each possible accommodation will have on the validity and reliability of the assessment instrument. IEP team discretion will have to be bounded by decisions reached on the statewide or districtwide level. These decisions, in turn, should be made on the basis of professional psychometric standards.

The author acknowledges that this is a facile statement. As discussed in Question 9, at this point the development of nationally recognized psychometric standards to apply to participation of students with disabilities in general statewide and districtwide assessments lags far behind the legal mandate.

7. Can a student with a disability receive accommodations for statewide or districtwide assessments that he does not receive for classroom (in-school) testing?

Yes. In theory, a student's IEP or Section 504 team may decide that test accommodations not used in class may be needed to help a student with a disability demonstrate his ability on an assessment. In practice, though, it's not rocket science: Assessment modifications typically parallel in-school testing accommodations provided for an individual student.[16]

6 : 5

Some states may have a policy under which assessment accommodations for both IDEA-eligible students with disabilities and those with Section 504 Accommodations Plans are provided only if they have been provided in the classroom. For example, the Washington State Commission on Student Learning has taken the position that no accommodation should be used for the first time on a state-level assessment.[17]

But, in the author's view, the better approach is the one adopted by the State of Michigan:

Any student with a disability may be considered for an accommodation. And while it is important to consider those accommodations that were used for instruction or testing in the past, a student may not be denied an accommodation solely on the basis that an accommodation was not used before.[18]

In either case, it is likely that a student with a disability will receive the same accommodations for in-school testing and statewide and districtwide assessments. However, like all generalizations, there are exceptions.

As we discuss in greater detail in Question 9, not every in-school testing accommodation offered to a student with a disability can be appropriately provided for a standardized test administered as part of a statewide or districtwide assessment.

Approaching the issue from the other end of the tunnel, the decision of the hearing officer in *Birmingham Board of Education* (20 IDELR 1281) is a good example of when a disabled student may be entitled to assessment accommodations that he has not previously received for in-school testing. In *Birmingham* the state's "Student Assessment Program Policies and Procedures for Students of Special Populations" contained what the hearing officer referred to as the "prior practice" requirement. "Modifications that can be made [for an assessment] are those approved accommodations on the accommodations checklists. The accommodations must be ones that the student has been receiving on a regular basis, and prior practice is included in the student's IEP/504 Plan."

In most instances, this general policy served well the individual needs of students with disabilities. In this instance it did not.

The IEP team for the 11th-grade student with a learning disability in reading had determined that the student could take the state's high school graduation exam, and that all parts of the test would be read aloud to him with the exception of the reading subtest. However, the IEP itself only documented the need for oral testing as an in-class test accommodation for English, science and social studies courses. Applying the state guidelines, a state oversight committee refused to allow the school district to have the mathematics subtest of the exit exam read aloud to the student.

The hearing officer refused to apply the state guidelines in a mechanical way. He explored at length how the assessment's mathematics subtest had far more in common with the student's in-class English tests than his in-class math tests in terms of how the student's reading deficits impacted his ability to display his knowledge of the core subject.

It is the opinion of this Hearing Officer that the unique needs of the student, as determined by the IEP [team] in determining whether or not an accommodation should be granted to that student in taking the [minimum competency test], outweigh and exceed the public's expectation of a certain level of competency based upon Congress' direction and our Court's decisions indicating that the unique needs of the student should be addressed and accommodations granted so as to not penalize students with unique needs. In this particular case this Hearing Officer does not believe that the scales are unduly tipped in favor of the student or that the student is given an unfair advantage by being provided the reading accommodation on the math portion of the [minimum competency test]. This is consistent with the balancing done by the IEP [team] in granting the accommodation.

20 IDELR at 1289.

8. How should an IEP team proceed when called upon to make decisions regarding appropriate accommodations for a student with a disability taking a statewide or districtwide assessment?

Of course, IEP team members must look to state law and local policies for the precise directives that apply in their particular circumstances. Nevertheless, as a general matter, IEP team members should do the following: Become knowledgeable about both the student and the test. Consider how the student's disability impacts his ability to demonstrate his mastery of the tested material and what accommodations should be provided to place the student on an equal footing with nondisabled students without giving the student an unfair advantage or destroying the validity of the test.

IEP team members looking to document their understanding of, and compliance with, the federal law governing testing accommodations provided for students with disabilities taking state or district-wide assessments should consider the following suggestions as food for thought:

- Be prepared to fully explain the nature of a student's disability, and why a particular accommodation is necessary.

- Don't assume all students with disabilities need accommodations, or that certain accommodations are "foregone conclusions."

- Educational programs for students with disabilities must teach the skills being tested, in the format they're being tested.

- Generally, accommodation needs should be apparent long before the student takes a "high stakes" standardized test.

- Don't provide accommodations that affect the test's validity. Your policy should provide for accommodations when necessary for individual students.

- Accommodation decisions should be made by people familiar with the student and his or her educational program, as well as people familiar with the purpose of the test, what the scores mean, and what relevant policies are.

- Make sure students, parents, teachers and administrators understand your policy on accommodations and know how conflicts will be resolved.[19]

9. Can an accommodation that compromises the reliability or validity of the assessment instrument be considered an appropriate accommodation?

No, an accommodation that affects validity or reliability is not an appropriate accommodation.

As discussed in Question 5, the IDEA regulations at 34 C.F.R. § 300.138(a) do not establish legal standards for identifying the range of assessment accommodations that are "appropriate accommodations," leaving those determinations to states and local school districts. Those decision-makers, in turn, will undoubtedly rely upon generally accepted principles of psychometrics concerning test reliability and validity when establishing guidelines for the administration of assessment tests to students with disabilities. They'll have a tough time for the next few years, though. "Little research exists on the validity of specific accommodations on the validity of achievement tests."[20]

We briefly explain test validity and reliability, as a general matter, in connection with determining whether a particular accommodation is appropriate below.

A test instrument is reliable when it produces consistent results with respect to whatever skill, knowledge or competency it is intended to measure. When considering whether accommodations are

6 : 7

appropriate for norm-referenced tests (tests that compare the performance of the test-taker against the performance of the national group of test-takers selected by the test publisher), inter-rater reliability, the extent to which students taking different forms of the same test receive the same scores for substantively similar performance, is a particular concern.

Variation in administration, including accommodations, makes it difficult to reliably compare student performance. This is the reason the Educational Testing Service, the publisher of the SAT, is standing firm in its refusal to grant certain accommodations requested by examinees with disabilities. See Question 17 in chapter 9 for a further discussion of (now) pending litigation concerning this issue.

Test validity is a different issue. A test instrument is valid when it actually measures what it is intended to measure. Content validity is a primary concern when criterion-referenced assessments are being used to determine whether students have mastered the state's core curriculum in terms of knowledge.

In this regard, note that a critical issue being considered by many states is whether standardized, norm-referenced tests must be replaced by criterion-referenced tests developed to assess mastery of the state's approved curriculum and ability to apply that mastery. New Hampshire and Nevada are just two of the states that have expressed reservations about the continuing viability of norm-referenced testing for student assessments.[21]

In this regard, the New Jersey Department of Education has proposed new regulations to require that only criterion-referenced tests be used for statewide assessments. It explains its rationale below:

> New Jersey assessments are criterion referenced and are standardized to ensure reliability and validity. This means that students are appropriately assessed against fixed criteria and that test administration procedures are consistent statewide. Unlike norm-referenced commercial achievement tests, New Jersey assessments will not compare students to each other. Instead, students will receive individual scores evaluating their achievement with respect to the Core Curriculum Content Standards, The state's standardized criterion-referenced approach directly aligns the assessment program with the Core Curriculum Content Standards. In effect, the statewide assessment system establishes the performance levels for the Core Curriculum Content Standards.[22]

10. What measures, if any, are provided in the IDEA to prevent states and school districts from "bubbling out" the scores of students with disabilities taking statewide or districtwide assessments?

The IDEA regulations establish reporting requirements that compel inclusion of scores achieved by students with disabilities.

Assessment of student achievement is an integral aspect of accountability and an essential tool for evaluating how well school districts, buildings, and staff are performing. It is therefore not surprising that, historically, students with disabilities have been excluded from assessments being conducted for purposes of, among other things, evaluating school performance. Concluding that such exclusionary practices "short-changed" students with disabilities by giving states the flexibility to set "low expectations" for them and offer them "less challenging curriculum,"[23] Congress included a directive for participation of students with disabilities in statewide and districtwide assessments in the 1997 IDEA Amendments. 20 U.S.C. § 1412(a)(17)(A).

Ordering participation is not enough, however. If states or school districts are permitted to exclude the scores of the students with disabilities who take the assessment, from the state or school district score aggregations, the IDEA participation mandate is meaningless.

This practice, sometimes referred to as "bubbling out," is kept in check by the reporting requirement set out in the IDEA regulations at 34 C.F.R. § 300.139(b), which provide, in pertinent part:

(b) Combined reports. Reports to the public under paragraph (a)[24] of this section must include-

(1) Aggregated data that include the performance of children with disabilities together with all other children; and

(2) Disaggregated data on the performance of children with disabilities.

Acknowledging that commenters correctly noted that this regulatory requirement exceeds the reporting requirements imposed by the statute (at 20 U.S.C. § 1412(a)(17)(B)), DOE explained its rationale below:

> In order to ensure that students with disabilities are fully included in the accountability benefits of State and districtwide assessments, it is important that the State include results for children with disabilities whenever the State reports results for other children. When a State reports data about State or districtwide assessments at the district or school level for nondisabled children, it also must do the same for children with disabilities.[25]

11. Is out-of-level testing an appropriate accommodation?

Not according to the opinion expressed in interpretive guidance by DOE. As discussed in Question 9 in chapter 7, DOE has opined that it considers out-of-level testing "modified administration."[26]

Generally speaking, "modified administration" is understood to mean changes in the content mastery being measured, or modified scoring of test results. This is distinct from what is commonly termed "accommodated administration." The latter involves administration with appropriate, or reasonable, accommodations, such as changes in test setting, scheduling, timing, presentation format, or response format that do not change the content mastery being tested or the meaning of the scores. See Question 5 for a further discussion of the differences between modified administration and accommodated administration.

Illinois is one state that has gone on record as taking the position that out-of-level testing is not appropriate accommodation for statewide assessments.[27]

12. Must a student with a disability receive all the accommodations he receives for classroom (in-school) testing as appropriate accommodations for statewide or districtwide assessments?

No, not always, according to OCR. Additional considerations relating to test reliability of the statistical aggregation of students' scores or content validity may come into play in connection with statewide or districtwide assessments.

As also discussed in Question 7, IEP teams would do well to start with the premise that test accommodations approved for in-school testing are also appropriate accommodations when the student participates in a statewide or districtwide assessment. But, as Illinois State education officials explain, IEP teams have to subject that premise to further analysis before making a final determination.

> In general, accommodations listed as appropriate within the student's IEP for classroom tests or local assessments are probably appropriate for state tests as long as three criteria are met. First, the accommodation should allow the test to reflect the student's proficiency in the area tested, not the disability reflected addressed in the IEP. Second, the accommodation should not compromise the purpose of the test ...[.] Third, the accommodation should not compromise test security.[28]

In *Virginia Department of Education*, 27 IDELR 1148 (OCR, Region XI 1997), OCR supported a state's refusal to provide an accommodation approved for in-school testing for a statewide assessment. In that instance the student's IEP specified that, as a general matter, items on reading tests would be read aloud. However, because state guidelines promulgated in connection with administration of the Stanford 9 (a norm-referenced test used for student assessment) barred use of that accommodation, the student's IEP team would not allow the student to take the test with that particular accommodation. The school district offered other options, including taking an alternate test, but the parents elected to file a complaint with OCR seeking to compel the school district to read all subtests aloud to the student.

OCR supported the school district's compliance with the guidelines. The test had to be given in given in exactly the same way (i.e., standard administration) for the test results to be reliable for their intended use, comparison of student performance in the Commonwealth to the performance of students at the same grade levels nationwide. For this reason, the parent could not compel the district to let the student take the test with the accommodation included in his IEP. Because the school district did not intend to use the test to assess the student's individual performance or make decisions about his programming or placement, it had no obligation under Section 504 to provide an alternate test to the student.

To like effect, in *Florida State Department of Education*, 28 IDELR 1002 (OCR, Region IV 1998), OCR supported the school district's refusal to allow a student with a disability the opportunity to have a proctor read and explain certain sections of a statewide high school competency test. The student's IEP allowed the reading and explanation of test materials to the student, but identified "flexible scheduling, flexible setting and oral presentations within test guidelines" as the only approved modifications for statewide assessments. Because the state had determined that reading or explaining the communications section of the state competency test would compromise test validity, test guidelines specifically barred this accommodation. Accordingly, OCR found that neither the establishment of the bar in the testing guidelines nor the application of the guidelines to this student in particular violated Section 504 or the ADA.

In conclusion, the author cannot overstate how much work needs to be done on the state and local level to determine what accommodations will be determined to be appropriate for purposes of meeting the participation requirements of the IDEA. Two excerpts from the expert testimony presented by the parties in *Doe v. National Board of Medical Examiners*, 16 NDLR ¶ 132 (E.D. Pa. 1999), discussed in detail in Question 17 in chapter 3, explain:

> Regarding the quality of research, I believe that given the constraints of sample sizes, many different types and degrees of disabilities, and many different accommodations, the bulk of the research has been of good quality. It is true that the profession [pyschometrics] can still not make definitive statements about the equivalence or validity of scores obtained under all circumstances; but there is legitimate reason to question whether that can ever be done.[29]

***

> Despite the history of attempts to modify tests for [disabled] people, significant problems remain. First, there have been few empirical investigations of the effects of special accommodations on the resulting test scores or on their reliability and validity. Strictly speaking, unless it has been demonstrated that the psychometric properties of a test, or type of test, are not altered significantly by some modification, the claims made for the test by its author or publisher cannot be generalized to the modified version. The major reason for the lack of research is the relatively small number of [disabled] test takers.[30]

As indicated above, the key concepts that come into play when considering whether a specific assessment accommodation should be provided for students with disabilities are reliability and validity. We explain each briefly in Question 9.

13. Does a student with a disability have an individual right to participation with appropriate accommodations in statewide or districtwide assessments that are not "high stakes" (or even any stakes) for the student?

There is little published guidance on this issue. Very limited published OCR guidance suggests that parents have no rights under Section 504 to challenge decisions concerning participation in assessments not used to evaluate or place the student. A parent's rights under the IDEA are also unclear.

According to the National Research Council:

> Distinctions among the various purposes of assessments become critical in light of [Section 504 and ADA] legal rights. Some assessments, for example, are designed mainly for the accountability of schools and school systems. Others are an integral part of learning, instruction, and curriculum. Some tests are used for making high-stakes decisions about individual students, including tracking, promotion or retention in grade, and awarding a high school diploma or certificate of mastery. Each use raises its own set of legal issues with different implications. As a general rule, the greater the potential harm to students, the greater the protection to which they are entitled, and the more vulnerable the assessment to legal challenge.[31]

Generally, our detailed legal analysis of the pertinent regulatory provisions of Section 504 and the IDEA supports the conclusion of the National Research Council.

The exclusion of students with disabilities from assessments because of disability violates Section 504, Title II of the ADA and the IDEA. If an accommodation is required for a student with a disability to participate in an assessment, that accommodation must be provided. *Joint Policy Memorandum on Assessments*, 27 IDELR 138 (OSEP 1997). In fact, the 1997 IDEA Amendments expressly require the inclusion of students with disabilities in both statewide and districtwide assessments. 20 U.S.C. § 1412(a)(17)(A).

The premise of federal law mandating participation of students with disabilities is that students with disabilities, as a group, will benefit from inclusion. As articulated by one state educational agency:

> [F]ederal statute requires the full participation of students with disabilities in state-mandated testing programs. Lawmakers recognize that it is more likely that students with disabilities will be provided with learning opportunities equal to their non-disabled peers if the academic achievement of students with disabilities is assessed in the same way as the achievement of non-disabled students. This applies especially when test results are used for accountability purposes, since such uses encourage schools to direct instructional attention and resources toward students who will be tested and for whom results will be reported.[32]

But does this group benefit translate into an individual benefit for each student with a disability? And, if you answer "yes," we have two more questions for you. First, does this "benefit" translate into a "right" to be included in statewide and districtwide assessments? In many states, assessment test results are used only for purposes such as curriculum planning, improvement of instruction, or program evaluation. But, in some instances the tests are high stakes for the school, being used as an element of school performance evaluation.

When that is the case, our second question arises. What is the remedy for unlawful exclusion when the assessment is not a "high-stakes" test from the student's perspective? That is, the test results will not be used as an exit exam (for graduation with a regular high school diploma), grade level promotions, diagnosis or placement.

In *Virginia Department of Education*, 27 IDELR 1148 (OCR, Region XI 1997), OCR answered these questions from the perspective of Section 504, taking the position that when an assessment is not used for educational decision-making relating to the individual student, the student is not denied a benefit or service. He has no rights under Section 504. Thus, there is no basis for a claim of disability discrimination.

The parent of a disabled student filed the complaint in *Virginia Department of Education* claiming that the district discriminated against the student by not allowing him to take a standardized test with an accommodation included in the student's IEP, having the reading portions of the test read aloud. The district offered alternatives, including taking an alternate test and being excused from participation, but the parent rejected them all.

OCR declined to take any action, however. It held that the district's action did not implicate any statute or regulation enforced by OCR. Key to OCR's position was the fact that the assessment was used to measure academic achievement across the country, but not for educational or placement reasons with regard to the individual student.

In contrast, if the assessment were also being used for purposes of placement in district programs, then Section 504 and ADA concerns would arise. This important distinction was drawn in *Chatham (GA) County School District*, 30 IDELR 727 (OCR, Region IV 1999), in which OCR investigated a complaint that a school district's policies discriminated against students with disabilities in administering standardized tests. Specifically, the complaint alleged that a disabled student who required certain accommodations, such as the use of Braille, verbal reading of test items, and testing out of level, would receive an invalid score on the Iowa Test of Basic Skills (ITBS), a norm-referenced test.

In this instance, a particular school district program established achievement of a certain score on the ITBS as one of four criteria for admittance. Although a student had to meet only three of the four criteria for admission, OCR found that the school district had never admitted a student who did not have a valid norm-referenced achievement score. As a result OCR opined that it had "Section 504 and Title II concerns that the District's practice for admitting students into the Search Program is adversely affecting students with disabilities who request accommodations for the ITBS." A voluntary settlement agreement providing for alternate testing resolved the complaint.

It is not clear if the IDEA gives a parent the right to challenge at due process decisions concerning participation in general statewide or districtwide assessments that are not used to make educational decisions. Under 34 C.F.R. § 300.507 a parent has the right to file for due process to challenge a proposal to initiate (or a refusal to initiate or change) the identification, evaluation[33] or educational placement of the student or the provision of FAPE to the student. An assessment that has no implications for identification, placement or the provision of special education or related services does not seem to be within the jurisdictional authority of due process hearing officers.

14. What specific assessment accommodations generally will be considered appropriate?

As discussed in Question 5, what is appropriate for any one student taking a particular assessment will vary based on a multifactorial analysis. The student's disability, the test instrument, the test scoring methodology, the state and school district, all these are among the variables that the IEP team must take into account.

That said, based on the author's review of assessment information provided by the states, the following specific accommodations appear to considered appropriate (in appropriate circumstances):

Presentation of Test Questions

- Large print/magnifying equipment
- Braille

- Test questions read to student (except tests of reading comprehension)
- Test instructions read to student with verification that student understood
- Test instructions simplified or explained with examples
- Interpreter/amplification equipment (for hearing-impaired)
- Masks or markers (to focus attention)

Student Test Performance and Response

- Student permitted to use a place marker
- Dictated by student to a scribe (also referred to as an amanuensis) or tape recorded (except writing skills assessments)
- Student permitted to use voice-actuated or other assistive technology
- Student permitted to use calculator (except tests of numeric calculations)
- Student permitted to use spell-checker or grammar-checker (except when testing grammar or spelling)

Timing or Scheduling

- Administer with extended time
- Administer in short periods, with rest breaks
- Administer on a day or time of day that takes into account student's medical or disability-related needs

Setting

- Administer individually
- Administer in a carrel
- Administer with a noise buffer
- Administer in an alternate setting
- Administer in a small group setting
- Administer with the student seated in the front of the room
- Administer with the student facing the test administrator

15. Are states required to ensure participation of students with disabilities attending public charter schools in statewide or districtwide assessments?

Yes. There is no explicit exemption of public charter schools in the IDEA requirement for participation of students with disabilities attending public charter schools.

Charter schools are created by a public agreement between the individuals and entity proposing to operate the school and the responsible state or local governmental entity. While the details will vary, based on governing state law, the general rule is that the operators of a charter school agree to meet certain accountability standards (i.e., educational outcomes or student performance standards) in exchange for relief from a variety of *state* laws and regulations.

6 : 13

However, no state has the authority to waive compliance with federal laws, including the IDEA. Section 1412(a)(17)(A) of the IDEA directs states to include children with disabilities in general state-wide and districtwide assessments, (with appropriate accommodations, where necessary). The IDEA explicitly applies to students with disabilities who attend public charter schools, whether the school is considered under the enabling state law to be a part of a school district or not. In the latter case, the charter school is treated as its own school district for purposes of coverage under the IDEA. 34 C.F.R. §§ 300.2(b)(ii), 300.3(h).

16. Are states required to ensure participation of students with disabilities attending private schools in statewide or districtwide assessments?

States must comply with the IDEA's assessment mandate with regard to publicly placed private school students. They are public school students, albeit attending a private school, and 20 U.S.C. § 1412(a)(17)(A) contains no explicit exemption.

Generally speaking, the IDEA does not govern students enrolled by their parents in private school. There is no basis in the statute upon which jurisdiction over private schools that are not receiving IDEA funding can be asserted. 34 C.F.R. § 300.2. Contrast this to Section 504, which governs any private school, that is a direct or indirect recipient of federal funding, and Title III, which governs all non-parochial private schools.

However, students with disabilities who have been publicly placed in private schools or facilities are covered by the IDEA. Under the IDEA states and school districts are responsible for ensuring that private schools that accept publicly placed students extend those students all IDEA "rights and protections." 34 C.F.R. § 300.2(c)(1). The same "rights and protections" are extended to students who are privately enrolled because their parents allege a denial of FAPE. 34 C.F.R. § 300.2(c)(2).

But is participation in a statewide or districtwide assessment a right or protection? As we discuss in Question 13, there is no explicit exploration of this issue in either the regulations or DOE's interpretive guidelines.

Assuming, for the sake of argument, participation in statewide or districtwide is not an IDEA right for privately-placed students, another section of the IDEA regulations suggests that inclusion of such students in assessments remains a state and local school district (or educational service agency)[34] obligation. Section 300.401(b) obligates a state placing a student with a disability in a private school or facility to ensure that the placed student "[i]s provided an education that meets the standards that apply to education provided by the SEA and LEAs (including the requirements of this part[.]"

Discussion accompanying the publication of the final IDEA regulations, set out below, suggest that DOE had compliance with the assessment mandate (including alternate assessments) in mind.

> The IDEA Amendments of 1997 made a number of changes to reinforce the importance of the participation of children with disabilities in the regular education curricula and the need for students with disabilities to have the opportunity to receive the same substantive content as nondisabled students. These include provisions that ... require the participation of children with disabilities in the same general State and districtwide assessments as non-disabled students. ...

> SEAs must ensure that public agencies that place children with disabilities in private schools as a means of providing FAPE make sure that the education provided to those publicly-placed children with disabilities meets all standards that apply to educational services provided by the SEA and LEA that are necessary to provide FAPE.[35]

17. Does the parent of a student with a disability have the right to exclude his child from participation in statewide or districtwide assessments or alternate assessments?

The IDEA does not explicitly address this issue. Because the team decides issues related to a disabled student's participation in general assessments (34 C.F.R. § 300.347(a)(5)), it is at least arguable that a parent may resort to due process to challenge a determination that participation is appropriate for the student. See Question 13 in this regard.

To the extent, though, that a parent wants the student excluded for reasons unrelated to appropriateness, state law controls. In Massachusetts, for example, parents have no legal basis to refuse to permit participation.[36] Michigan law, on the other hand, contains a "parent exemption."[37]

18. Does the IDEA require states to conduct statewide or districtwide assessments of students with disabilities who are limited-English proficient in their native language?

No, not explicitly. Another federal law imposes that requirement upon states and school districts, however.

Unlike the IDEA regulations at 34 C.F.R. § 300.532(a)(1)(ii), which concern evaluations for eligibility, the regulations mandating participation in statewide or districtwide assessments do not impose special requirements concerning assessment of students with disabilities who are limited-English proficient (LEP). *See* 34 C.F.R. §§ 300.138, 300.347(a)(5).

An extended discussion of required assessment accommodations for students who are limited-English proficient is beyond the scope of this publication. But have no doubt that the same native language requirements established by Title VI of the Civil Rights Act of 1964, discussed in Questions 18 and 19 in chapter 2, apply when participation in statewide or districtwide assessments are involved. Pursuant to Title VI, general assessments will have to be translated into the student's native language in appropriate instances. States will not be permitted to exclude students with disabilities from participation on the basis of their status as either LEP or SPEDLEP (special education LEP) students.

19. What is the NAEP?

The NAEP is the National Assessment of Educational Progress, a national assessment of student achievement administered by the National Center for Education Statistics (NCES). Also called the Nation's Report Card, the NAEP is the "only nationally representative and continuing assessment of what America's students know and can do."[38]

Federal legislation at 20 U.S.C. § 9010 authorizes periodic testing — at least once every two years — of students in reading, mathematics, science, writing and history, and other fields. Assessments are conducted on the state, regional and national levels. On the national level, the so-called Main Assessment measures educational achievements of fourth-grade, eighth-grade, and 12th-grade students in the various content areas.

The NAEP is not a high-stakes test for students. Under the program, all results are aggregated; all data related to individual students and their families is confidential. 20 U.S.C. § 9010(c)(1).

Section 9010(d)(1) states that participation in regional (Northeast, Southeast, Central, and West) and national assessments is "voluntary." The NAEP Guide promulgated by NCES is more specific, stating that "[p]articipation is voluntary for states, school districts, schools, teachers, and students."[39] Because the assessment involves students' responding to background questions about themselves and their schools, as well as questions addressing specific academic topics, parental consent is required prior to participation. As of October 1999, all states except Alaska and South Dakota have elected to participate.[40]

20. Must students with disabilities be included in NAEP assessments?

The law is not clear, but DOE policy favors inclusion, with accommodations, if needed, in most instances.

The legislation authorizing the NAEP (20 U.S.C. § 9010(b)) does not address selection of participating students with any specificity, beyond requiring use of "sampling techniques that produce data that are representative[.]" NAEP assessments are not general assessments. Representative samples of students are selected to participate. 20 U.S.C. § 9010(b). Nor do they have direct educational consequences for the students who do participate. For these reasons it is not clear if the inclusion mandate of the 1997 IDEA Amendments at 20 U.S.C. § 1412(a)(17) or the non-discrimination requirement of Section 504 apply.

DOE sets out its accommodation policy for both students with disabilities and students with limited English proficiency in its NAEP Guide, informal guidance that does not have the force of law. The policy is brief and summary in nature.

We produce it verbatim below:

NAEP intends to assess all students selected to participate. However, some students may have difficulty with the assessment as it is normally administered because they are students with disabilities (SD) or limited English proficient (LEP).

Because it is committed to increased inclusion, the National Center for Education Statistics (NCES) formally tested new policies with the 1996 assessment. Under these guidelines, school administers were encouraged even more than in the past to include students with disabilities or limited English proficiency if any doubt about excluding the student existed.

When a school identifies a student as having a disability or limited English proficiency, the teacher or staff member who is most familiar with the student completes an SD/LEP questionnaire to determine whether or not the student takes part in the assessment.[41]

21. Who decides which accommodations a student with a disability should receive when participating in an NAEP assessment?

It appears that accommodations are selected for use in assessments being used as part of a state, regional or national level NAEP assessment on the same basis as discussed in Question 5 with respect to participation in general statewide or districtwide assessments. That is, the determination in each instance depends upon the student's individual circumstances, tempered by the need to preserve the validity and reliability of the test instrument. According to NCES:

Beginning with the 1996 national assessment, NAEP implemented a two-part modification of procedures to increase inclusion in NAEP assessments. First, revised criteria were developed to define how decisions about inclusion should be made. Second, NAEP provided certain accommodations that were either specified in a student's Individual Education Plan (IEP) or frequently used to test the student. The accommodations varied depending on the subjects being assessed.[42]

22. Does the federal Goals 2000 assessment requirement specify the accommodations states must provide to allow participation by students with disabilities?

No. But the Goals 2000 legislation does generally encompass the dual requirements that accommodations meet individual needs while still preserving the reliability and validity of the assessment instrument.

In 1994 Congress enacted the Goals 2000: Educate America Act. The legislation established a program of federal grants to states agreeing to implement strategies to improve "teaching and learning and students' mastery of basic and advanced skills in core content areas, such as English, mathematics, science (including physics), history, geography, foreign languages, the arts, civics and government, and economics." 20 U.S.C. § 5881 *et seq.*

In order to demonstrate eligibility for an award, a state must design a state improvement plan that includes "state content standards." 20 U.S.C. § 5886(c). In the opinion of the National Research Council, the language of the law clearly includes inclusion of students with disabilities, including students with severe cognitive impairments, in both improved content and performance standards.

The state improvement plan must also provide for assessments that measure student mastery of those standards. 20 U.S.C. § 5886(c)(1)(B). "All students with diverse learning needs" must participate in the assessments. 20 U.S.C. § 5886(c)(1)(B)(i)(III)(aa). Clearly, students with disabilities should be understood to be encompassed within that directive.[43] However, the legislation leaves the specifics of inclusion up to the states and there are no regulations. The only statutory guidance provides that states must offer "adaptations and accommodations necessary to permit such participation," 20 U.S.C. § 5886(c)(1)(B)(i)(III)(bb).

> The legislation is not specific with regard to how the integration of students with disabilities into state content or performance standards should be accomplished or what expectations are appropriate for them. An analysis of the legal issues surrounding students with disabilities and standards-based reform prepared for the committee [proposing the Goals 2000 legislation] argues that the omission may reflect recognition of problems inherent in singling out particular groups of students for differential treatment. They conclude, however, that 'the absence of any express exceptions for children with severe cognitive impairments, coupled with Goals 2000's repeated emphasis on 'all children,' suggests that states participating in [the grant program] should design their content and performance standards in such a way as to reflect outcomes desirable for that population, too.'[44]

In selecting accommodations and adaptations, states presumably must adhere to all guidelines for the assessments themselves. Specifically, the assessments must remain valid, nondiscriminatory and reliable. 20 U.S.C. § 5886(c)(1)(B). They must also remain consistent with relevant, nationally recognized professional and technical standards for such assessments. 20 U.S.C. § 5886(c)(1)(B)(IV).

Endnotes

1   See Chapter 8 with respect to exit examinations.

2   Julia K. Landau, J.D., Janet R. Vohs, B.A., Carolyn A. Romano, J.D., *All Kids Count,* note 14, *infra.*

3   See Question 22 in this regard.

4   JAY P. HEUBERT, ROBERT M. HAUSER, EDS., HIGH STAKES: TESTING FOR TRACKING, PROMOTION, AND GRADUATION 189 (National Academy Press 1999).

[5] *Id.,* at 195.

[6] *Id.,* at 191.

[7] Author's review of state educational agency material. E.g., "Overview of the MCAS Program," note 36, *infra.*

[8] See Question 1 in chapter 8.

[9] 64 *Fed. Reg.* 12564 (1999).

[10] Assessing Special Education Students (ASES) Work Group Council of Chief State School Officers, "Determining When Accommodated Test Administrations Are Comparable to Standard Test Administrations" <http://www.coled.umn.edu/NCEO/Accommodations/brief.htm> University of Minnesota (October 18, 1999).

[11] See Questions 1 and 2 in chapter 1.

[12] "Determining When Accommodated Test Administrations Are Comparable to Standard Test Administrations," *supra,* note 10.

[13] Montana Office of Public Instruction, *Assessment Handbook, Volume 1* (Feb. 1999).

[14] Julia K. Landau, J.D., Janet R. Vohs, B.A., Carolyn A. Romano, J.D., *All Kids Count,* <http://www.fscn.org/text/peer-text/assess.htm> Federation for Children with Special Needs (September 1, 1999).

[15] 64 *Fed. Reg.* 12565 (1999).

[16] The straight-to-the-point conclusion of Indiana State Special Education Director Paul Ash, included in *Assessment Accommodations: What You Should Do,* THE SPECIAL EDUCATOR®, vol. 10, iss. 21 (May, 27, 1995).

[17] "Guidelines for Inclusion and Accommodations for Special Populations on State-Level Assessments" <http://www.k12.wa.us/reform/specialaccomm/accomm.html> Office of Superintendent of Public Instruction (November 17, 1999).

[18] "Guidelines and Procedures" <gopher://gopher.mde.state.mi.us/00/serv/meap/hsprof/part02%09%09%2B> Michigan Department of Education (November 16, 1999).

[19] These suggestions were made by Denise B. Azar, associate general counsel in the Alabama Department of Education, in *Assessment Accommodations: What You Should Do,* THE SPECIAL EDUCATOR®, *supra,* note 16.

[20] HIGH STAKES: TESTING FOR TRACKING, PROMOTION, AND GRADUATION, note 31 (citation omitted), *infra.*

[21] See, e.g., "NHEIAP FAQ" <http://www.state.nh.us/doe/Assessment/nheiap.htm> New Hampshire Department of Education (November 17, 1999) and "Proposed Code" <http://www.state.nj.us/njded/proposed/standards/> New Jersey Department of Education (November 17, 1999).

[22] "Proposed Code," *supra,* note 21.

[23] *See* Joint Policy Memorandum on Assessments, 27 IDELR 138 (OSEP 1997).

[24] 24 Paragraph (a) states:

> (a) General. In implementing the requirements of §300.138 [participation in assessments], the SEA shall make available to the public, and report to the public with the same frequency and in the same detail as it reports on the assessment of nondisabled children, the following information:
>
> (1) The number of children with disabilities participating —
>
> (i) In regular assessments; and
>
> (ii) In alternate assessments.
>
> (2) The performance results of the children described in paragraph (a)(1) of this section if doing so would be statistically sound and would not result in the disclosure of performance results identifiable to individual children —
>
> (i) On regular assessments (beginning not later than July 1, 1998); and
>
> (ii) On alternate assessments (not later than July 1, 2000).

[25] 64 *Fed. Reg.* 12565 (1999).

[26] *Id.*

[27] "Frequently Asked Questions" <http://www.isbe.state.il.us/isat/FAQnew.htm> Illinois State Board of Education (November 16, 1999).

[28] *Id.*

[29] William A. Mehrens, *Flagging Test Scores: Policy, Practice and Research* (1997), from Defendant's Exhibit 22 at p. 40.

[30] *Standards for Educational and Psychological Testing*, from Plaintiff's Exhibit 11 at p. 78.

[31] JAY P. HEUBERT, ROBERT M. HAUSER, EDS., HIGH STAKES: TESTING FOR TRACKING, PROMOTION, AND GRADUATION 198 (National Academy Press 1999).

[32] "MCAS: Requirements for Participation of Students with Disabilities" <http://www.doe,mass.edu/mcas/guides/spedm-cas.htm> Massachusetts Department of Education (September 1, 1999).

[33] Keep in mind that "evaluation" is a term of art under the IDEA (34 C.F.R. § 300.500(b)(2)). An assessment, for purposes of 20 U.S.C. § 1412(a)(17)(A), is not an evaluation.

[34] Educational service agencies include the agencies that used to be called "intermediate educational units."

[35] 64 *Fed. Reg.* 12600 (1999).

[36] "Overview of the MCAS Program" <http://www.doe.mass.edu/mcas/1098facts.html> Massachusetts Department of Education (November 16, 1999).

[37] "Questions and Answers About the MEAP Tests Taken in the Spring of 1998" <http://mde.state.mi.us/reprots/meap/spring98/resultsqa.pdf> Michigan Department of Education (November 16, 1999).

[38] "What is NAEP?" <http://nces.ed.gov/nationsreportcard/site/whatis.asp> National Center for Education Statistics (December 14, 1999).

[39] "The NAEP Guide" <http://nces.ed.gov/nationsreportcard/particip/> National Center for Education Statistics (December 14, 1999).

[40] "NAEP Participation" <http://nces.ed.gov/nationsreportcard/guide/quest3.shtml> National Center for Education Statistics (December 14, 1999).

[41] "The NAEP Guide" <http://nces.ed.gov/nationsreportcard/guide/ques7.shtml> National Center for Education Statistics (December 14, 1999).

[42] *Id.*

[43] LORRAINE M. MCDONNELL, MARGARET J. MCLAUGHLIN, PATRICIA MORISON, EDS., EDUCATING ONE AND ALL: STUDENTS WITH DISABILITIES AND STANDARDS-BASED REFORM 25 (National Academy Press 1997).

[44] MCDONNELL, MCLAUGHLIN & MORISON, EDS., *supra*, note 43.

Chapter 7

ALTERNATE ASSESSMENTS

1. What is an alternate assessment?

The term "alternate assessment" appears in the IDEA at 20 U.S.C. § 1412(a)(17)(A). Beginning not later than, July 1, 2000, all students with disabilities who cannot participate in statewide and districtwide assessment programs must participate in "alternate assessments."

Like the general statewide and districtwide assessments, alternate assessments are designed or selected by states. The IDEA requires only that there be such an animal as an alternate assessment: States or school districts develop guidelines for the participation of students with disabilities in alternate assessments and the alternate assessments themselves. That's enough of a new requirement to keep states and school districts busy for years to come, however. Prior to enactment of the 1997 IDEA Amendments only six states had conducted alternative assessments for students with disabilities.[1]

IDEA regulations at 34 C.F.R. § 300.138(b)(2) state that states or local school districts must develop alternate assessments in accordance with 34 C.F.R. § 300.138(b)(1). Section 300.138(b)(1), discussed in greater detail in Question 4, requires development of guidelines for the participation of children with disabilities in alternate assessments for those children who cannot participate in State and districtwide assessment programs."

One interesting issue that DOE raises indirectly in its comments accompanying the publication of IDEA final regulations is the distinction that should be made between "modified administration of a test" and "an alternative (sic) test."[2] See Question 8 in this regard.

2. When is a state (or district) permitted to exclude a student with a disability in a general statewide (or districtwide) assessment?

The expectation is that, with the provision of appropriate accommodations, most students with disabilities will be able to participate in all general statewide or districtwide assessments. However, reason dictates that there will be some students with disabilities so severe that participation, even with accommodations, will be either impossible or meaningless.

Under 34 C.F.R. § 300.138(b) states must ensure that the SEA or school districts, as appropriate, develop guidelines for the participation in alternate assessments of children with disabilities who cannot participate in statewide and districtwide assessment programs. IEP teams must then ground their determinations about individual students with disabilities on those guidelines. 34 C.F.R. § 300.347(a)(5).

In its *Joint Policy Memorandum on Assessments*, 27 IDELR 138, 139 (OSEP 1997), DOE identified likely candidates for exclusion the "small number" of students with disabilities who have "significant cognitive impairments." But it is incorrect to conclude that DOE has established a categorical approach to exceptions to participation or opined about when exclusions are appropriate. "In some cases, alternate assessments may be necessary, depending on the needs of the child, and not the category or severity of the child's disability."[3]

The author is not aware of any published decisions challenging a state's proposed guidelines as being inconsistent with the IDEA.

3. Who decides when a student with a disability should participate in an alternate assessment?

A student's IEP team makes the final decision for an individual student with a disability. That decision must reflect an informed evaluation of the individual circumstances of the student and must also be consistent with state or school district guidelines.

Each state or local school district, as appropriate, must develop guidelines for the participation of students with disabilities who cannot participate in statewide and districtwide assessment programs in alternate assessments. 34 C.F.R. § 300.138(b)(1). Following those guidelines, IEP teams decide on an individual basis if a particular student with a disability cannot participate in statewide and districtwide assessment programs, even if provided with appropriate accommodations. The IDEA is clear that all students who cannot participate in general assessment programs must participate in an alternate assessment. 20 U.S.C. § 1412(a)(17)(A).

Implementing regulations at 34 C.F.R. § 300.347(a)(5)(ii) provide as follows:

> If the IEP team determines that the child will not participate in a particular State or districtwide assessment of student achievement (or part of an assessment), a statement of -
>
> (A) Why that assessment is not appropriate for the child; and
>
> (B) How the child will be assessed.

Accord, Joint Policy Memorandum on Assessments, 27 IDELR 138 (OSEP 1997) (decision as to which students will not participate must be made by each individual student's IEP team).

4. Does the IDEA establish standards about when an alternate assessment is appropriate for a student with a disability?

Both the IDEA statute and regulations are silent on this issue, by design. But a federal requirement can be teased out of DOE interpretive guidelines. If application of a state or local school district guideline results in more than a small percentage of the population of students with disabilities participating in alternate assessments, the standards used to get to that result are suspect.

IDEA regulations at 34 C.F.R. § 300.138 require state or local level development of guidelines for participation of alternate assessments. Discussion accompanying the publication of final regulations stressed DOE's intent to impose only minimum regulatory requirements. No further regulations will be forthcoming, according to DOE. Instead, DOE intends to work with State and local education personnel, parents, experts in the field of education and others interested in the area of assessment to identify the best practices that could serve as the basis for a technical assistance document.[4]

The issue of the development of particular standards or guidelines for participation in alternate assessments is not primarily a legal one, as DOE sees it. But it will become one for sure if a state develops guidelines for the participation of students with disabilities in alternate assessments that result in more than a "relatively small percentage" of students with disabilities being left out of statewide or districtwide assessments. In the author's view, this is the implied threat found in discussion accompanying the publication of IDEA final regulations:

> As provided in § 300.347(a)(5), the IEP team must determine whether a child with a disability will participate in a particular State or districtwide assessment of student achievement, and if the child will not, the IEP must include a statement of why that assessment is not appropriate for the child and how the child will be assessed. If IEP teams properly make individual decisions about participation of each child with a disability in general State or districtwide assessments, including the use of appropriate accommodations, and modifications in administration (including individual modifications, as appropriate), it

should be necessary to use alternate assessments for a relatively small percentage of children with disabilities.[5]

The Kansas State Department of Education, for example, has estimated that (based on 1998 data) approximately eight percent of students with disabilities may need to participate in alternate statewide or districtwide assessments.[6] The Louisiana Department of Education, on the other hand, expects that 20 percent of its students with disabilities will be taking alternate assessments.[7] Apparently these two states are developing significantly different standards for alternate assessments. Between the two, Louisiana's estimated participation seems out-of-kilter.

Don't be surprised if in the next few years DOE begins to investigate those states or school districts with higher-than-average percentages of students with disabilities excluded from general assessments.

5. If no student with a significant cognitive impairment participates in statewide or districtwide assessments has the state violated the IDEA?

There is no definitive answer. In the absence of authoritative administrative interpretation or case law, the author's best advice is to document the reasons why an alternate assessment is needed for a particular student very carefully, anticipating that some day either DOE or a litigant will be reading that documentation with a gimlet eye.

Categorical exclusions are inconsistent with the IDEA. 20 U.S.C. § 1414(d)(1)(A)(v)(II). "Alternate assessments should not be assumed appropriate only for those students with significant cognitive impairments."[8] Conversely, alternate assessments should not be assumed to be appropriate for all students with significant cognitive impairments. There is no exception to the individual review requirement of 34 C.F.R. § 300.347(a)(5) made when such students are concerned.

Nonetheless, it seems reasonable to conclude that students with significant cognitive disabilities, for example severe or profound mental retardation (as those terms are defined in the DSM-IV) are included in the universe of students with disabilities who should undergo alternate assessments. Exclusions of all such students from participation in regular assessments would seem to be permitted, provided each student's participation in alternate assessments has been determined appropriate by the student's IEP team consistently with 34 C.F.R. §§ 300.138, 300.347(a)(5).

6. Must an alternate assessment have the same format as the general statewide or districtwide assessments used in the jurisdiction?

The IDEA contains no directives about the format that an alternate assessment must take. Nothing in either the IDEA statute or its implementing regulations, 20 U.S.C. § 1414(d)(1)(A)(v)(II), 34 C.F.R. § 300.138, or in published interpretive guidance contain any specific requirements. That is up to state or local authorities.

States must begin conducting alternate assessments no later than July 1, 2000. 34 C.F.R. § 300.138(b)(3). As this publication is being written, states are now in the process of considering the form alternate assessments will take. They are not starting from ground zero, but perhaps close to it. Educators are now considering several possibilities, including functional behavioral checklists and assessment portfolios. Other possible assessment strategies include: unstructured teacher observation, structured teacher observation, surveys of parents and teachers, performance events and performance tests.[9]

7. Must an alternate assessment link the disabled student's IEP goals and objectives with the state's academic standards and measure achievement with reference to both?

There is no explicit requirement to that effect in either the IDEA statute or pertinent implementing regulations. 20 U.S.C. § 1414(d)(1)(A)(v)(II); 34 C.F.R. §§ 300.138, 300.347(a)(5). However, DOE has opined in interpretive guidance that "[a]lternate assessments need to be aligned with the general curriculum standards set for all students[.]"[10]

In some states, educators are developing alternate assessments that will represent an alignment of their state's academic content standards with the students' IEP goals and objectives. This promises to be either a challenging process or "a great, big headache," depending on your perspective.[11]

To date, the challenge is more pedagogical than legal. The author is not aware of any other published legal administrative guidance or decisions addressing this issue.

8. Must all students with disabilities who cannot participate in statewide or districtwide assessments with appropriate accommodations participate in an alternate assessment?

Some educators are starting to acknowledge that there are students with disabilities who cannot be included in general assessments with appropriate accommodations, but can participate with modified administration. The IDEA does not clearly address whether these students should be considered to be participating in general assessments or being assessed with alternate assessment instruments.

As discussed in Question 5 in chapter 6, the consensus among educators seems to be that the deviations from standard administration commonly classified as "accommodated administration" (changes in test setting, scheduling, timing, presentation format, or response) are appropriate accommodations. Those classified as "modified administration" (changes in the nature of the test, the content mastery being measured or the basis upon which the test is scored) are not.

From an educational perspective, an alternate assessment is *not* the same as modified administration of a general assessment.[12] Given that premise, there are five distinct possibilities when the participation of a student with a disability in statewide or districtwide assessments is being considered:

- Participation in a general assessment without accommodations.

- Participation in a general assessment with accommodated administration.

- Participation in a general assessment with modified administration.

- Participation in an alternate assessment.

- No assessment.

The fifth possibility — no assessment — is no possibility now. 20 U.S.C. § 1412(a)(17)(A).

But the language of the IDEA seems to allow students who can participate in general assessments with modified administration to slip under the radar screen. Section 1412(a)(17)(A) states that: (1) states must include children with disabilities in general State and districtwide assessments, if they can participate "with appropriate accommodations" and (2) states must conduct alternate assessments of children with disabilities who "cannot participate in State and districtwide assessment programs."

Taken literally, then, there is no clear IDEA statutory directive regarding students with disabilities who *could* participate in general assessments, if permitted to take the test with modified administration. It is for this reason that these disabled students have been termed "gap or gray-area kids."[13] It is not clear if they should be considered to be participating in general assessments or taking alternate assessments. Correct characterization is critical because it is only in the latter instance that the students' scores can be disaggregated.[14]

The language of the IDEA regulations suggests students who take statewide and districtwide assessments with modified administration are participating in general assessments. Specifically, 34 C.F.R. § 300.138(a) requires inclusion of students with disabilities in general State and districtwide assessment programs, with appropriate accommodations *and* modifications in administration, if necessary." This language appears to distinguish between appropriate accommodations (i.e., accommodated administration) and modified administration, requiring participation of disabled students who require either in general assessments.

Limited, and at best elliptical, support for this interpretation of the IDEA assessment requirement can be found in discussion accompanying the publication of IDEA final regulations. DOE appears to acknowledge therein that it recognizes that "appropriate modifications" of a general assessment, "modified administration" of a general assessment and alternate assessments are different things.[15]

In addition, an interpretation of the statute as compelling the participation in general assessments of disabled students who require modified administration is consistent with Congressional intent. If such students do not have to participate in general assessments, they can be more easily disregarded. We all know Congress did not have this in mind.

Admittedly, this response is less than clear. But so is the law — at least at this point. If you are unsure about how to proceed, recognize that you are in good company. Here is an example of how one state is wrestling with this issue, as shown by a question and answer representing its then-current interpretation of the IDEA assessment requirements.

Question: Will there be a modified assessment for students who even with accommodations are unable to take the standard assessment but who do not meet all of the eligibility criteria for the alternate assessment?

Response: At the present time, the need to develop a modified assessment is being studied. [The State Department of Education] continues to investigate the many assessment issues and student concerns related to a modified assessment.[16]

9. Is out-of-level testing an alternate assessment?

No, not according to DOE.

Out-of-level testing is generally understood to mean administration of a standardized test to a student who is at a different grade level than the grade level for which the test was designed. In the context of students with disabilities, out-of-level testing may involve a disabled student taking an assessment customarily given to younger nondisabled students.

The IDEA regulations at 34 C.F.R. § 300.138 do not address out-of-level testing. But in a surprising departure from its refusal to respond to commenters' specific questions, DOE took a position on this issue in discussion accompanying the publication of the IDEA final regulations.

The determination of what level of an assessment is appropriate for a particular child is to be made by the IEP team. It should be noted, however, that out-of-level testing will be considered a modified administration of a test rather than an alternate test[.][17]

10. Are there generally accepted criteria for identifying when a student with a disability should be subject to alternate assessment?

In the absence of federal guidelines, states are charged with developing their own legal standards. The author expects that states' criteria will coalesce as each state adopts standards premised on generally accepted psychological and educational principles. The eligibility criteria for alternate assessment adopted by the state of Kansas appear to be consistent with federal requirements and best practice and we thus present them as an example.[18]

In Kansas, alternate assessment is appropriate only when *all* of the following is the case for a particular student with a disability:

- The student is IDEA-eligible and is receiving services under an IEP.

- The student's "demonstrated cognitive abilities and adaptive behavior require substantial adjustment to the general curriculum."

- The objectives in the student's IEP mainly relate to functional capabilities rather than academic progress.

- The student primarily requires direct and extensive instruction to acquire, maintain, generalize and transfer the skills done in the naturally occurring settings of the student's life (such as school, vocational/career, community, recreation, leisure and home).

In addition, no "mixing and matching" of regular assessments and alternate assessments is permitted. If a student can participate in one regular state assessment on some basis, then a way will have to be found for him to participate in all.

Endnotes

[1]   JAY P. HEUBERT, ROBERT M. HAUSER, EDS., HIGH STAKES: TESTING FOR TRACKING, PROMOTION, AND GRADUATION 197 (National Academy Press 1999) (citation omitted).

[2]   64 *Fed. Reg.* 12565 (1999).

[3]   *Id.*

[4]   64 *Fed. Reg.* 12564 (1999).

[5]   *Id.*

[6]   "Frequently Asked Questions & Answers Assessing Students with Disabilities and the Kansas State Assessments" (November 1998) <http://www.ksbe.state.ks.us/sss/faq.html> Kansas State Department of Education (October 19, 1999).

[7]   "Louisiana's School and District Accountability System" <http://www.doe.state.la.us/DOE/account/Policy/acct-main.html> Louisiana Department of Education (November 16, 1999).

[8]   64 *Fed. Reg.* 12565 (1999).

[9]   See *Alternate Assessments: Accounting for Students With the Most Severe Disabilities*, THE SPECIAL EDUCATOR®, vol. 14, iss. 20 (January 1, 1999).

[10]   64 *Fed. Reg.* 12564 (1999).

[11]   The latter viewpoint is the conclusion articulated by an educator, who preferred to remain nameless, in *Alternate Assessments: Accounting for Students With the Most Severe Disabilities*, THE SPECIAL EDUCATOR®, *supra*, note 9.

[12]   See, e.g., Assessing Special Education Students (ASES) Work Group Council of Chief State School Officers, "Determining When Accommodated Test Administrations Are Comparable to Standard Test Administrations" <http://www.coled.umn.edu/NCEO/Accommodations/brief.htm> University of Minnesota (October 18, 1999).

[13]   "Alternate Assessments: Allowing All Students to Participate in Large-Scale Assessments" <http://ici2.coled.umn.edu/ntn/audio/1999/jun.html> National Transition Network (November 23, 1999).

[14]   See Question 10 in chapter 6 regarding test score aggregation requirements under the IDEA.

[15]   64 *Fed. Reg.* 12565 (1999).

[16]   "Frequently Asked Questions & Answers Assessing Students with Disabilities and the Kansas State Assessments," *supra*, note 6.

[17]   64 *Fed. Reg.* 12565 (1999).

[18]   "The Kansas Alternate Assessment Status Report" June 1999, <http://www.ksbe.state.ks,us/sss/status_report.html> Kansas State Department of Education (September 1, 1999).

Chapter 8

HIGH SCHOOL EXIT EXAMINATIONS

1. Do federal laws regulate high school exit exams?

Yes, courts have ruled that when a state requires that a student pass an exit exam to graduate high school with a regular high school diploma, it triggers the students' constitutional right to procedural due process. Similarly, the rights of students under Title VI of the Civil Rights Act of 1964 and Section 504 are also implicated. We discuss Section 504 (and IDEA) issues in Questions 2 to 6; the balance of this response concerns federal laws affecting both disabled and nondisabled students.

The high school graduation requirements of at least 20 states include a requirement that a student achieve a passing grade on standardized tests that measure mastery of what are commonly called core subjects, e.g., English, mathematics, science or social studies. These standardized tests are often referred to as "exit exams." Until recently, most exit exams were "minimum competency tests," requiring students to demonstrate mastery of eighth-grade reading and mathematical skills. Now, as we discuss in more detail in Question 8, some states are raising the stakes. Because of their criticality to the test-takers, exit exams are often called "high-stakes tests."

In *Brookhart v. Illinois State Board of Education*, EHLR 554:285 (7th Cir. 1983) the court grounded its opinion on the legality of exit exams on the deferential posture that is the norm when federal courts are called upon to examine educational decisions made by states and local school districts. "The school district's desire to ensure the value of its diploma by requiring graduating students to attain minimal skills is admirable, and the courts will interfere with educational policy decisions only when necessary to protect individual statutory or constitutional rights."

In *Debra P. v. Turlington*, 644 F.2d 397 (5th Cir. 1981) the Court of Appeals addressed allegations that the state's exit exam requirement violated both federal statutory and constitutional rights.

With regard to individual statutory rights, the court supported the right of a class of African-American students to bring a claim under Title VI of the Civil Rights Act of 1964 and its implementing regulations. Title VI bars discrimination against students in the provision of educational services on the basis of race, color or national origin. The students' challenge alleged that the state's high school exit examination discriminated against African-American students, who had a disproportionately high failure rate.

In evaluating the students' claims the court adopted the disparate impact analysis established by controlling judicial authority in connection with Title VI. The court held that, even assuming an exit exam has a discriminatory impact on African-American students, a school district may continue to use the test if it demonstrates that the exit exam is an integral part of the state's academic program. *Accord, Larry P. v. Riles*, EHLR 557:433 (9th Cir. 1986).

The Fifth Circuit also opined in *Debra P.* that an exit examination requirement also might have constitutional dimensions. There is no federal constitutional right to an education. Whether a student has such a right, and if so, the contours of the right, are a matter of state law, specifically the state constitution, as well as state laws and regulations governing public education. However, assuming state law creates a property interest in education, the rights of students to procedural due process under the Fourteenth Amendment are implicated when an exit examination is a state-created requirement for graduation.

In addition, the Seventh Circuit Court of Appeals in *Brookhart v. Illinois State Board of Education*, EHLR 554:285 (7th Cir. 1983) also recognized a liberty interest in receipt of a diploma "sufficient to invoke the procedural protections of the due process clause of the 14th Amendment to the U.S. Constitution."

According to both courts, procedural due process in connection with conditioning graduation with a regular high school diploma upon achieving a passing grade on an exit exam entails the following:

- States must give students "adequate notice" that they will be required to pass an exit examination in order to earn a high school diploma. The notice must advise students what is considered to be a passing score and what will happen if a student does not pass. What is adequate notice? We discuss this in greater detail in Question 6.

- The test must be "fair," that is, the state must teach what it tests. Put into educational jargon, the test must have "curricular validity." If the purpose of the test is to determine whether a student has mastered the subject matter as part of a student's eligibility for a diploma, the content of the exit exam must be correlated to what the state has afforded its students an opportunity to learn.

The National Governor's Association clarifies curricular validity in this way:

Curricular validity has come to mean the consistency between the test content and what is found in the curricular materials and what is being taught in classrooms. In *Debra P. v. Turlington*, [the State] demonstrated curricula validity by commissioning a study by a private firm and carried out by the state department of education and local school districts that surveyed curricular materials, teachers, district personnel and students. The court accepted the results of the study, which provided a cross-sectional sample, as evidence that the content of the exit exam was being taught in Florida classrooms.[1]

2. Is a state required to validate statewide tests required for graduation for students with disabilities?

The answer appears to be "no."

The IDEA requires that "standardized tests" used in connection with evaluating a student with a disability be validated for the specific purpose for which they are used. 34 C.F.R. § 300.532(c)(1). However, the IDEA regulations, by their terms, do not address validation of tests taken by all students, including students with disabilities, to ascertain proficiency on statewide standards. They concern only testing and assessment used in connection with establishing whether a student meets the eligibility requirements of 34 C.F.R. § 300.7.

The same is true under Section 504 regulations. OCR gave a detailed explanation of its position on this issue in *Georgia Department of Education*, EHLR 352:480 (OCR, Region IV 1987), which addressed allegations that the state should have validated the Georgia Basic Skills Test (GBST) for students with learning disabilities. Because all students were required to pass the GBST in order to obtain a regular high school diploma, the complainant charged that failing to validate the test for students with learning disabilities was discrimination on the basis of disability.

OCR supported the state, however. Nothing in the Section 504 regulations was found to create an obligation to validate the test separately for students with learning disabilities. OCR rejected the applicability of 34 C.F.R. § 104.35(b)(1), (3) to the GBST. That section, which specifies that tests must be validated for the specific purpose for which they are used, applies only to tests used for individual evaluation and placement (provision of FAPE).

OCR similarly found that 34 C.F.R. § 104.4, a more general prohibition on methods of test administration, which have the effect of discriminating on the basis of disability, did "not mandate test validation with respect to any or all categories of handicapping conditions."

To the best knowledge of the author, no court has addressed the particular Section 504 challenge to exit exams or minimum competency tests analyzed by OCR in *Georgia Department of Education*. The student-plaintiffs in *Brookhart v. Illinois State Board of Education*, EHLR 554:285 (7th Cir. 1983) urged the court to rule that both Section 504 and the IDEA require all tests to be validated separately for students with disabilities. The court refused to take the bait, though, ruling against the students on narrower "less intrusive" grounds. We discuss the court's ruling in *Brookhart* in Question 3.

3. Is a state requirement that a student pass an exit examination or minimum competency test in order to graduate with a regular high school diploma inconsistent with the IDEA?

No. Even though some IDEA-eligible students with disabilities will not be able to pass the test because of their disabilities, denial of a regular high school diploma is not equivalent to denial of FAPE in all instances. *Brookhart v. Illinois State Bd. of Ed.*, EHLR 554:285 (7th Cir. 1983).

The *Brookhart* decision concerned the claims of a group of IDEA-eligible students (one student was physically disabled, one was multiply disabled, four were educable mentally disabled and eight had learning disabilities) who failed the state minimum competency test and were accordingly denied regular high school diplomas. The students claimed their failure to pass the exam was the foreseeable consequence of their IEPs not providing for instruction in the subject matter covered by the test. For this reason they claimed they had been denied FAPE. They also alleged they had been discriminated against on the basis of disability and denied due process.

The court affirmed the lower court decision in favor of the school district on the students' IDEA claims. Denial of diplomas to students with disabilities who are unable to achieve the educational level necessary to pass a minimum competency test is not a denial of FAPE, assuming the school district can establish the following:

- The lack of exposure to the subject matter that will be covered in the exam resulted from a determination by the student's IEP team that the subject matter was inappropriate for the student in light of his disabilities.

- The student has received special education and related services in accordance with an IEP designed to provide a meaningful educational benefit.

Although not bound to follow the decision of the *Brookhart* court, the hearing officer in *Birmingham Board of Education*, 20 IDELR 1281 (SEA Ala. 1994) came to the same conclusion with respect to whether failure to prepare disabled students to pass the state's exit exam is a denial of FAPE. The hearing officer opined that, when an IEP team determines that the student's education program should not include instruction in a subject that is the subject of the state's minimum competency test (i.e., reading, language or mathematics), the student should not take the test. This is the case even though the student will, thus, be ineligible to receive a regular high school diploma upon graduation.

According to the hearing officer, assuming the following is the case, the IEP team's decision that the student is not a candidate for the exit exams is not a denial of FAPE:

- The IEP team considers all available data, including but not limited to assessment data and teacher evaluations, in the course of deciding that the education program for the student should not include instruction in the competencies subject to minimum competency testing;

- The IEP team must revisit its decision annually; and

8 : 3

- The exemptions agreed to by the IEP team must be documented fully in the student's IEP.

In addition to their allegation of denial of FAPE, the students in *Brookhart* claimed that the requirement that a student with a disability pass a minimum competency test was inconsistent with 34 C.F.R. § 300.532(f). That regulation contains the caveat that no single procedure be used as the sole criterion for determining an appropriate educational program. As discussed in Question 2 in connection with test validation, the pertinence of that regulation with reference to exit exams is questionable. In any event, at some point during the litigation the students conceded that passing the exit exam was not the sole criterion for graduation.

4. Is a state requirement that a student pass an exit examination or minimum competency test in order to graduate with a regular high school diploma inconsistent with Section 504?

No, a requirement that a student with a disability pass an exit examination or minimum competency test in order to receive a regular high school diploma is not discrimination on the basis of disability, providing the school district permits students with disabilities to take the exam with reasonable accommodations.

The Supreme Court's decision in *Southeastern Community College v. Davis*, EHLR 551:177 (1979) is the controlling law in this regard. However, if the requested accommodation calls for "substantial modifications" of an academic program, the accommodation is not reasonable, as a matter of law, and does not have to be provided. Section 504 does not require an academic program to compromise its integral criteria in order to accommodate a student with a disability.

In *Brookhart v. Illinois State Board of Education*, EHLR 554:285 (7th Cir. 1983) the Seventh Circuit relied on the reasoning in *Southeastern Community College* in adjudicating the claims of students with disabilities who did not pass the state minimum competency exam, required for graduation with a regular high school diploma.

The court distinguished between the reasonable accommodations that disabled students have the right to receive when taking minimum competency tests and those that are unreasonable.

With regard to the former, the court had this to say:

[A]n otherwise qualified student who is unable to disclose the degree of learning he actually possesses because of the test format or environment would be the object of discrimination solely on the basis of his handicap. ... [F]ederal law requires administrative modification to minimize the effects of plaintiffs' handicaps on any future examinations.

EHLR at 288.

But administrative modifications were not at issue in this case, the court noted.

Plaintiffs in this case have no grounds on which to argue that the contents of the M.C.T. [minimum competency test] are discriminatory solely because handicapped students who are incapable of attaining a level of minimal competency will fail the test. Altering the content of the M.C.T. to accommodate an individual's inability to learn the tested material because of his handicap would be a 'substantial modification,' as well as a 'perversion' of the diploma requirement. A student who is unable to learn because of his handicap is surely not an individual who is qualified in spite of his handicap. Thus denial of a diploma because of inability to pass the M.C.T. is not discrimination under Section 504.

EHLR at 288.

5. Can a student with a disability receive an accommodation for an exit examination if he has not received that accommodation during the course of his schooling?

Probably not. In some instances a student may not be able to have the benefit of an accommodation he has received in the classroom if the accommodation impacts test validity. But it is at least equally unlikely that a student with a disability will be entitled to receive an accommodation for the sole purpose of taking the exit exam.

An accommodation that might help just about anyone — disabled or nondisabled — is extended time to complete the exam. But decision-makers have shot down requests for relaxation of time limits when the accommodation has never been part of a student's menu of services and modifications. *See, e.g., Board of Educ. of the Wappingers Cent. Sch. Dist.*, 27 IDELR 517 (SEA N.Y. 1997).

Similar reasoning has been adopted when evaluating requests for other accommodations made for the first time for exit exams. The hearing officer in *Mobile County Board of Education*, 26 IDELR 695 (SEA Ala. 1997), for example, held that the policies and procedures used by the SEA in granting or denying a requested accommodation were reasonable and designed to prevent an exit exam from being invalidated. Under those policies students with disabilities were entitled to use on an exit exam any test accommodation that had been a part of a student's instructional program for at least a year, as long as use of the accommodation would not invalidate the test. Consistent with that policy, the 18-year-old student with a learning disability was not permitted to have the language and math portions of the standardized test he was required to pass to graduate read aloud. The request was denied because the student had never received the requested accommodation during his academic career.

6. Is the advance notice for exit exams as a diploma requirement the same time period for both disabled and nondisabled students?

No definitive answer can be found in Section 504, the IDEA or interpretive case law. But there is limited judicial guidance suggesting that an extended period of time may be appropriate for a student with a disability in some instances. In any event, best practice involves broad dissemination of information about graduation standards and accommodations to students with disabilities and their parents.

When a student has not been provided adequate advance notice about exit examination requirements he may be able to establish that his due process rights have been violated. *Debra P. v. Turlington*, 644 F.2d 397 (5th Cir. 1981). However, the *Debra P.* court did not identify a particular amount of time that will be deemed adequate. Nor has any other court established a specific period that will be appropriate in all instances.

As discussed in Question 3, the *Brookhart* court refused to hold that the class of students with disabilities were denied FAPE because they were instructed to meet IEP objectives, rather than to master the curricula covered by the state's newly instituted exit exam. Nor was the court willing to agree that the state had an obligation to alter the content of the test to allow disabled students who lacked the cognitive skills to master the content to receive passing grades. But on one other point the court supported the students' claims. Denying students adequate notice of any new diploma requirement, e.g., sufficient time to prepare for new diploma requirements violates due process because it is "fundamentally unfair." EHLR 554 at 289.

When students with disabilities are involved, the court opined that what one might ordinarily consider a fairly long period of time might be inadequate for an individual student. In the particular instance before it, the court held that a year to a year-and-a-half was not adequate advance notice for the student-litigants. "[I]n an educational system that assumes special education students learn at a slower rate than regular division students," a year and a half at most to prepare for the [test] is insufficient." EHLR 554 at 290.

Practical tips for providing adequate notice about testing and diploma requirements include the following:

- Develop and distribute widely an appropriate advance notice for parents and students regarding choices in making decisions about testing, grading and modifications.

- Be sure parents understand the difference between accommodations which lower or fundamentally alter regular education (including regular high school diploma) standards and those which do not. This is necessary in order to allow parents to make informed choices regarding these accommodations.

- Address in the student handbook issues regarding access to courses at all curriculum levels and issues relating to accommodations and modifications of regular education classes for students with disabilities and other identified students. The handbook should specify that all modifications which lower or substantively alter course standards, expectations and requirements need to be made by a student's IEP team and included in the student's IEP.[2]

7. Can a state modify the requirements for award of a regular high school diploma to a student with a disability?

Yes. As discussed in more detail in Question 4, a state does not have to lower its substantive standards for award of regular high school diplomas to students with disabilities in order to comply with Section 504 or the IDEA. On the other hand, though, according to OCR, nothing in Section 504 or the ADA prohibits states from electing to lower standards in individual cases. "There are no restrictions in either Section 504 or Title II that would prohibit a school district from modifying or adjusting graduation requirements, consistent with the student's IEP." *Letter to Runkel*, 25 IDELR 387, 390 (OCR, Region VIII 1996).

The administrative decision in *Kingsway Regional Board of Education*, 18 IDELR 1322 (SEA N.J. 1992) illustrates how a state may allow a school district to award a regular high school diploma to a student with a disability who did not meet state requirements for graduation. In that instance the IEP of a student specifically exempted a student identified as behaviorally disordered from the Mathematics, P.E./Health/Safety and Career Education state requirements. Graduation was conditioned upon completion of IEP goals.

8. Do all states require students to pass a statewide exit examination in order to receive a regular high school diploma?

No. But we are now in the age of "standards-based" education. According to many educators and government officials, those standards can no longer be local. Even national standards might not be enough for our students to compete in a global economy. So the trend appears to be toward universal adoption of a competency standard as an additional requirement (besides successful completion of a specified number and range of courses) for award of a regular high school diploma.

But we're not there yet. We identify and briefly describe current (as of the date referenced in the citation) requirements on a state-by-state basis below.

In this regard, we note at the outset that it may be impolitic in some quarters to continue to refer to these standardized testing requirements for graduation as "minimum competency requirements." The summary of Hawaii's exit examination requirements includes a discussion of why that state has taken exception to the whole concept of minimum requirements.

Alabama

The class of 2001 will be the first that will have to pass the state's new Alabama High School Graduation Exam (AHSGE) in order to receive a regular high school diploma. Unlike the previous exam, which was on an eighth-grade level, the AHSGE measures whether students have mastered eleventh-grade level mathematics, reading, language, and science (core courses).[3]

Alaska

Beginning with the graduating class of 2002, students will have to pass Alaska's new (1997) High School Qualifying Examination in order to earn a regular high school diploma. Students who do not receive a passing grade on the examination, but otherwise meet the requirements for graduation, will receive a certificate of attendance. The test will measure the students' mastery in reading, writing and mathematics.[4]

Arizona

The state adopted Arizona's Instrument to Measure Standards (AIMS) as part of its program for standards-based education and accountability. The test will be given to students in grades three, five and eight. An exit-level version of the test will also serve as an exit examination for graduation with a regular high school diploma. Pursuant to a state statutory directive, students must demonstrate mastery in the areas of at least reading, writing, and mathematics, as evidenced by passing scores in AIMS tests, in order to graduate. A student will first take the test in 10th-grade and have up to four retake opportunities during the next two years. The tests are being field-tested now. The first graduating class for whom the test will be "high stakes" is the Class of 2002.[5]

Arkansas

In 1999 Arkansas passed legislation authorizing the creation of a program aimed at improving the "academic preparation of public high school students for secondary education." One aspect of that program was provision of services intended to increase the scores of graduating students taking the statewide ACT assessment. The ACT assessment measures skills in English, reading, math, and science reasoning and is required for admittance to most in-state colleges and universities. There is, however, no requirement that all high school seniors take the ACT in order to earn a regular high school diploma.[6]

California

In 1999 the state legislature authorized development of a high school exit examination. The statute reads, in pertinent part: "The Superintendent of Public Instruction, with the approval of the State Board of Education, shall develop a high school examination in language arts and mathematics in accordance with the statewide academically rigorous content standards adopted by the State Board of Education[.]" The purpose of the exam is to "ensure that pupils who graduate from high school can demonstrate grade level competency in reading, writing, and mathematics." Development is still in its earliest stage. No decisions have been made yet about either the test content or its format, although, of necessity, the test will be criterion-referenced in nature with its content reflecting state-approved curricula.[7]

8 : 7

Colorado

Swimming against the tide, Colorado does not have statewide standards for graduation. "Each local school board defines graduation requirements for its district. These vary from district to district. The state considers a graduate to be any student who has met the graduation requirements of his or her local school district."[8] This is not to say that Colorado does not acknowledge the importance of conducting statewide assessments of students' mastery of the core curricula. The state's CSAP (Colorado State Assessment Program) assesses student performance in math, reading, reading & writing, and science at the third, fourth, fifth, seventh, eighth and 10th-grade levels. According to the state DOE, CSAP is not intended to provide detailed information about any one student or measure performance in a "punitive" way.[9]

Connecticut

Legislation enacted in 1995 mandated administration of a statewide assessment with challenging state goals to all publicly enrolled 10th-grade students. By law that test, the Connecticut Academic Performance Test or CAPT, cannot be used as the sole criterion for the award of a regular high school diploma or promotion to a higher grade. While the test is, therefore, not an exit exam, students still have a personal stake in the results. Students are awarded Certificates of Mastery for each subject area in which they at least meet state goals. Test results are reported on the students' official school transcripts. Colleges and prospective employers may take them into account. The tested areas are mathematics, language arts (response to literature and editing), science and interdisciplinary.[10]

Delaware

Delaware does not have an exit examination requirement. Since 1998 secondary school students participate in the Delaware Student Testing Program (DSTP) in reading, writing, mathematics, science and social studies in the 10th-grade and in the 11th-grade. The purpose of the test is measurement of school districts vis-à-vis student performance. It is their accountability that is at issue.[11]

District of Columbia

The sole requirement for graduation with a regular high school diploma is successful completion of 23.5 Carnegie Units, representing the achievement of passing grades in the required distribution of courses.[12]

Florida

Florida conditions graduation with a regular high school diploma upon meeting statewide standards that include achieving a passing grade on the High School Competency Test (HSCT). The test is described as a "basic skills" test, assessing whether the student can demonstrate minimum competency in mathematics and communications (i.e., reading and writing). The state has responded to the national movement toward higher standards by elevating slightly the states' minimum grading requirements. In 1997 the legislature increased the minimum cumulative GPA requirement for graduation from 1.5 to 2.0, reduced course credit given for low-level coursework, and raised the minimum numeric percentage grade two points (from 75 to 77) for letter grade C and 5 points (from 65 to 70) for letter grade D.[13]

Georgia

In 1991 the state introduced the requirement that all students must pass "basic skills tests" in reading, writing and mathematics in order to earn a regular high school diploma. The subject matter and the objectives of the Georgia High School Graduation Tests (GHSGT) have both been enhanced since that time. Since 1998 students have been required to pass tests in English language arts, mathematics, writing, social studies and science. Further, acquisition of minimum skills is no longer enough. The law changing the testing requirements states that the GHSGT must "include process and application skills as assessed in a range of academic content and shall exceed minimum and essential skills by extending the assessments' range of difficulty." Students must pass all five tests in order to receive a Georgia regular high school diploma. Failure to pass even one will limit a student (assuming all other graduation requirements are met) to receipt of a Certificate of Performance.[14]

Hawaii

Hawaii is bringing in the new millennium by suspending use of the Hawaii State Test of Essential Competencies (HSTEC) as a requirement for earning a regular high school diploma, effective with the class of 2000. At first blush, a state that proposes to do away with mastery requirements seems to be totally out of touch. But the increasing importance of high standards is exactly the reason why the state DOE concluded that a test, which measured achievement of only "minimal standards," had become "inappropriate." Another problem, according to the state Office of Accountability and School Instructional Support, was the multiple-choice format of the test. "Research on assessment emphasizes the importance of including performance-based assessments in any series of tests."[15]

Idaho

There is no statewide exit examination required for graduation with a regular high school diploma. But Administrative Rules of the State Board of Education effective starting school year 1998-1999 seem to give local school districts the authority to design and implement their own, subject to state approval. "All students must meet locally established subject area exiting standards (using state standards as minimum requirements) demonstrated through various measures of accountability including examinations or other measures."[16]

Illinois

Legislation enacted in July 1999 amended statewide testing requirements. Under the new law the Prairie State Achievement Examination (PSAE) tests 11th-grade students in reading, writing, mathematics, science, and social science. Under the prior law a passing grade on PSAE was required to graduate with a high school diploma. Under the new law, a student's receipt of a regular high school diploma is no longer contingent upon receipt of a passing score on the PSAE. However, students with qualifying scores may earn a Prairie State Achievement Award for each subject tested. A student's highest score and performance levels are noted on his transcript for consideration by colleges or prospective employers. The PSAE should be distinguished from the Illinois Standards Achievement Tests (ISAT), which are administered periodically to students throughout their elementary and secondary schooling to measure achievement relative to statewide goals for content mastery, called the Illinois Learning Standards. The PSAE is a separate 11th-grade test, not a part of the ISAT.[17]

Indiana

Indiana does not have an exit examination requirement, although it does have in place a statewide assessment program (Indiana Statewide Testing for Educational Progress or ISTEP+) for testing students in language arts and mathematics at various points in the elementary and secondary school years.[18]

Iowa

This state does not have an exit examination requirement.[19]

Kansas

This state does not have an exit examination requirement.[20]

Kentucky

Students in Kentucky are not required to earn a passing score on an exit examination in order to graduate with a regular high school diploma. Starting in the year 2002 Kentucky's minimum requirements for graduation with a regular high school diploma are more rigorous. The legislature increased the minimum requirements for graduation from 20 to 22 credits. But it continued to make completion of the minimum number of credits the sole requirement for graduation.[21]

Louisiana

The Graduation Exit Examination (GEE) has been a graduation requirement since 1991. The test has five components: Written Composition, English Language Arts, Mathematics, Science and Social Studies. Students take the first three parts in 10th-grade; the latter two the next year. There are five retest opportunities, including an additional retest opportunity in June of what would be a student's senior year.[22]

Maine

Maine adopted a program of state and local assessments in 1996 that included testing of 11th-grade students. But it does not use the assessment as an exit examination.[23]

Maryland

Students who enter the ninth-grade in the school year starting in 2001 (and in the normal course of events will be graduating in the spring of 2005) will be the first class whose graduation with a regular high school diploma depends upon passing the Maryland High School Assessments. As an initial matter the assessment components will address content mastery in English, algebra or geometry, and government. Local school districts have the option to also test in the area of biology. Trial testing will begin in 2000, but the test will not then be "high stakes" from the student's perspectives. The State Board delayed by one year the original implementation schedule, citing the need for additional time and trial testing in order to allow the DOE to develop a "more accurate picture of the scores [that can be expected during the first year of 'real' testing]." In stating that its goal in delaying implementation is to better establish "challenging, yet attainable, passing scores" the State Board concisely describes the precise delicate balance that educators across the country try to achieve in conditioning graduation upon successful performance on an exit examination.[24]

Massachusetts

The Massachusetts Comprehensive Assessment System (MCAS) Program was implemented in response to the legislative directive in the Education Reform Law of 1993. The MCA is a statewide assessment program that includes, but is not limited to, use of the assessment as an exit examination. Beginning with students expected to graduate in 2003, passing grades on the 10th-grade level MCAS tests is a requirement for a regular high school diploma. Four testing areas, based upon the content in the state's Curriculum Framework, are now identified: English Language Arts; Mathematics; Science & Technology; and History and Social Science. The results are expressed in terms of four possible performance levels — advanced, proficient, needs improvement, or failing — so it is not simply a determination of whether the student has met minimum requirements.[25]

Michigan

Michigan does not require that students earn passing grades on an exit examination in order to receive a regular high school diploma. However, a graduating student can earn endorsements on the basis of superior test performance on the "MEAP (Michigan Educational Assessment Program) High School Test." When students are in 11th-grade they are tested in mathematics, science, reading, writing and social studies. Prior to 1998 test performance that reflected acquisition of basic skills resulted in endorsement. Governing law and DOE regulations were changed at that time, however, to allow students to earn one of three possible levels of endorsement. Level 1 indicates that the student exceeded Michigan Standards; Level 2 that his performance met the standards; and Level 3 that the student's performance was at the basic skill level. "[T]he State Board of Educators ... believe that basic skills are no longer sufficient for student success following graduation and that it was important to continue to identify and recognize student performance that meets or exceeds Michigan standards." A student can graduate with a Level 3 endorsement, or even without an endorsement at all. However, a student who graduates without an endorsement is certainly in a different position with colleges and potential employers than a student who can point to a Level 1 or Level 2 endorsement.[26]

Minnesota

In 1993 Minnesota introduced novel statewide graduation requirements that go exit examinations one better in attempting to measure the amount and quality of knowledge and skills a student is taking away from his public school education. New state Graduation Standards have two components. In addition to any local school district requirements students must meet to earn a regular high school diploma, students must also meet state-imposed Basic Standards and High Standards. According to the state Department of Children, Families & Learning[27] "the new state requirements focus on results. They define what students must know and must be able to do in order to graduate from a public high school in Minnesota."

The author's review of the state departments of education public information indicates that no other state is doing anything quite like what Minnesota proposes to do with public high school students, starting with the class of 2002. Accordingly, we excerpt extensively from the departmental explanation of the new graduation requirements below:

Standards are clearly defined expectations against which individual student achievement and progress may be judged. They outline what a student needs to both know and do in a particular subject.

The Basic Standards are the 'safety net' that ensure high school graduates have a minimum competency in reading, mathematics and writing. Students show they meet the Basic Standards by passing the basic skill tests first administered in the eighth-grade in reading and mathematics; 10th-graders take a writing test.

The High Standards define what students should know, understand and be able to do to demonstrate a high level of achievement. The High Standards are organized into ten learning areas. ... Public high school students from the class of 2002 and beyond must complete 24 of 48 possible standards from ten learning areas. Some standards are required for all students, while in some learning areas students may choose the standards they wish to complete.

Students complete a standard when they complete all the work locally required for that standard. Student achievement of the High Standards is assessed by locally designed assignments, that, taken together as a 'package,' show whether a student has learned and can apply the knowledge and skills outlined in the standard. These assignments ask students to apply their knowledge in real-world situations.

In short, Minnesota embraces the concept as requiring more than passing grades and accumulation of sufficient credits to demonstrate readiness to graduate. At the same time it has emphatically rejected standardized testing, the customary mode of testing. "In order to succeed, our children need to do more than memorize facts and regurgitate them for a test. Knowing and doing must go hand in hand."[28]

Mississippi

The Functional Literacy Examination (FLE) serves as this state's exit examination. As modest in aspirations as its name suggests, the FLE — an eighth-grade level test given to 11th-grade students — is identified by the state's DOE as the "only" requirement for earning a regular high school diploma. The FLE tests in the areas of reading, mathematics and written communications. Unlike most tests used to establish eligibility for graduation, the FLE is an untimed test. Any student who fails to achieve a passing score the first time is entitled to retake the test at least three more times.[29] The state DOE asserts that the FLE is to be phased out in favor of a new Subject Area Testing Program (SATP). The four subject areas are Algebra I, Biology, U.S. History from 1877 and English II (with a writing assignment). "Probably" the FLE will be used for another three years. "Eventually" students will be required to take tests in all four subject areas in order to receive a regular high school diploma. Clearly this changeover to a new exit examination program is in the embryonic stages. (The author is not trying to make fun of the state DOE; the quoted language is verbatim.[30])

Missouri

The state does not have an exit examination requirement for graduation. Minimum state requirements for award of a regular high school diploma are based upon earning a specified number of units of credits in several subject areas.[31]

Montana

This state does not have an exit examination requirement for graduation.[32]

Nebraska

The state does not have an exit examination requirement. In fact, it is just now (late 1999) in the process of developing academic standards in reading/writing, math, science, history and social sciences and an assessment process to measure student achievement toward those standards.[33]

Nevada

Students must pass both parts (Mathematics and English) of an 11th-grade level minimum proficiency examination in order to graduate with a regular high school diploma. If a student fails either part of the test in 11th-grade the test can be taken up to more three times prior to graduation and once after graduation. Students who are not able to pass the test prior to high school graduation, but otherwise meet state and local school district requirements for graduation receive a Certificate of Completion. OCR addressed complaints about alleged discrimination in the administration of the mathematics portion of the test in *Nevada State Department of Education*, 25 IDELR 752 (OCR, Region X 1996), addressed in Question 4 in chapter 1.

New Hampshire

This state has an assessment program that includes testing of 11th-graders since 1993. The results of the test are reported on an individual student basis. However, the test results are not used to determine whether a student has met state and local graduation requirements.[34]

New Jersey

Students must pass all three sections of the New Jersey Grade 11 High School Proficiency Test (HSPT11), Reading, Mathematics, and Writing, in order to earn a regular high school diploma. As of 1999 the state Department of Education is proposing new regulatory changes to implement its Core Curriculum Content Standards (adopted in 1996) and related statewide assessment system. One aspect of the proposed regulations is the phase-out of the HSPT11 in favor of the High School Proficiency Assessment (HSPA), under which a graduating student must be able to demonstrate proficiency in all the content areas covered by the aforementioned Standards. The first students to be subject to the new requirement will be those graduating in 2007. According to the state DOE the proposed regulations reflect the shift from minimum competency to higher expectations for all students.[35]

New Mexico

Students must pass the state's high school minimum competency examination in order to receive a regular high school diploma. The test has six parts: reading, writing, language arts, mathematics, science and social studies. Students are given four chances, starting in the 10th-grade, to pass the test before the end of their 12th-grade year. Either the test is surprisingly easy or the state's schools are really doing a bang-up job. Historically, ninety-seven percent of seniors pass.[36]

New York

High school students in New York have long had to take a series of "commencement level examinations" or "Regents Competency Tests" in connection with graduation. The tests have served as both a minimum competency examination for award of a regular high school diploma and, for students whose scores indicated higher levels of achievement, qualifying exams for the award of endorsed or Regents diplomas.

That testing system is being phased out and will be replaced in its entirety for students graduating after June 2004. During the phase-in period the passing score for a regular high school diploma will be raised 10 points. After that period, i.e., for students entering ninth-grade in 2001, a student will have to achieve a passing score in all 5 Regents examinations (English, mathematics, global history and geography, United States history and government, and science). Superior achievement, as indicated by test performance, will continue to be endorsed or recognized on diplomas and noted on students' transcripts.[37]

North Carolina

In 1997 the state legislature directed the state DOE to develop a plan to implement, among other things, high school exit exams. The exit exam will not exist in a vacuum, though. It is to be part of a system of statewide student accountability standards, with curriculum content and achievement standards for elementary, middle school and high school age students. Effective with the graduating class of 2003, students will have to earn a passing score on an "exit exam of essential skills" in order to receive a regular high school diploma. The exam tests whether students meet statewide standards, called gateways. The exam will be given in the spring of a student's 11th-grade year and will assess the "knowledge gained up to that point." That knowledge is in the particular areas of English/reading/grammar, mathematics through Algebra I, science and social studies. With regard to those subject matter areas, the test assesses the following competencies: communication, using numbers, problem solving (application) and processing information. In other words, the exit exam assesses both what a student knows and what he is able to do.[38]

North Dakota

This state does not require students achieve a passing score on an exit examination in order to earn a regular high school diploma.[39]

Ohio

A student must achieve passing scaled scores on the 12th-Grade Proficiency Tests in order to graduate with a regular high school diploma. The five tests cover reading, mathematics, citizenship, science and writing. Passing scores were increased most recently in 1998, although the requirements for honors were not changed.

You will not see "citizenship" often identified as an area being tested in an exit exam. It's not history, *per se*, nor is it quite social science, either, although that may be the subject it most closely resembles. Here is what the state DOE has to say about it:

The student will:

1. Understand the rationale, consequences, and applications of the Constitution, including the Bill of Rights and other amendments, as the supreme law of the land.

2. Identify factors that have contributed to America's cultural pluralism, including historical, racial, ethnic, religious, and linguistic backgrounds of this nation's people.

3. Locate major bodies of water, continents, and significant places in the United States, and important regions and countries of the world.

4. Read maps, charts, or graphs to draw conclusions regarding natural resources and topography of the U.S. and the world.

5. Understand that geographic locations affect the political and economic systems of the world.

6. Understand the following economic concepts:

    a. Individuals and households exchange their resources for the income they need to buy goods and services.
    b. Individuals and business firms use resources to produce goods and services and generate income.
    c. Markets allocate goods and services.
    d. Competition affects markets.
    e. Local, state, and national governments play important roles in a market economy.

7. Understand principles of traditional, market, and command economies (as applied in nations of the world).

8. Distinguish the constitutional relationship among the several levels of government regarding reserved powers, delegated powers, concurrent powers, elastic clause, and powers denied the government.

9. Understand and apply the principles of separation of powers and checks and balances.

10. Compare and contrast the U.S. representative democracy with other types of governments around the world.

11. Understand that lawmaking is influenced through formal and informal processes (recall, referendum, initiative, legislative committees, lobbying).

12. Understand that the evolution of democratic principles (e.g., civil rights, widening franchise) can occur through civil disobedience.

13. Understand the roles of political parties in a democratic process.

14. Describe the ways officials can be elected, appointed, or removed from office.

15. Know the purposes of and the qualifications for voting in Ohio's primary and general elections.

16. Identify significant features of the 14th amendment (due process and equal protection of the laws).

17. Identify the legal responsibilities of citizenship.

18. Demonstrate the ability to use information that enables citizens to make informed choices.

    a. Analyze sources to obtain information.
    b. Compare and contrast points of agreement and disagreement among sources.
    c. Evaluate the reliability of available information.
    d. Identify and weigh alternative viewpoints.

19. Recognize that local and national issues can be related to those confronting the global society.

20. Recognize that a nation's foreign policy may have a worldwide impact.[40]

Oklahoma

Under the 1999 Oklahoma School Testing Program Act high school students must complete an end-of-instruction test in English II and United States History in order to graduate with a regular high school diploma, beginning with the school year 2000-2001. Tests in Biology I and Algebra I are additional requirements, beginning the next school year. The legislation directs the state DOE, in the interest of economy, to adapt tests that are used by other states to assess competency or otherwise commercially available, assuming the tests are criterion-referenced and have contents consistent with state approved curriculum.[41]

Oregon

Under the state's assessment program, called the Oregon Statewide Assessments, 10th-grade students take tests in reading, writing, mathematics, science and social studies. Starting in school year 2000-2001, 10th-grade students whose test results reflect mastery of 12th-grade standards are awarded a Certificate of Advanced Mastery. That is the carrot. But as yet there is no stick, at least as far as the students are concerned. According to the state DOE, passing the test is not required for graduation (unless a school district decides otherwise).[42]

Pennsylvania

There is no state exit examination. Local control is a key element of this state's approach to education. As explained by the Commonwealth's DOE:

> The philosophy of local control has a strong tradition in Pennsylvania. Each school district, through a locally developed strategic plan unique to its community, outlines how it will meet the state's curriculum regulations, including requirements for high school graduation, what academic standards will apply, and how it will assess the individual achievement of its students.[43]

Rhode Island

This state does not have an exit examination requirement.[44]

South Carolina

The High School Exit Examination has been a part of the state's Basic Skills Assessment Program (BSAP) since 1990. The examination, which is first administered in 10th-grade, assesses students' performance in reading, mathematics and writing. Those who do not achieve passing scores the first time have at least four other opportunities to bring their scores up. Starting in 2003, the current exit examination will be replaced by a new test instrument, the PACT Examination, which is part of the newly adopted Palmetto Achievement Challenge Tests (PACT) assessment program.[45]

South Dakota

This state does not have an exit examination requirement.[46]

Tennessee

Students must achieve passing scores on the TCAP Competency Test in order to graduate with a regular high school diploma. The test, which measures student competency in mathematics and language arts (spelling, language, and reading), is given for the first time in the fall of the student's ninth-grade year. Not surprisingly, the state has taken action to "raise the academic bar" for high school students by requiring that students demonstrate mastery of subject matter studied after eighth-grade. The last scheduled administration of the TCAP Competency Test will be in the summer of 2004. Starting with "entering freshmen" (the state DOE's chosen formulation) in the 2001-2002 school year, the exit examination is the more rigorous Gateway Tests.[47] Students will be required to take an 11th-grade Writing Test, as well as end-of-course tests in the following subjects: Math Foundations II, Algebra I, Geometry, Algebra II, Physical Science, Biology, Chemistry, English I, English II, and U.S. History. Passing grades in the English II, Algebra I and Biology tests are a requirement for graduation with a regular high school diploma.[48]

Texas

Achieving a passing score on an exit examination has long been a state requirement for the award of a regular high school diploma. Under legislation enacted in 1995 publicly enrolled students can elect to take one of two exit-level tests in order to meet the exit examination requirement. The exit-level Texas Assessment of Academic Skills (TAAS) tests in reading, mathematics and writing are still being used. As an alternative, a student may apply for graduation with a regular high school diploma on the basis of achieving satisfactory scores on end-of-course assessments in English II, Algebra I and either of Biology I or United States History. As a matter of state law, a student who is eligible for graduation on the basis of his performance on the end-of-course (EOC) tests is not required to take the exit level TAAS test. On the other hand, students who pass the TAAS tests must still take the EOC exams. Further, "mix and match" remains just a fashion concept, in so far as the exit exams are concerned. Students cannot combine results on TAAS or EOC subtests to assemble an ensemble of the required passing grades. "For example, a student is not allowed to meet the graduation requirements by passing TAAS reading and writing tests and the end-of-course examination for Algebra I."[49]

Utah

This state has an assessment program that includes exit-level testing of secondary school students but does not use the results of the testing as a requirement for award of a regular high school diploma.[50]

Vermont

This state does not have an exit examination requirement.

Virginia

The Class of 2004 (school year 2003-2004) will include the first students whose graduation depends upon passing end-of-course tests that measure mastery of the state's academic standards, called the Standards of Learning (SOL). Field-testing of the new tests began in 1998. The SOL tests measure students' achievements in five core content areas: English, Mathematics, Science, History/Social Science, and Computer Technology. The state DOE is in the process of determining what a passing score should be and how many subject matter exams a student will have to pass in order to earn a regular high school diploma. The SOL tests replace the Literacy Passport Test (LPT) as the state's exit examination. Given to ninth-graders, the LPT program measured students' knowledge and skills in reading, writing, and mathematics. Adopting the same goals and reasoning as Tennessee, the state DOE has changed the timing of its exit exam from testing students as they start ninth-grade to testing them as they complete (or nearly so) their secondary school education. As DOE declares, it has opted for "increased academic rigor."[51]

Washington

Washington does not now require graduating students to pass an exit examination. But students graduating in the Class of 2006, and thereafter, will be required to pass assessments designed to demonstrate mastery of "essential academic learning requirements." Students who do so will earn a Certificate of Mastery, a requirement for high school graduation. The legislation empowering development of the program of required assessment states:

> [S]uccessful completion of the high school assessment shall lead to a certificate of mastery. The certificate of mastery shall be obtained by most students at about the age of sixteen, and is evidence that the student has successfully mastered the essential academic requirements during his or her educational career. The certificate of mastery shall be required for graduation but shall not be the only requirement for graduation.[52]

West Virginia

This state does not have an exit examination requirement.[53]

Wisconsin

This state does not have an exit examination requirement.[54]

Wyoming

In 1998 the state enacted legislation directing establishment of a statewide system of academic standards, assessments and accountability. The resulting Wyoming Comprehensive Assessment System, or WYCAS, will test fourth-grade, eighth-grade and 11th-grade students in reading, writing, and mathematics. The purposes of the testing at all three levels relate to school improvement and performance review, but will not serve as a high-stakes test, from the student's perspective.[55]

Endnotes

[1]   "High School Exit Exams: Setting High Expectations," Sept. 1, 1998 web site at <http://www.nga.org/Pubs/Issue Briefs/1998/980901ExitExams.asp> NGA On-line (September 9, 1999).

[2]   *Testing, Grading Modifications: Helpful Hints for Tough Tasks,* THE SPECIAL EDUCATOR®, vol.13, iss. 7 (Oct. 3, 1997).

[3]   "Results of the Alabama High School Pre-Graduation Exam Grade 10 Spring 1999" <http://www.alsde.edu> Alabama State Department of Education (November 15, 1999).

[4]   "The Alaska High School Graduation Qualifying Examination" <http://www.educ.state.ak.us/tls/assessment/gradexam-faq.html> Alaska State Department of Education (November 15, 1999).

[5]   "Academic Standards & Accountability" <http://www.ade.state.az.us/standards/brochure/htm> Arizona Department of Education (November 15, 1999).

[6]   "Student Assessment" Arkansas Department of Education <http://arkedu.state.ar.us/assessment.htm> Arkansas Department of Education (November 15, 1999).

[7]   "High School Exit Examination (HSEE)" <htpp://www.cde.ca.gov/cilbranch/sca/hsee/hsee.html> California Department of Education (November 15, 1999).

[8]   "Definition of Selected Terms" <http://www.cde.state.co.us/cdemgmt/rvdefine.htm> Colorado Department of Education (November 15, 1999).

[9]   "CSAP: What It Is ... And What It's Not" <http://www.cde.state.co.us/cdedepcpm/ascspwht.htm> Colorado Department of Education (November 15, 1999).

[10]   "Connecticut Academic Performance Test" <http://www.state.ct.us'sde/capt/proovr.doc> Connecticut Department of Education (November 15, 1999).

[11]   "Delaware Student Testing Program" <http://www.doe.state.de.us/aab/DSTP-intro.html> Delaware Department of Education (November 15, 1999).

[12]   "High School Graduation Requirements" <http://www.k12/dc.us/dcps/curriculum/curriculum_frame.html> District of Columbia Public School System (November 15, 1999).

[13]   "High School Graduation Requirements (January 1999)" <http://www.firn.edu/doe/doehome.htm> State of Florida Department of Education (November 15, 1999).

[14]   "Georgia High School Graduation Tests (GHSGT)" <http://www.doe.k12.ga.us/sla/ret/ghsgtabout.html> Georgia Department of Education (November 15, 1999).

[15]   "Assessment Resource Center of Hawaii" <http://www.arch.k12.hi.us/student/hstec.htm> Hawaii State Department of Education (November 15, 1999).

[16]   "Graduation Requirements" <http://www.sde.state.id.us/instruct/SchoolAccount/gradreq.htm> Idaho Department of Education (November 15, 1999).

[17]   "Prairie State Achievement Examination" <http://www.isbe.state.il.us/isat/prairiestatenews.htm> Illinois State Board of Education (November 15, 1999).

[18]   "Division of School Assessment" <http://www.doe.state.in.us/assessment/welcome.html> Indiana Department of Education Access Network (November 15, 1999).

[19]   Julia K. Landau, J.D., Janet R. Vohs, B.A., Carolyn A. Romano, J.D., *All Kids Count* <http://www.fscn.org/text/peertext/akcia.htm> Federation for Children with Special Needs (September 16, 1999).

[20]   *Id.*

[21]   "Minimum requirements for high school graduation" <http://www.lrc.state.ky.us/KAR/704/003/305.htm> Kentucky Department of Education (November 16, 1999).

[22]   "Questions and Answers About the Graduation Exit Examination" <http://www.doe.state.la.us/DOE/account/exitexam.asp> Louisiana Department of Education (November 16, 1999).

[23]   "Maine Educational Assessment" <http://janus.state.me.us/education/mea/mea.htm> Maine Department of Education (November 16, 1999).

[24]   "Letter from the State Superintendent of Schools (April 1999)" <http://www.msde.state.md.us/hsimprovement/parentletter6th7th4-99.html> Maryland State Department of Education (November 16, 1999).

[25]   "Overview of the MCAS Program" <http://www.doe.mass.edu/mcas/1098facts.html> Massachusetts Department of Education (November 16, 1999).

[26]   "MEAP Q & A" <http://www.mde.state.mi.us/reports/meap/spring98/resultqa.pdf> Michigan Department of Education (November 16, 1999).

[27]   Minnesota no longer has a State Department of Education.

[28]   "Minnesota's Graduation Standards" <http://cfl.state.mn.us/GRAD/faq.htm> Minnesota Department of Children, Families & Learning (November 16, 1999).

[29]   "The Mississippi Assessment System" <http://www.mde.k12.ms/acad/osa/FLEUPD.htm> Mississippi Department of Education (November 16, 1999).

[30]   "Mississippi Curriculum Content Assessment Program (July 30, 1999)" <http://www.mde.k12.ms.us/acad/osa/mccap.htm> Mississippi Department of Education (November 16, 1999).

[31]   "Graduation Requirements for Students in Missouri's Public Schools" <http://www.dese.state.mo.us/divschsvc/surpervision/graduat.htm> Missouri Department of Elementary and Secondary Education (November 17, 1999).

[32]   Julia K. Landau, J.D., Janet R. Vohs, B.A., Carolyn A. Romano, J.D., *All Kids Count* http://www.fscn.org/text/peertext/akcmt.htm Federation for Children with Special Needs (September 16, 1999).

[33] "Academic Standards" <http://www.edneb.org/IPS/Issu/STBRDPROC.html> Nebraska Department of Education (November 17, 1999).

[34] "Assessment General Information" <http://www.state.nh.us/doe/Assessment/assess,e1.htm> New Hampshire Department of Education (November 17, 1999).

[35] "Standards and Assessments" <http://www.state.nj.us/njded/schools/achievement/1998/hsptsum.htm> and <http://www.state.nj.us/njded/proposed/standards/> New Jersey Department of Education (November 17, 1999).

[36] Lynn Schainberg, "New Mexico: Building on a Base" <http://www.edweek.org/sreports/qc99/states/policy/nm-up.htm> Education Week on the Web (November 17, 1999).

[37] "Revised Graduation Requirements" <http://nysed.gov/regents/brgrad.pdf> New York State Board of Regents (November 17, 1999).

[38] "Student Accountability Standards Frequently Asked Questions" <http://www.dpi.state.nc.us/student_promotion/faq.html> North Carolina Public Schools Infoweb (November 17, 1999).

[39] Julia K. Landau, J.D., Janet R. Vohs, B.A., Carolyn A. Romano, J.D., *All Kids Count* <http://www.fscn.org/text/peertext/akcnd.htm> Federation for Children with Special Needs (September 16, 1999).

[40] "Ohio Proficiency Tests Update Center" <http://www.state.oh.us/proficiency/twelfth.htm> Ohio Department of Education (November 17, 1999).

[41] "Oklahoma Requirements for State Graduation" <http://www.sde.state.ok.us/pro/grarequir.html> Oklahoma Department of Education (November 17, 1999).

[42] "State Test: Information for Parents" <http://www.ode.state.or.us/edact/Parentinfo.htm> Oregon Department of Education (November 17, 1999).

[43] "Standards and Assessments" <http://www.pde.psu.edu/pssa/esstand.html> Pennsylvania Department of Education (November 17, 1999).

[44] Julia K. Landau, J.D., Janet R. Vohs, B.A., Carolyn A. Romano, J.D., *All Kids Count* <http://www.fscn.org/text/peertext/akcri.htm> Federation for Children with Special Needs (September 16, 1999).

[45] "Results of the 1999 High School Exit Exam" <http://www.state.sc.us/sde/reprots/exit1999/index.html> South Carolina Department of Education (November 18, 1999).

[46] Julia K. Landau, J.D., Janet R. Vohs, B.A., Carolyn A. Romano, J.D., *All Kids Count* <http://www.fscn.org/text/peertext/akcsd.htm> Federation for Children with Special Needs (September 16, 1999).

[47] "TCAP/Competency Test (TCAP/CT)" <http://www.state.tn.us/education/tscompetency.htm> Tennessee: Sounds Good to Me(tm) Department of Education (November 18, 1999).

[48] "Gateway Testing Initiative" <http://www.state.tn.us/education/cigateway.htm> Tennessee: Sounds Good to Me(tm) Department of Education (November 18, 1999).

[49] "Welcome to the Division of Student Assessment" <http://www.tea.state.tx.us/student.assessment> Texas Education Agency (November 18, 1999).

[50] Julia K. Landau, J.D., Janet R. Vohs, B.A., Carolyn A. Romano, J.D., *All Kids Count* <http://www.fscn.org/text/peertext/akcut.htm> Federation for Children with Special Needs (September 16, 1999).

[51] "Questions Parents Frequently Ask about Virginia's Standards of Learning (SOL)" <http://www.pen.k12.va.us/VDOE/PolicyPub/Parents> Virginia Department of Education (November 18, 1999).

[52] "Certificate of Mastery Recommendations" <http://www.k12.wa.us/reform/com/Intro.html> Office of Superintendent of Public Instruction (November 18, 1999).

[53] Julia K. Landau, J.D., Janet R. Vohs, B.A., Carolyn A. Romano, J.D., *All Kids Count* <http://www.fscn.org/text/peertext/akcwv.htm> Federation for Children with Special Needs" (September 16, 1999).

[54] *Id.*

[55] "Facts About the Wyoming Comprehensive Assessment System" <http://www.asme.com/wycas/WDEPP/facts.htm> Wyoming Department of Education (November 18, 1999).

Chapter 9

GRADUATION AND FAPE

1. How does a student with a disability exit the special education system?

There are four basic alternatives. Other possibilities, such as termination of eligibility and return to a regular education program or incarceration, are not pertinent to this publication.

1. A student with a disability could receive a "regular" high school diploma, with the term "regular" meaning a diploma identical to that for which students without disabilities are eligible, upon meeting state and school district graduation requirements. *See* 34 C.F.R. § 300.122(a)(3)(i).

2. A student with a disability could also exit the special education system through receipt of a certificate of completion, modified diploma, fulfillment of an IEP, or some similar mechanism. *See* 34 C.F.R. § 300.122(a)(3)(ii).

3. Even if a student with a disability cannot meet the requirements for a regular high school diploma or a modified diploma (or similar certification, as identified above), he will exit the educational system when he reaches the maximum age for receipt of special education services. *See* 34 C.F.R. §§ 300.121, 300.122.

4. As is the case for nondisabled students, a student with a disability may elect to withdraw from school without completing the education program, i.e., the student could drop out of school.

2. What role does an IEP team play in making decisions about graduation?

Decisions about graduation are not specifically included among the topics that must be discussed by IEP teams and documented in the written IEP. 34 C.F.R. §§ 300.346, 300.347. Nonetheless, IEP teams may play a role in reviewing decisions about when to graduate the student and what type of degree he will receive as a matter of best practice, and, in some instances, state law.

As OSEP observed in *Letter to Anonymous*, 22 IDELR 456 (OSEP 1994) the issue of whether a student with a disability will receive a regular high school diploma or a certificate of attendance when he graduates from school is not addressed by the federal regulations. As the court in *Livingston v. De Soto County School District*, 18 IDELR 656 (N.D. Miss. 1992) explained, the IDEA does not establish whether a student with a disability should receive a special education certificate or a regular high school diploma. IEP teams decide the special education and services a school district must provide to a student with a disability in order to provide him with a meaningful benefit. Whether that IEP leads to the student earning a regular high school diploma or a certificate depends on the student's individual circumstances and generally applicable state law.

In *Letter to Richards*, 17 EHLR 288, 289 (OSEP 1990) OSEP summarized the role of the IEP team in graduation decisions. "The proper function of the IEP team [is] to conduct a review of the child's IEP at an appropriate time before the child receives a diploma to assure that graduation requirements will be met, and that the goals and objectives in the IEP will be completed." Because there may be states where the IEP team is not authorized to make decisions about graduation, the IDEA establishes a prior notice requirement in order to keep parents in the loop. 34 C.F.R. § 300.122(a)(3)(iii).

That said, graduation always will be an unavoidable topic of discussion by the IEP team of a high school student with a disability. The anticipated date of graduation and type of diploma to be awarded is the predicate for the IEP team's identification of transition service needs (34 C.F.R. § 300.347(b)(1)) and required transition services (34 C.F.R. § 300.347(b)(2)). In addition, to the extent a student's disability impacts his ability to earn a regular high school diploma, meeting graduation requirements may become an IEP goal. 34 C.F.R. § 300.347(a)(2). See Question 3 in this regard. When a student with a disability must achieve passing scores in exit examinations in order to earn a diploma, the IEP team is charged with making decisions about testing accommodations. 34 C.F.R. §§ 300.347(a)(3), 300.347(a)(5). We discuss high school exit examinations in chapter 8.

In this regard, state law may contain an explicit directive to IEP teams to consider when a student will graduate and what type of diploma he will receive at that time. For example, the student's IEP team in *Birmingham Board of Education*, 20 IDELR 1281 (SEA Ala. 1994) was charged with determining what type of "exit document" the student would receive upon graduation. In that instance, the IEP team decided that a regular high school diploma was an appropriate goal for the student. (The due process proceeding addressed the ensuing dispute about what testing accommodations the student should receive for the exit examination.) To the same effect, the state regulations described in *Quaker Valley School District*, 30 IDELR 634 (SEA Pa. 1999) required IEP teams to include in the student's IEP a plan for the completion of necessary credits for graduation developed at least 3 years prior to the anticipated year of graduation.

When decisions about graduation are made a part of a student's IEP, parents have an accelerated avenue for invoking due process, besides in response to a notice of proposed graduation. 34 C.F.R. § 300.507. Given the length of time it can take for a dispute that is not resolved to the parties' satisfaction at due process to wend its way through the courts, earlier identification of a disputed issue can be a boon to all concerned. The 1992 district court decision in *Livingston v. DeSoto County School District*, *supra*, for instance, resolved the parents' dispute with the school district about whether the student should receive a regular high school diploma or a special education certificate. The year of the proposed graduation was 1989.

3. Can an IEP team identify graduation with a regular high school diploma as an IEP goal?

Yes. Attainment of a regular high school diploma can be an appropriate IEP goal, assuming the student requires special education or related services in order to receive a regular high school diploma upon graduation.

A few published administrative decisions have addressed assertions by parents of students with learning disabilities that graduation with a regular high school diploma is not an appropriate IEP goal. The thrust of the parents' arguments is that achievement of such a goal is not enough. The students' goals should be more challenging. (And, as a necessary corollary, the services provided by the school district must be more extensive.) *In Re: D.B.*, 26 IDELR 1061 (SEA Vt. 1997), *Birmingham Board of Education*, 20 IDELR 1281 (SEA Ala. 1994) and *Huntsville City Board of Education*, 18 IDELR 1243 (SEA Ala. 1992) are three examples. The hearing officer in *In Re: D.B.* explained well why a parent is not likely to prevail on such a claim.

> In the oft-cited language of the U.S. Supreme Court in *Board of Education of Hendrick Hudson School District v. Rowley*, a special education program is sufficient under the law if it is 'reasonably calculated to enable the child to receive educational benefits.' ... In this case the District has amply demonstrated that its IEPs for the student incorporate reasonable goals, expectations, and objectives for the student in light of his disability. Nothing in student's evaluations suggest that it is reasonable to expect that the student can be 'accelerated' up to grade level with a more intensive academic program. As pointed out by the dis-

trict, the student's learning disability will be life-long. The goal of his IEP is for him to acquire the basic skills necessary for graduation from high school and entry into the job market or postsecondary training. Although this goal may not, in the parent's words, 'maximize his potential,' the evidence shows that it is appropriate and realistic — and, thus, all that the law requires.

26 IDELR at 1064.

4. Must a school district award a regular high school diploma to a student with a disability because he has achieved all his IEP goals?

No, state law and school district policy establishes diploma requirements. A school district is not required to award a regular high school diploma to a student with a disability that has not met the requirements for a regular high school diploma, even if the student has met his IEP goals. *Special Sch. Dist. of St. Louis County (MO)*, 16 EHLR 307 (OCR, Region VII 1989).

On the other hand, a state or school district may elect to award a regular high school diploma to a student with a disability on the basis of his achievement of IEP goals. "There is nothing in either Section 504 or Title II (of the ADA) that would prohibit a school district from modifying graduation requirements, consistent with the student's IEP." *Letter to Runkel*, 25 IDELR 387, 391 (OCR, Region VIII 1996).

According to the National Research Council in findings reported in 1997, in several states special education students are exempted from state or local graduation requirements. "Completion of IEP goals is a sufficient condition for receipt of a [regular] high school diploma or its equivalent."[1]

5. Must a school district graduate a student with a disability who has met all the requirements for award of a regular high school diploma?

Yes and no, depending upon whether you consider the issue in terms of disability discrimination under Section 504 or the provision of FAPE under the IDEA.

If a student with a disability meets all state and school district requirements for award of a regular high school diploma, then he cannot be denied a diploma purely and simply because he has a disability. That is discrimination on the basis of disability of the rankest kind, clearly prohibited under Section 504. *See, e.g., Letter to Runkel*, 25 IDELR 387 (OCR, Region VIII 1996); *Letter to Anonymous*, 22 IDELR 456 (OSEP 1994).

The IDEA, however, does not compel a school district to graduate a student with a disability who has met the requirements for award of a regular high school diploma, assuming the parents and school district agree to continue the student's secondary education. (Inevitably there are occasions when they don't agree. See Question 6 in this regard.) Establishment of appropriate substantive standards for graduation is entirely a matter of state law for both disabled and nondisabled students. *See, e.g., Letter to Anonymous, supra.* Section 300.122(a)(3)(i) of the IDEA regulations only relieves school districts of the obligation to provide FAPE to students who have graduated with a regular high school diploma.

6. Does a school district violate the IDEA if it awards a regular high school diploma to a student with a disability who has not met his IEP goals?

No. The IDEA does not make achievement of a disabled student's IEP goals a prerequisite for award of a regular high school diploma. In fact, the statute does not establish standards for graduation, as a general matter. *See, e.g., Letter to Richards*, 17 EHLR 288, 289 (OSEP 1990).

Some students whose IEPs include, for example, behavioral goals, may meet the state's academic requirements for award of a regular high school diploma without achieving all IEP objectives. However, when the student's parents want the student to graduate with his class and get on with his life, a challenge to the district's recommendation to graduate a student who has failed to achieve his IEP goals is (excuse the expression) academic.

But when a student with a disability does not have promising prospects, parents are poised to contest readiness for graduation. Under such circumstances parents have alleged that a school district violated its duty under the IDEA to provide FAPE when it awarded a duly earned regular high school diploma. Without exception, they lose. The decision-makers in *Daugherty by Daugherty v. Hamilton County Schools*, 26 IDELR 127 (E.D. Tenn. 1997) and *In re Child with Disability*, EHLR 401:220 (SEA Va. 1988), for example, ruled to that effect.

In Child with Disability the parents appealed the school district's decision to terminate special education services for an 18-year-old student with learning and emotional disabilities who had been awarded a regular high school diploma on the basis of his academic performance. The parents claimed that the school district should not have graduated the student and terminated services when the student had not met his IEP goals and objectives related to "fundamental interpersonal skills."

The hearing officer rejected the parents' expansive view of the school district's obligations. He held that, while the school district was responsible for formulating and pursuing IEP goals and objectives, it was not bound to fulfill them. It could elect to terminate special education services to disabled students who had met all regular education graduation requirements, but had not achieved their IEP goals and objectives.

The hearing officer in *Hamilton County School*, 23 IDELR 772 (SEA Tenn. 1996), *affirmed in Daugherty by Daugherty v. Hamilton County Schools*, 26 IDELR 127 (E.D. Tenn. 1997), similarly rejected the plea for provision of additional services for a 20-year-old student with an emotional disturbance. The student completed the academic and credit requirements of his IEP, but did not have the same success with the social and independent living skills goal of his IEP. The parent demanded compensatory education in the form of further placement in a structured environment and additional vocational training and programming to improve the student's independent living skills.

Accepting that the student had not met his goals, the hearing officer nonetheless supported the district. Because the student had met all academic requirements for graduation, the school district was entitled to terminate services under the IDEA, which was not superceded by a more rigorous state law. The hearing officer opined that the student's inability "to enter the mainstream of society" did not create an obligation for the school district to provide postsecondary educational services.

State law may permit deferral of graduation for students who have not met their IEP goals, notwithstanding their having earned a regular high school diploma. When both the school district and the parents agree that a 12th-grader who could graduate should nonetheless remain in school for another year, there appears to be nothing in the IDEA to thwart their preference. The student in *Chuchran v. Walled Lake Consolidated School*, 20 IDELR 1035 (E.D. Mich. 1993), *aff'd* 22 IDELR 450 (6th Cir. 1995), for example, could have graduated with a regular high school diploma with his class in 1988, but opted to continue to attend school through the 1992-1993 school year. That student, who had muscular dystrophy, required tracheal suctioning, required the use of a ventilator, and assistance by a nurse or paraprofessional.

And, as the hearing officer in *Hamilton County School* noted, some parents may be able to make a better argument at due process for deferral of graduation under state law. For example, at a due process concerning the district's refusal to fund a "14th" year of secondary education, the principal in *Morse v. Henniker School District*, EHLR 508:361 (SEA N.H. 1987) testified that he believed that the school district was morally, but not legally, obligated to fund such a program. Prior to funding a residential placement at the Landmark school for the "13th" year program of a student with a learning disability, the student's IEP team had concluded that the "student's needs for special education were beyond what she had gotten in high school." Budgetary constraints were the decisive factor when continuation for a second year was the issue. The hearing officer reminded the district that neither morality nor funding played a part. Under controlling state law, the IEP team of a student with a disability could defer graduation of a student with a disability (who had not reached the maximum age of eligibility) until such time as the student no longer required special education. *Accord, Wexler v. Westfield Bd. of Educ.*, EHLR 557:283 (3d Cir. 1986); *Appleton Area Sch. Dist.*, 27 IDELR 682 (SEA Wis. 1998); *Mason City Community Sch. Dist.*, 21 IDELR 248 (SEA Iowa 1994); and *East Orange Bd. of Educ.*, EHLR 507:500 (SEA N.J. 1986).

7. Can a school district award a regular high school diploma to a student with a disability covered under the IDEA to whom it has not provided transition services?

No. If a district were able to graduate a student with a disability without providing transition services, the school district would be able to violate its duty to provide FAPE with immunity. All published decisions concerning this issue have taken the position that IDEA-eligible students cannot be graduated until they receive appropriate transition services. Those who are graduated without such services are entitled to post-graduation relief.

On the judicial level, the decision in *J.B. v. Killingly Board of Education*, 27 IDELR 324 (D. Conn. 1995) recognized a disabled student's right to relief when a school district fails to provide appropriate transition services prior to awarding a regular high school diploma. In this case the student was a 20-year-old young man with language and learning disabilities, a conduct disorder, mixed specific developmental disorder, attention deficit disorder, multiple personality disorder and a history of sexual misconduct who had been placed in a residential treatment program. The school district awarded him a diploma in 1995 as a result of his completion of the required amount of academic credits. In response to a complaint filed by the student a hearing officer ordered the district to provide up to two years of compensatory education. The court on appeal affirmed this order.

The administrative decision in *Novato Unified School District*, 22 IDELR 1056 (SEA Cal. 1995) also concerned a claim that a school district awarded a regular high school diploma to an emotionally disturbed student without providing adequate transition services. Specifically, the parents asserted that the student did not receive the full amount of residential placement in his home community promised by the district. They sought compensatory education, including further transition services and residential placement in his home community, for up to two years as relief. The hearing officer found that the district had provided the student with only two of the three elements of transition services, instruction and development of employment and other post-school adult living objectives. He had not received the third element, community experiences in his local community, prior to his graduation. Given the student's long period of residence in a locked mental health facility, these omitted services were, in fact, the most critical. Although the student had thus established his right to compensatory education as a matter of law, the hearing officer limited relief to a brief additional period of residential placement because the school district had furnished the necessary transition services after his graduation.

Mason City Community School District, 21 IDELR 248 (SEA Iowa 1994) is another due process decision about a student with a disability who did not receive adequate transition services. The school district in *Mason City* proposed graduation of a 19-year-old student with cerebral palsy, mild quadriplegia, and adjustment, language, and developmental disorders for whom it had not developed a transition plan. The only assistance the district offered the student with regard to post-graduation life was a graduation checklist. It did not contact outside agencies until four months prior to the student's anticipated graduation. According to the administrative law judge (ALJ), the district's efforts at transition planning were both procedurally and substantively inadequate. The ALJ forbid the district from proceeding with the student's graduation as planned. Instead the school district was ordered to comply with federal directives concerning adequate transition services, including parental participation in development of a transition services plan.

8. Does graduation with a regular high school diploma terminate the eligibility of a student with a disability under the IDEA?

Yes. The 1999 IDEA regulations contain the first explicit statutory or regulatory statement that graduation with a regular high school diploma ends a student's eligibility for Part B services. Section C.F.R. § 300.122(a)(3)(i) states: "The obligation to make FAPE available to all children with disabilities does not apply with respect to the following: ... Students with disabilities who have graduated from high school with a regular high school diploma."

The regulations affirm DOE's long-standing interpretation of the statute. *See, e.g., Letter to Richards*, 17 EHLR 288 (OSERS 1990). They are consistent with earlier court decisions, as well. *See, e.g., Gorski v. Lynchburg Sch. Bd.*, EHLR 441:415 (4th Cir. 1989); *Wexler v. Westfield Bd. of Educ.*, EHLR 557:283 (3d Cir. 1986).

Conversely, graduation with a special education diploma or certificate of mastery does not terminate a disabled student's eligibility to receive educational programming under the IDEA. A student with a disability who does not earn a regular high school diploma continues to be covered under the IDEA until he reaches the maximum age of eligibility. See Question 9 in this regard.

9. Does graduation with a special education diploma or certificate of competency terminate IDEA eligibility?

No, receiving a special education diploma is like checking into "The Hotel California" — "you can check out anytime you like, but you can never leave." In other words, a student with a disability who graduates with a special education diploma remains IDEA-eligible, or potentially able to receive IDEA services and protections, until aging-out.

In the influential *Gorski v. Lynchburg School Board*, EHLR 441:415 (4th Cir. 1989) the court opined that a student with a disability was entitled to receive services under the IDEA until the student was awarded a high school diploma or reached the maximum age of eligibility, whichever occurred first. The court did not distinguish between receipt of a regular high school or special education diploma; the student in that instance had been awarded a special education diploma. The issue remained fuzzy.

DOE made the author's job at lot easier when it clarified this issue in the 1999 IDEA regulations. To the extent *Gorski* permitted a school district to terminate the eligibility of a student who received a special education diploma, it has been repudiated by Section 300.122(a)(3)(i)(ii). That section provides that a school district's obligation to provide FAPE to a graduating student with a disability continues if that student does not receive "a regular high school diploma."

In discussion accompanying the publication of the 1999 final regulations DOE stated:

[I]f a high school awards a student with a disability a certificate of attendance or other certificate of graduation instead of a regular high school diploma, the student would still be entitled to FAPE until the student reaches the age at which eligibility ceases under the age requirements within the State or has earned a regular high school diploma.[2]

10. May a school district continue to provide special education services to a student with a disability after graduation with a regular high school diploma?

A school district has no responsibility for continuing to provide special education services to a student with a disability after award of a regular high school diploma. That student is no longer enrolled. That is the clear relief from continuing obligation to provide FAPE given in 34 C.F.R. § 300.122(a)(3)(iii).

However if a school district wishes to serve students with disabilities who have graduated but remain in a position to benefit from continued services, the IDEA won't stand in the way. Part B funds may even be used. DOE discussion at 34 C.F.R. § 300.122 accompanying the publication of final regulations advised as follows:

> An SEA or LEA may elect to use Part B funds for services for a student with a disability who has graduated with a regular high school diploma but who is still within the State-mandated age range for Part B eligibility, but may not include the student in its Part B child count.[3]

Unlike services for private school children with disabilities (34 C.F.R. §§ 300.450-300.462), services for students with regular high school diplomas are not even a group entitlement. As far as the IDEA is concerned, states have almost complete discretion in deciding what Part B services will be provided to which graduates.

There are, however, two limitations. For one thing, students must not be older than the maximum age of eligibility under the IDEA. For another, the services must qualify as special education or related services. This is because FAPE is defined in terms of the provision of only preschool, elementary and secondary education. 34 C.F.R. § 300.13.

As numerous courts have ruled, postsecondary services are distinguishable from preschool, elementary and secondary education services. As a result they cannot be characterized as either special education or related services. Numerous courts have ruled that postsecondary services are not encompassed within the IDEA. School districts have no obligation to provide them. *E.g., Daugherty by Daugherty v. Hamilton County Schs.*, 29 IDELR 699 (E.D. Tenn. 1998); *Yankton Sch. Dist. v. Schramm*, 24 IDELR 704 (8th Cir. 1996); *Gorski v. Lynchburg Sch. Bd.*, 1988-1989 EHLR 441:415 (4th Cir. 1989); and *Cronin v. Bd. of Educ. of East Ramapo Sch. Dist.*, 15 EHLR 441:124 (S.D.N.Y. 1988).

So what *are* postsecondary services? Nowhere in the IDEA is the term defined. In the hope that the author is not the only one who doesn't think the meaning of the term is obvious, we attempt to separate the mules from the donkeys in Question 22.

11. Is graduation with a regular high school diploma a change in placement under the IDEA?

Yes. IDEA regulations at 34 C.F.R. § 300.122(a)(3)(iii) state: "Graduation from high school with a regular diploma constitutes a change in placement, requiring written prior notice in accordance with [34 C.F.R.] § 300.503." As a necessary implication, a parent wishing to challenge the decision to award a regular high school diploma has access to due process in accordance with 34 C.F.R. § 300.507(a)(2) or mediation in accordance with 34 C.F.R. § 300.506(a).

Neither the prior statute nor regulations had a provision substantially similar to Section 300.122(a)(3)(iii). But the importance of parental notification of intent to graduate has been acknowledged by courts for decades. In *Stock v. Massachusetts Hospital School*, EHLR 555:550 (Mass. 1984) the state Supreme Court agreed with the school district defendants that there was no explicit statutory directive or authoritative judicial decision to support the parents' interpretation of the law. But that was the extent of its agreement. The court explained its reasoning in language that remains eloquent.

> It seems obvious, however, that graduation, because it will cause the termination of a student's participation in special education programs, can hardly be characterized as anything other than a change in placement. ... No change in placement seems quite so serious nor as worthy of parental involvement and procedural protections as the termination of placement in special education programs.

EHLR at 552.

12. What are the IDEA content requirements for prior notice of intent to graduate a student with a disability with a regular high school diploma?

There are no specific requirements concerning the information the school district must disclose in the prior notice to parents of intent to graduate with a regular high school diploma or when the school district must provide the notice. The general requirements set out in 34 C.F.R. § 300.503 govern, leavened by any controlling state law or local policy, and common sense.

As to contents, Section 300.503 requires communication of the following:

- A statement that the school district proposes to award a regular high school diploma. 34 C.F.R. § 300.503(b)(1).

- An explanation of why the school district proposes to award the diploma, i.e., the standard for graduation that the student will have met by the anticipated graduation date. 34 C.F.R. § 300.503(b)(2).

- A description of any other options that the school district considered, along with an explanation of why they were rejected. For example, the district may have considered whether the student should remain in school for an additional year in order to receive additional special education services or programming. See Question 9 in this regard. 34 C.F.R. § 300.503(b)(3).

- A description of each evaluation procedure, test, record, or report the school district has considered in proposing to award to the student a regular high school diploma. 34 C.F.R. § 300.503(b)(4).

- A description of any other factors that are relevant to the district's proposal. 34 C.F.R. § 300.503(b)(5).

- A statement that the parents (or perhaps the student, depending on the age of the student and controlling state law regarding transfer of IDEA rights when a student reaches the age of majority) have IDEA procedural safeguards with respect to this proposed change of placement, and the means by which a copy of a description of the procedural safeguards can be obtained. 34 C.F.R. § 300.503(b)(6).

- Sources for parents to contact to obtain assistance in understanding the provisions of this part. 34 C.F.R. § 300.503(b)(7).

13. What are the IDEA timeline requirements for prior notice of intent to graduate a student with a disability with a regular high school diploma?

No specific timeline is set out in the regulations at 34 C.F.R. § 300.122(a)(3). DOE's discussion accompanying the publication of IDEA final regulations in 1999 state that under section 300.122(a)(3) a school district should give parents notice within a "reasonable time" before graduation to "ensure that parents are appropriately informed to protect the rights of their child ... "[4]

Adequate notice of intent to graduate is also a component of a student's right to procedural due process under the Fourteenth Amendment and 42 U.S.C. § 1983. We discuss the constitutional dimensions in greater detail in Question 6 in chapter 8.

14. Is graduation with a certificate of attendance or special education diploma a change in placement under the IDEA?

No, graduation with a special education diploma is not a change in placement for purposes of the IDEA. In this way the IDEA parts ways with Section 504. OCR considers any graduation a "significant change in placement" for purposes of triggering the procedural safeguards established by the Section 504 regulations at 34 C.F.R. § 104.35. *Letter to Runkel*, 25 IDELR 387 (OCR, Region VIII 1996).

IDEA regulations at 34 C.F.R. § 300.122(a)(3)(iii) provide that graduation from high school with a regular diploma is a change in placement. They say nothing about graduation with any other kind of diploma. The implication seems obvious.

But those uncomfortable with interpreting the law simply on the basis of negative inference, should note the following. In discussion accompanying the publication of final regulations, DOE stated more directly that it did not consider "exiting or graduating a student with a disability with a diploma that is different from the diploma granted to students who do not have disabilities [to be] a change in placement requiring notice under § 300.503."[5]

15. Must a school district provide prior notice if it proposes to award a student with a disability a special education diploma?

Yes. According to OCR, to do otherwise would be discrimination on the basis of disability in violation of 34 C.F.R. § 104.4(b). The IDEA does not have its own prior notice requirement, however Section 504 applies to IDEA-eligible students.

In *Special School District of St. Louis County (MO)*, 16 EHLR 307 (OCR, Region VII 1989), OCR opined that a school district must provide notice to the parents "in advance" when successful completion of the IEP will not result in receipt of a regular high school diploma. The parents' receipt of notice will then trigger their rights to initiate due process to challenge the district's decision. In due process, the burden will be placed upon the school district to demonstrate that the student's disability results in his not being able to meet generally applicable requirements for graduation with a regular high school diploma.

When the IDEA is implicated, graduation with a special education diploma is not identified as a change in placement, as is graduation with a regular high school diploma. 34 C.F.R. § 300.122(a)(3). Neither does award of the special education diploma allow a district to unilaterally terminate services. For these reasons, as DOE explained in discussion accompanying the publication of the IDEA final regulations, prior notice to parents (in accordance with 34 C.F.R. § 300.503) is not required when graduating a student with a special education diploma.[6]

16. Must a school district reevaluate an IDEA-student with a disability prior to graduation with a high school diploma?

It appears that a school district is not required to reevaluate the student as a matter of course. Nevertheless, parents appear to retain the right to demand reevaluation.

IDEA regulations at 34 C.F.R. § 300.534(c)(1) state that a school district must evaluate a student with a disability before determining that the student is no longer IDEA-eligible. Paragraph (c)(2) makes an exception to the requirement for an evaluation set out in paragraph (c)(1) when the proposed termination of eligibility is "due to graduation with a regular high school diploma, or exceeding the age eligibility for FAPE under State law."

Section 300.534(c)(2) does not, however, address the parent's right to demand that the district conduct a reevaluation. 34 C.F.R. § 300.536(b). It is difficult to conceptualize many situations in which a parent might respond to a proposal to graduate the student with a regular high school diploma with a demand for a reevaluation. One scenario that has appeared in published decisions relates to college-bound students who wish to present a recent evaluation as part of a request for college-level accommodations. We discuss this issue in chapter 3.

17. Does graduation with a regular high school diploma moot a claim for denial of FAPE?

Limited judicial authority suggests that a disabled student's receipt of a regular high school diploma does not moot a claim for denial of FAPE brought under the IDEA, although it may limit the relief available. The author has not neglected to consider *Wexler v. Westfield Board of Education*, EHLR 557:283 (3d Cir. 1986). In that decision the United States Court of Appeals for the Third Circuit rejected the parent's claim that under the IDEA a school district was responsible for the student's education until he reached age 21, notwithstanding his prior receipt of a diploma acknowledged by the parent to be properly awarded. "A case is moot, and hence not justifiable, if the passage of time has caused it completely to lose its character as a present, live controversy of the kind that must exist if the court is to avoid advisory opinions on abstract propositions of law."[7]

Generally speaking, a claim for injunctive relief under the IDEA becomes moot when a student ages-out. *Honig v. Doe*, EHLR 559:231 (1988). However, the weight of judicial authority allows claims for compensatory education and tuition reimbursement to proceed even when the student is older than the maximum age of eligibility. *Board of Educ. of Oak Park & River Forest High Sch. Dist. 200 v. Illinois State Bd. of Educ.*, 23 IDELR 1118 (7th Cir. 1996); *Pihl v. Mass. Dep't of Educ.*, 20 IDELR 668 (1st Cir. 1994); and *Lester H. v. Gilhool*, 16 EHLR 1354 (3d Cir. 1990). All three courts interpreted the IDEA as empowering courts to grant a remedy in the form of compensatory education to students with disabilities who are beyond the statutory age of entitlement for special education services.

A student with a disability also loses entitlement to services and protections of the IDEA when he receives a regular high school diploma. 34 C.F.R. § 300.122(a)(3)(i). According to the courts in *Capistrano Unified School District v. Wartenberg*, 22 IDELR 804 (9th Cir. 1995) and *Bean v. Conway School District*, 18 IDELR 65 (D. N.H. 1991) the judicial precedents and reasoning concerning students who have aged-out apply equally well to students who have graduated with a regular high school diploma. The claims of students who accept award of a regular high school diploma may proceed to the same extent as the claims of students who have reached the maximum age of eligibility. That is, claims for injunctive relief are moot, but those seeking relief in the form of compensatory education and tuition reimbursement are not.

Unfortunately, neither decision clearly sets out the rationale for the court's decision. The court's decision in *Capistrano* seems to have been an application of "the law of the case" (prior admissions by the parties) and provides no explanatory guidance. The student in that case had graduated, twice in fact, by receiving diplomas from both his regular high school and the school he attended during placement in a mental health facility. The court ruling in *Conway School District* also fails to explore whether there is a meaningful difference in the status of a student who has aged-out, as compared to one who has graduated with a regular high school diploma. Its reasoning was premised upon the Second Circuit's now discredited opinion in *Mrs. C. v. Wheaton*, 16 EHLR 1394 (2d Cir. 1990).[8]

Keep in mind, though, that a student with a disability who earns a regular high school diploma may face an uphill battle when he claims denial of FAPE, over and above defeating a motion to dismiss on the basis of mootness. See Question 21 in this regard.

18. Can a parent assert IDEA due process to challenge the award of a regular high school diploma to a student with a disability?

Yes, it appears that due process is an appropriate forum for challenges to decisions to award a regular high school diploma, even when the diploma has been awarded on the basis of the student's meeting generally applicable state and local school district-established standards.

Graduation with a regular high school diploma is a change in placement triggering a district's obligation to comply with the prior notice requirement of 34 C.F.R. § 300.503. 34 C.F.R. § 300.122(a)(3)(i).

As a general matter, a parent can request due process or mediation in connection with a proposed change of placement for which the school district has provided prior notice. 34 C.F.R. §§ 300.506, 300.7. By implication, then, a parent has the right to request due process after receiving a notice of proposed graduation with a regular high school diploma in accordance with 34 C.F.R. § 300.122(a)(3)(i). DOE discussion accompanying the publication of the final regulations confirms this inference:

> The parents would have the option, as with any public agency proposal to change the educational program or placement of a child with a disability, to seek to resolve a disagreement with the proposal to graduate the student through all appropriate means, including mediation and due process hearing proceedings.[9]

On the other hand, as OSEP has consistently opined in published policy letters, state law (including local school district policy) — not the IDEA — is the sole source of substantive standards for high school graduation. *E.g., Letter to Anonymous*, 22 IDELR 456 (OSEP 1994).

Thus, it is not intuitively obvious (at least not to the author) how hearing officers can reconcile their obligation to determine if it is appropriate for a student with a disability to be graduated with a regular high school diploma with their powerlessness to make or alter state graduation standards.

The review officer in *Arlington Central School District*, 28 IDELR 1130 (SEA N.Y. 1998), for example, interpreted his authority to review the district's decision to award a regular high school diploma quite narrowly. The student in *Arlington Central School District* was a resident of New York who had been publicly placed in a residential school in New Hampshire. When he had earned sufficient academic credits to receive a regular high school diploma in accordance with New Hampshire law, the school district graduated him. The parent filed for due process, alleging that the student should not have been graduated until he had earned a sufficient number of academic credits to meet the more rigorous New York state standards.

In dismissing the parent's claim, the review officer noted that the parent had not submitted documentation to support her allegation that the requirements for a New Hampshire diploma were not as rigorous as the requirements for a New York diploma. But he also went on to opine that it wouldn't have affected the outcome even if she had.

> [Parent's] concerns about the academic standards required by the State of New York or the State of New Hampshire for receipt of a regular education high school diploma are not matters that either the hearing officer or I could address in a proceeding of this nature, which must be limited to the program and services provided by [the school district].

28 IDELR at 1134.

When a school district awards diplomas to students with disabilities on the basis of attainment of IEP goals, then a hearing officer is on more familiar ground when called upon to review a decision to graduate a disabled student.

For example, when the parents in *Mount Abraham Union School*, 21 IDELR 972 (SEA Vt. 1994) challenged the district's decision to graduate a residentially-placed student, the hearing officer examined the student's test scores and reviews to determine if the student had reached the levels identified in his IEP for graduation. Determining that the student had met his IEP goals, the hearing officer denied the parents' request for additional services. A further factor in favor of the school district was its compliance with the procedural safeguards of the IDEA. The parents had been notified of each significant change in placement prior to graduation and had not challenged any.

To similar effect, the review officer in *Quaker Valley School District*, 30 IDELR 634 (SEA Pa. 1999) supported the school district's assertion that it had properly graduated a 19-year-old student with an emotional disability in accordance with the standards and objectives set out in her IEP.

Although the parents claimed the student was still entitled to special education services, the hearing officer found that the student had been properly graduated. The district had planned for the student's graduation through changes in the IEP. The student had satisfied all credit requirements contained in her IEP. The district's decision to graduate her was consistent with its graduation policy. Affirming the decision of the hearing officer, the review panel found no evidence that the student was graduated with insufficient credits. To the contrary, the panel cited ample evidence that, three years before graduation, the student's IEP contained a plan for completion of course credits in anticipation of graduation.

19. Can a student with a disability assert stay-put pending resolution of a challenge to the school district's proposed graduation with a regular high school diploma?

Yes, the consensus seems to be that stay-put is a procedural safeguard available for the protection of disabled students challenging award of a regular high school diploma.

The stay-put provision of the IDEA, directing a district to maintain a student with a disability in his current educational placement during the pendency of any administrative or judicial proceeding, is found at 34 C.F.R. 300.514(a). There is no exception made for due process proceedings concerning a disputed graduation proposal.

Prior to publication of the 1999 final regulations, there was uncertainty about whether award of a regular high school diploma was a change in placement. Courts went both ways. Now that the regulations at 34 C.F.R. § 300.122(a)(3)(iii) answer this question in the affirmative (and make it clear that a district cannot terminate services unilaterally for students who are awarded special education diplomas), the field of pertinent published decisions narrows considerably.

Of those semi-finalists, the most authoritative ruling is *Cronin v. Board of Education*, EHLR 441:124 (S.D. N.Y. 1988). In that case the school district argued that the student's right to stay-put ended when it issued his high school diploma, but the court held that stay-put was available to students challenging proposals to graduate.

> [School district] defendants argue that because [the student] was validly issued a high school diploma, he no longer falls within the protection of the Act. The Commissioner of Education rejected this argument when he stated that the pendency provisions of the education law could not be avoided by the conferral of a high school diploma that is the subject of an appeal. The Court agrees, finding that defendants' interpretation would render the stay-put provision meaningless because the school district could unilaterally graduate handicapped children. The primary issue before this Court is whether [the student] was properly graduated. Until that issue is ultimately decided Bruce is entitled to remain at [his last-agreed placement] in accordance with protection provided by the stay-put provision. [The district's] interpretation would render the stay-put provision meaningless because the school district could unilaterally graduate handicapped children. The primary issue before this Court is whether [the student] was properly graduated. Until that issue is ultimately decided [the student] is entitled to remain at [his last-agreed placement] in accordance with protection provided by the stay-put provision.

EHLR at 127, footnote 4.

Administrative decision-makers have endorsed the interpretation of the stay-put provision adopted by the *Cronin* court. *Bret Harte Union High School Dist.*, 30 IDELR 1014 (SEA Cal. 1999); *Arlington Central Sch. Dist.*, 28 IDELR 1130 (SEA N.Y. 1998); and *Piscataway Bd. of Educ.*, 26 IDELR 1362 (SEA N.J. 1997). All reasoned that, because graduation with a regular high school diploma is a change in placement, parents have the right to assert stay-put when challenging at due process.

Timing is everything, though, when a parent asserts stay-put in connection with a challenge to graduation. The parents in *Arlington Central* filed for due process to challenge the student's graduation during the student's senior year. The review officer ordered the district to continue to fund the student's residential placement during the course of the proceedings. The student in *Mount Abraham Union School*, 21 IDELR 972 (SEA Vt. 1994) had already graduated when the parents filed their challenge to the district's decision. The hearing officer denied the parents' request for continued services during the tendency of the proceedings. The student's stay-put was "out the door."

In any event, note that there may be only a limited amount of instances, such as continuation of a residential placement for an emotionally disturbed student, when a parent chooses to invoke stay-put while contesting award of a regular high school diploma. Consider, for example, the high school student with a learning disability and other health impairment (chronic fatigue syndrome) whose parents challenged the decision of the student's graduation. One month after graduation the hearing officer issued a stay-put order. In order to comply, the school district "invited" the student to return to high school. The student opted to enroll as a freshman in college instead. Because the student was performing at the college level, the hearing officer agreed with the student that a return to high school would be, well, silly.

20. Are special education hearing officers empowered to rescind a regular high school diploma awarded to a student with a disability?

Yes. According to limited judicial authority, a state may authorize recession of regular high school diplomas by due process hearing officers.

Because receipt of a regular high school diploma ends a disabled student's entitlement to services under the IDEA, parents seeking provision of additional services as compensatory education must claim that the school district did not properly award the diploma. However, as the court noted in *Max M. v. Thompson*, EHLR 555:431 (N.D. Ill. 1984) it is not clear as a matter of logic or law whether revocation of a student's diploma is a prerequisite to receipt of compensatory services under the IDEA.

Similarly, the court in *Puffer v. Raynolds*, 17 EHLR 618 (D. Mass. 1988) affirmed the order for provision of remedial services to a student who had received a regular high school diploma, but declined to grant her request to have her diploma rescinded. "To rescind [the student's] diploma ... would be a disruptive remedy that would only serve to derail further [the student's] post-graduate educational path." 17 EHLR at 626.

That said, if a parent makes a demand for recession of a diploma awarded on the basis of the student meeting generally applicable graduation requirements, a hearing officer may entertain the claim and grant the requested relief. *See, Max M., supra*. The *Puffer* court held to the same effect. The court closely analyzed the numerous substantive and procedural objections to the decision made by the state advisory commission granting the student's request for rescission of her diploma. It found no fault with the fact that the decision was made in the course of a special education administrative proceeding.

As a related matter, in *Stock v. Massachusetts Hospital School*, EHLR 555:550 (Mass. 1984) the state Supreme Court upheld the judicial rescission of the diploma of a student with a disability as a remedy for the district's failure to provide prior notice of graduation. The court also reviewed the decision to graduate the student as a matter of substance, concluding that, at the time of graduation, the student lacked the "sufficient learning and skills to merit award of a high school diploma under existing standards."

21. Can a student with a disability who graduates with a properly awarded regular high school diploma successfully claim the school district failed to provide a meaningful educational benefit?

Courts have not reached a consensus. Passing from grade to grade without special education services or programming does not necessarily mean a student with a disability is not entitled to FAPE. 34 C.F.R. § 300.121(e). Similarly, the author believes the better view is that meeting the requirements for a regular high school diploma does not always mean a student has received FAPE.

Board of Education v. Rowley, EHLR 553:656 (1982) contains the Supreme Court's only discussion of the relationship of graduation with a regular high school diploma to receipt of FAPE.

The Act requires participating States to educate handicapped children with nonhandicapped children whenever possible. When that 'mainstreaming' preference of the Act has been met and a child is being educated in the regular classrooms of a public school system, the system itself monitors the educational progress of the child. Regular examinations are administered, grades are awarded, and yearly advancement to higher grade levels is permitted for those children who attain an adequate knowledge of the course material. The grading and advancement system thus constitutes an important factor in determining educational benefit. *Children who graduate from our public school systems are considered by our society to have been 'educated' at least to the grade level they have completed, and access to an 'education' for handicapped children is precisely what Congress sought to provide in the Act.* (emphasis added and footnotes omitted)

EHLR at 668.

The Court seemed to be leaning in the direction of opining that graduation with a bona fide regular high school diploma, at the least, presumptively establishes provision of FAPE. But such a conclusion is, of course, based solely on *dicta*. And the famous footnote 25, which appears at the end of the excerpt, sets out the Court's cautioning against adopting a bright-line rule equating passing from grade to grade without receiving a meaningful educational benefit.

Keeping in mind the Court's directive to consider the issue of educational benefit on an individual basis, the court in *Puffer v. Raynolds*, 17 EHLR 618 (D. Mass. 1988) provided a thoughtful analysis of the relationship between a student's properly awarded regular high school diploma and the school district's obligation to provide FAPE.

In *Puffer* the court affirmed the hearing officer's finding that the disabled student's diploma had been validly issued; the student had attended the regular education program and had passed all her courses without any special education assistance. But the court also agreed that the student should have been identified as a student with a disability and provided special educational under an IEP. "These two findings, a valid diploma and a procedurally defective attempt at special education services are not entirely inconsistent," the court found. "[The student] succeeded despite [the school district's] failure to follow the regulations for serving children in need of special education. She earned a valid diploma but that does not mean that she did not need services[.]" 17 EHLR at 625.

22. What are postsecondary services?

"Postsecondary services" is not a term of art; it is not defined in the IDEA. A definition by negative inference is that postsecondary services are not special education or related services provided in connection with preschool, elementary or secondary education. 34 C.F.R. § 300.13.

Distinguishing postsecondary services from secondary education services is crucial when identifying the specific services, if any, a school district must provide as compensatory education to students who have graduated or have otherwise completed their secondary education. The same issue arises if states and school districts elect to provide additional IDEA-funded services to disabled students who have graduated with regular high school diplomas.[10]

The author's review of the LRP Publications data base shows an increasing number of published disputes about the nature of compensatory services that a school district can be ordered to provide as compensatory education for a disabled student who has gone on to attend college. We discuss this issue in greater detail in Questions 18-20 in chapter 3.

23. Is reevaluation prior to proposing graduation with a regular high school diploma required under Section 504?

Not necessarily. OCR does not interpret the Section 504 regulations as imposing such a requirement.

As OCR has reminded school districts hundreds of times, a school district must conduct an evaluation of any student who, because of disability, needs or is believed to need special education or related services before taking any action with respect to initial placement or any subsequent significant change in placement. 34 C.F.R. § 104.35(a)-(c).

Graduation is indeed a "significant change in placement" for purposes of Section 504, OCR explained in *Letter to Runkel*, 25 IDELR 387 (OCR, Region VIII 1996). But that doesn't dictate that a reevaluation always be conducted. Addressing whether procedural safeguards are required when a student with disabilities graduates from high school, OCR responded thusly:

> Clearly, the graduation of a special education student receiving an education in accordance with an IEP constitutes a "significant change in placement." Under Section 504 and Title II, the student's most recent IEP should anticipate the student's graduation by describing the criteria that must be met by the student in order to do so. If this criteria is achieved, however, there is no explicit Section 504 or Title II requirement that expressly provides that a formal determination must be made on this point by an evaluation team[.]

25 IDELR at 390.

24. Under Section 504 must a school district send a notice of procedural safeguards to the parents of a high school senior with a disability who will be graduating with his class and receiving a regular high school diploma?

No, although OCR considers graduation a significant change in placement, the agency does not read into 34 C.F.R. § 300.104.35(a)-(c) a requirement for notice of procedural safeguards in all cases.

In *Letter to Runkel*, 25 IDELR 387 (OCR, Region VIII 1996) OCR seemed to recognize that sometimes enough is enough. No one's interests are served by the propagation of superfluous paperwork. If "there is no question" that parents have already been advised of their procedural safeguards at an IEP meeting convened to discuss the student's graduation, then it's not necessary to provide yet another procedural safeguard notice. But if you want to err on the side of duplicative notices, OCR advises that "it would certainly be acceptable to do so." 25 IDELR at 390.

Endnotes

[1] JAY P. HEUBERT, ROBERT M. HAUSER, EDS., HIGH STAKES: TESTING FOR TRACKING, PROMOTION, AND GRADUATION 193 (National Academy Press 1999) (citation omitted).

2   64 *Fed. Reg.* 12556 (1999).

3   *Id.*

4   *Id.*

5   *Id.*

6   *Id.*

7   LAURENCE H. TRIBE, AMERICAN CONSTITUTIONAL LAW § 3-11, at 83 (2d ed. 1988) (internal quotations omitted).

8   The court ruled that compensatory education is a remedy only for gross violations of the IDEA, or those evidencing bad faith on the part of the school district.

9   64 *Fed. Reg.* 12556 (1999).

10   See Question 10.

Chapter 10

POMP AND CIRCUMSTANCE

Graduation Ceremony

1. Are students with disabilities who graduate with special education diplomas entitled to participate in the graduation ceremony?

Yes. Section 504 prohibits school districts from limiting participation in graduation ceremonies to students who graduate with regular high school diplomas.

The source of the prohibition is 34 C.F.R. § 104.4, which bars discrimination on the basis of disability with respect to, among other things, grades, class ranking, honor rolls, graduation, and diplomas. When graduation requirements are at issue, the law does not compel states to abandon generally applicable standards for the awarding of regular high school diplomas.[1] Participation in the graduation ceremony itself is another matter. No matter what type of diploma a student with a disability will be receiving, he has the right to participate in the same graduation ceremony as the students in his school who are receiving regular high school diplomas.

In technical terms, a student with a disability who meets his state's requirements for graduation from secondary school is "qualified" to participate in the same graduation ceremony he would participate in if he did not have a disability. Excluding a qualified person with a disability from participation is unlawful discrimination.

As OCR opined in *Letter to Runkel*, 25 IDELR 387 (OCR, Region VIII 1996):

> Under Section 504 or Title II, a student who has met graduation requirements, irrespective of age, cannot be treated differently on the basis of disability. A qualified student with a disability is eligible to participate in whatever graduation ceremony a student of similar age without disabilities would be eligible to participate.
>
> Section 504 or Title II does not address participation of a student with disabilities in a separate graduation service or activity. Section 104.34 (c), Comparable facilities, may apply, if a separate service or activity is undertaken by the school district. Eligible students with disabilities cannot be precluded, in any event, from participation in the school district's main graduation ceremony, if the student wishes to do so.

25 IDELR at 391.

2. Does Section 504 grant to non-graduating "seniors" with disabilities the right to participate in the graduation ceremony?

By custom, graduation ceremonies are for presentation of diplomas. Nonetheless, some students earn and receive diplomas even if they do not attend graduation ceremonies. Conversely, in some school districts students who are not receiving diplomas "walk in" graduation ceremonies. Generally, the decision whether to allow non-graduating "seniors" to participate in commencement exercises with age peers is a matter of state or local law or policy. In limited instances, Section 504 or IDEA may govern decisions about the participation of non-graduating "seniors" with disabilities.

As an initial matter, one thing is clear. Both the parents and the school district need to be on the same page about what it means for a student with a disability to be participating in the graduation ceremony. Consider the circumstances related by the hearing officer in *Bret Harte Union High School District*, 30 IDELR 1014 (SEA Cal. 1999).

The school district in *Bret Harte* proposed that an 18-year-old student with a disability graduate with the rest of his class. At an IEP meeting held in May of the disabled student's 12th-grade or senior year, the parent went on record as disagreeing with the school district's proposal. She contended that the student was entitled to additional years of special education programming. The parent also inquired whether the student could "walk through" the graduation ceremony without actually graduating. A district official said no. No one was ever permitted to walk through the ceremony without graduating. As the student's mother testified at a due process hearing, several days after the meeting she received a telephone call from a different district official. This representative advised that the student could attend the graduation ceremony, with "no strings attached."

Believing that the school district was now amenable to both providing additional services and allowing the student to participate in the ceremony, the student doffed his cap and gown to participate in the graduation ceremony. But surprise! The student was awarded a high school diploma; the school district refused to enroll the student for the next school year. Thus the parent was compelled to submit this textbook case of miscommunication (which reminds the author of how Miss Piggy tricked Kermit into marriage in *The Muppets Take Manhattan*) to resolution at due process.[2]

As a matter of policy, some school districts may elect to limit participation in commencement exercises to graduating students as a way of expressing the significance of the graduating seniors' accomplishment. For example, the high school principal in *Frank S. v. School Committee of the Dennis-Yarmouth Regional School District*, 29 IDELR 707, 711 (D. Mass. 1998) testified in administrative proceedings why participation of non-graduates was contrary to school policy. "'We have never allowed any students in my eleven years at Dennis-Yarmouth Regional High School to receive a blank diploma at our ceremony. To me graduation is a public statement that those students participating have fulfilled all academic requirements and have met the necessary standards for a diploma.'"

Section 504 does not appear to prohibit blanket exclusion of all non-graduating "seniors." In *Central Kitsap (WA) School District No. 401*, EHLR 352:119 (OCR, Region X 1985) OCR concluded that the school district had not discriminated against a student with a disability who participated in a separate graduation ceremony. It found that the criterion for participation in the regular graduation ceremony was neutral on its face with respect to disability. Any student, disabled or nondisabled, had to have earned the requisite amount of credit in order to participate in the ceremony conducted in connection with the awarding of regular high school diplomas.

Other school districts may adopt a more flexible approach, under which the particular circumstances of the non-graduating student with a disability are determinative. The sympathy vote, so to speak. Consider for example, how the hearing officer in *Appleton Area School District*, 27 IDELR 682 (SEA Wis. 1998) described a non-graduating senior with a disability who was permitted to participate in commencement exercises.

[T]he student Kinsley T. is an amiable nineteen-year-old who has hopes and dreams that are similar to those of her nondisabled peers. She wants to live independently, she wants to work at a job she enjoys, and she wants to have a social life. Each of those goals is understandable, indeed, desirable. Unfortunately, they are somewhat harder for Kinsley to achieve than for someone who does not face her challenges. Kinsley has spastic quadriplegia cerebral palsy and also has mild to moderate cognitive disability. Since the seventh grade, Kinsley has attended school in the Appleton Area School District. This past year, she achieved enough credits to graduate from North High School. However, when the IEP committee convened toward the close of the 1996-97 school year, it concluded that although Kinsley had sufficient credits to graduate, she had not yet mastered several of the goals and objectives outlined in her IEP.

27 IDELR at 683.

Contrast the decision to allow participation in *Appleton Area School District* with the decision against participation made by the review officer in *Randolph Central School*, 21 IDELR 776 (SEA Ind. 1994). "The Student's academic history was relevant to this consideration [participation in graduation ceremony], as was the Parent's behavior in preventing the School from providing educational services to the Student. The Parent's behavior was a substantial reason the Student was not eligible to receive a diploma and participate in the graduation ceremony." 21 IDELR at 778.

To the extent that the participation decision is discretionary, Section 504 is not implicated when disabled and nondisabled non-graduating seniors are treated in an even-handed manner. For that reason, OCR closed the complaint in *Lauderdale County (AL) School District*, 25 IDELR 161 (OCR, Region IV 1996) without awarding relief for the complainant or directing the school district to revise its policies. The complainant alleged that the school district discriminated against a non-graduating high school student on the basis of his disability when it refused to allow him to participate in the graduation ceremony. OCR's investigation disclosed several other students, including another student with a disability, were not allowed to participate in the graduation ceremony. Based on these circumstances, the parent could not establish discrimination on the basis of disability.

3. Does the IDEA give a non-graduating "senior" with a disability the right to participate in the graduation ceremony with his age-peers?

Very limited authority suggests that a student with a disability who meets the requirements for award of a regular high school diploma but is nonetheless continuing his secondary education for a 13th, or perhaps a 14th year, is entitled to participate in graduation ceremonies with his age peers.

The school district in *Frank S. v. School Committee of the Dennis-Yarmouth Regional School District*, 29 IDELR 707, 711 (D. Mass. 1998) refused to permit a non-graduating senior with a disability to participate in his age-peers' graduation ceremony. The student in that instance was continuing his education for a 13th year in order to receive additional transition services, but did not meet the minimum academic requirements for graduation, in any event. He was one course short.

The court declined to rule on a parent's IDEA complaint regarding participation, opining that the IDEA has no pertinence when a disabled student has not earned enough credits to receive a regular high school diploma. The court stated that the parent's complaint "regarding the District's refusal to permit [the student] to participate in a mock graduation ceremony raised an issue of discretionary school policy which is beyond the educational concerns of IDEA." 29 IDELR at 714.

Unlike the student in *Dennis-Yarmouth Regional School District*, the 19-year-old high school student with mental retardation in *Woodland Hills School District*, 30 IDELR 927 (SEA Pa. 1999) had earned more than the required minimum number of credits. Nonetheless, he was not graduating with his high school class. Instead, because he had not completed his IEP goals, he would be continuing his education and receiving his diploma when he reached age 21. The student's parents requested permission for their son to participate in his high school graduation ceremony, but the school district refused to grant their request. It relied on a state regulation that barred students who were not entitled to receive a diploma from participating. Ruling against the parents, who challenged the decision at due process, the hearing officer also appeared to consider the issue one solely of state law and local policy.

But the review panel gleaned an IDEA connection: IDEA regulations at 34 C.F.R. §300.306(a), entitled "Nonacademic services." That section states: "Each public agency shall take steps to provide nonacademic and extracurricular services and activities in the manner necessary to afford children with disabilities an equal opportunity for participation in those services and activities."

The review panel ruled that a school district violates that section of the regulations when it excludes students with disabilities who meet the general requirements for graduation (i.e., those applicable to nondisabled students) from "walking in" the graduation ceremony. This applies even when a disabled student is not receiving a regular high school diploma.

Responding to the school district's contention that graduation ceremonies are not covered by the cited regulation, the panel responded that the definitions of "nonacademic" and "extracurricular" in 34 C.F.R. §300.306(b) are broad. In fact, they overlap. The examples are non-exhaustive. In a footnote, the panel asserted that its interpretation of 34 C.F.R. § 300.306(a) was reinforced by the "overlapping federal policy in Section 504, which has parallel language about nonacademic and extracurricular activities[.]" 30 IDELR at 929, footnote 21.

The review panel made it clear, though, just how narrow its ruling was. It applied only to students who met the district's general requirements for graduation. It specifically stated that it did not find in the IDEA any general right to participate in graduation ceremonies without having met general graduation requirements. (Although the review officer opined in a footnote that he could cite no other decisions relating to participation in graduation ceremonies, the panel seems to have adopted the same reasoning as the *Dennis-Yarmouth Regional School District* court.)

For this reason, the panel in *Woodland Hills School District* noted that it did not agree with the contention of the parents that IEP teams have a role to play, as a matter of law. "Although making provisions in the IEP would, for a student who met the general requirements for graduation, optimally resolve the matter, the district's duty to provide equal opportunity in such activities exists where the IEP team has not made any such determination." 30 IDELR at 927, footnote 16.

States or school districts could opt to have the student's IEP or placement team decide whether the student may participate. For example, in *Appleton Area School District*, 27 IDELR 682 (SEA Wis. 1998) the student's IEP team decided that the student would be allowed to participate in the Class of 1997 graduation ceremonies, but would not receive her diploma. Similarly, a student's IEP team made the participation decision in *Chuhran v. Walled Lake Consolidated School*, 20 IDELR 1035 (E.D. Mich. 1993); *Piscataway Bd. of Educ.*, 26 IDELR 1362 (SEA N.J. 1997).

4. Are older students with disabilities entitled to participate in high school graduation ceremonies?

Yes, they are entitled to participate in 12th-grade graduation ceremonies to the same extent as older students who are not disabled.

Subject to state law and practice, the IDEA age range extends until age 22, assuming the student is not awarded a regular high school diploma before reaching the maximum age. 34 C.F.R. §§ 300.121, 300.122. In addition, a state may elect a special education mandate that exceeds the federal age range. A 21-year-old or 22-year-old student with a disability, or even an older student, could exit the system by earning a diploma, rather than simply aging-out.

Section 504 limits a school district's ability to exclude non-traditional age students with disabilities from customary commencement exercises for 12th-graders. In *Letter to Runkel*, 25 IDELR 387 (OCR, Region VIII 1996) OCR elucidated the right of disabled students who meet graduation requirements as a result of post 12th-grade education to participate in graduation ceremonies.

Under Section 504 or Title II, a student who has met graduation requirements, irrespective of age, cannot be treated differently on the basis of disability. A qualified student with a disability is eligible to participate in whatever graduation ceremony a student of similar age without disabilities would be eligible to participate.

25 IDELR at 391.

5. Is holding a separate graduation ceremony for students with disabilities necessarily illegal discrimination on the basis of disability?

No. Surprisingly, holding a separate graduation ceremony just for students with disabilities does not violated Section 504 in all cases. Holding two ceremonies at one school — one for students with disabilities and the other for nondisabled students — is, of course, prohibited. 34 C.F.R. § 104.4(b). But if a district can demonstrate an educational necessity for conducting a separate ceremony for some students with disabilities, the separate ceremony may be permitted.

According to OCR, neither Section 504 nor Title II addresses participation of a student with disabilities in a separate graduation service or activity. *Letter to Runkel*, 25 IDELR 387 (OCR, Region VIII 1996). In that guidance, however, OCR also stated that the comparable facilities requirement of 34 C.F.R. § 104.34(c) applies when a school district conducts a separate graduation ceremony. 34 C.F.R. § 104.34(c) states that a district operating a facility identifiable as being for students with disabilities must ensure that the facility and the services and activities provided therein are comparable to the other facilities, services, and activities provided by the district.

Thus in *Letter to Runkel* OCR seems to be taking the position that there might be instances when separate ceremonies are permitted. In *Aldine (TX) Independent School District*, 16 EHLR 1411 (OCR, Region VI 1990) illustrates the analysis OCR uses when considering whether, even assuming the comparable facilities requirement of 34 C.F.R. § 104.34(c) is met, separate commencement exercises are prohibited. The parent in *Aldine* claimed that the school district discriminated against severely disabled students being educated at a separate facility by scheduling graduation ceremonies for these students on a different date and at a different location than the graduation ceremonies for other students (both disabled and nondisabled).

The students at issue were low functioning; disruptive behavior (i.e., salivating, hollering or fighting) at the ceremony was a possibility for some. But the possibility of disruption was not enough for OCR. Because the school district had failed to demonstrate an educational necessity for separate graduation ceremonies for the severely disabled students at the separate facility, it had violated the non-discrimination provisions of the Section 504 regulations at 34 C.F.R. §§ 104.4(a), (b)(1)(iv), 104.34(b), and 104.37(a)(1).

The key for OCR was lack of individual assessment. OCR found that the student's IEP teams had not specifically discussed the individual needs of each potentially excluded student to participate in the regular graduation exercises. Nor had they considered whether there was a need for a separate graduation ceremony for that student.

The clear implication of *Aldine* is that the decision to hold separate graduation ceremonies for students in self-contained schools or facilities cannot be made on a facility-wide basis. OCR guidance in *Letter to Runkel*, 25 IDELR 387, 391 (OCR, Region VIII 1996) appears to be to the same effect. "Eligible students with disabilities cannot be precluded, in any event, from participation in the school district's main graduation ceremony, if the student wishes to do so."

In this regard, keep in mind that the physical accessibility standards of Section 504 and Title II of the ADA apply to graduation ceremonies. For example, in *Coventry (RI) Public School*, 20 IDELR 1081 (OCR, Region I 1993) OCR held that a school district which held its graduation ceremony at a theatre that could not be used by students with disabilities discriminated against students with disabilities in violation of Section 504 and Title II of the ADA. *Accord, West Warwick (RI) Pub. Sch.*, 20 IDELR 684 (OCR Region I 1993).

6. Can a school district exclude a student with a disability from commencement exercises as a sanction for disability-related misconduct?

There is no specific prohibition on excluding students with disabilities from high school commencement exercises as a sanction for disability-related misconduct in either the IDEA or Section 504.

In the first instance, exclusion from the graduation ceremony is likely not included in a school district's array of disciplinary sanctions, or approved for imposition in only the most extraordinary of circumstances.

10 : 5

To the extent such a harsh punishment (at least from the parents' perspective) is permitted, it is neither a significant change of placement for purposes of Section 504 nor a change of placement for disciplinary reasons under 34 C.F.R. § 300.519 of the IDEA. Because exclusion from the ceremony is not a removal from a student's then-current educational placement for more than 10 school days, there is no express requirement to conduct a manifestation determination (34 C.F.R. § 104.35(a), 34 C.F.R. § 300.523) and forbear from taking disciplinary action when the misconduct is disability-related.

Put another way, exclusion from the graduation ceremony seems far closer to a "restriction of privileges" that may be imposed without consideration of relatedness than a removal for more than 10 school days — at least from a legal perspective. See *Honig v. Doe*, EHLR 559:231 (1988) restriction of privileges.

This is not to say that parents have not challenged a school district's decision to exclude a student with a disability from participation in the graduation ceremony as a disciplinary sanction. In *Forsyth County (NC) School District*, 26 IDELR 757 (OCR, Region IV 1997), for example, the parent of an elementary school student with severe attention deficit hyperactivity disorder alleged that the school district discriminated against her daughter by refusing to allow her participation in the elementary school graduation ceremony. After investigation, OCR found that the student's poor behavior during practices caused the school district to decide to limit her participation in the ceremony. The parent had agreed with the district's decision to have the student participate in only a portion of the elementary school graduation ceremony.

The stakes were higher in *Turlock (CA) Union Joint High School District*, 29 IDELR 985 (OCR, Region IX 1998), but the result was the same: the school district's exclusion of a high school student with a disability from the regular high school graduation was not discriminatory.

The disabled student, who had attention deficit disorder, entered his freshman year at the school district's Turlock High School (THS), but was transferred before the year was out to another district school because of failure to follow school rules and his irregular attendance. A series of transfers in and out of various district programs did not improve the student's ability to follow the rules at THS. Finally, at the request of the student's parents, and with the concurrence of THS personnel, the student entered the THS Independent Study Program (ISP), completing all requirements to receive a diploma from THS. The student was awarded the same regular high school diploma as the graduating students at THS, but he was not permitted to attend the class trip or the senior prom, or to walk with his class at graduation.

After graduation, the parents filed a complaint with OCR alleging that the student had been excluded from participation in the graduation ceremony as a disciplinary sanction for misbehavior related to his disability. The school district countered that the student had been excluded because he was in the ISP Program. That program has its own graduation ceremony.

OCR agreed with the school district. All concerned, the school district, the parents, and the student, had agreed to the student's participation in the ISP program. Students were in the ISP for a variety of reasons; all students in the program, disabled and nondisabled alike, were subject to the same rules. "[The student] was denied participation in the class trip, the senior prom, and the THS comprehensive program graduation ceremony because he was in ISP. He was not treated differently than nondisabled students in the ISP, on the basis of disability." 29 IDELR 988.

Diplomas and Awards

7. Is every publicly enrolled student with a disability eligible to receive a regular high school diploma?

Yes, that is how OCR interprets the IDEA, Section 504 and Title II of the ADA. *Letter to Runkel*, 25 IDELR 387 (OCR, Region VIII 1996). But keep in mind that eligibility means no more for disabled students than it does for nondisabled students. Eligibility is not the same as guaranteed receipt.

Even when a student is not able to earn a regular high school diploma because of his disability, compliance with federal disability law does not compel waiver of all diploma requirements, in the sense of graduation requirements. There is no guaranteed right for every student with a disability to receive a diploma of graduation from high school. *Letter to Anonymous*, 22 IDELR 456 (OSEP 1994).[3]

Subtly different from the issue of modifying graduation requirements is the issue of awarding a student with a disability a document to signify successful completion of the student's secondary education in those instances when the student cannot meet the requirements for a regular high school diploma. Again, there is no right to receive a document called a diploma.

That was the sad truth the hearing officer in *Salem-Keizer School District*, 30 IDELR 1024 (SEA Or. 1999) had to convey to the parents of a 20-year-old student with mental retardation who was reading at the second grade level when she graduated from high school. Because the student had met graduation criteria based on the needs and abilities identified in her IEP, the school district awarded the student a certificate of attainment. The parents brought a due process action, challenging the IEP team's determination that the student was not able to work toward earning a regular high school diploma.

In upholding the determination of the IEP team, the hearing officer noted that all the parents really wanted was for the school district to have called the certificate of attainment a "modified diploma." As understandable as that wish might be on an emotional level, the hearing officer concluded that she had no authority under the IDEA to order the school district to change its terminology. "The school district is not, however, required to use that label, or any label including the word 'diploma,' for a document which does not signify completion of the legally mandated diploma requirements." 30 IDELR at 1032.

8. May a school district use different wording on a diploma awarded to a student with a disability?

In *Letter to Runkel*, 25 IDELR 387 (OCR, Region VIII 1996) OCR posed the above question and then answered it with a qualified "yes."

If a student with a disability meets all the standards established by the state for obtaining a regular high school diploma, any deviation in wording on that student's diploma is discrimination on the basis of disability. *Letter to Anonymous*, 25 IDELR 632 (OSEP 1996).

But what about the wording on a diploma awarded to a student with a disability who is only able to meet different graduation standards? According to OCR in *Letter to Runkel*, as the wording on the diploma for each student is "similar" in all "significant" respects, deviations from the declarations found on the regular high school diploma may be permitted for the diploma of a student with a disability meeting different standards.

All deviations must be "based upon objective criteria." No variation can be based on disability as a category of students. Accordingly, any different diploma wording that a state uses for diplomas awarded to students with disabilities "must be available to all students on a nondiscriminatory basis." *Runkel*, 25 IDELR at 391.

To illustrate, consider the voluntary resolution reached in the dispute over diploma policy discussed in *Moffat County (CO) School District RE-1*, 26 IDELR 28 (OCR, Region VIII 1996). That LOF resulted from a complaint brought by the parent of a student with a disability, alleging that the school district engaged in disability discrimination when it awarded different diplomas to students with disabilities. In response, the school district voluntarily agreed to change its diploma policy as follows. All students — including students with disabilities — who completed a specific number of credits and passed a state proficiency exam were entitled to receive a "Guaranteed" diploma. Students, again both disabled and nondisabled, who completed the required number of credits, but failed to pass the proficiency exam, were entitled to receive a different diploma.

As OCR recognized in *Runkel* there exist an infinite number of wording variations that school officials may want to use on a diploma. In that letter, OCR identified one possibility for alternative wording of diplomas that passes muster: "[E]ach diploma may contain language that refers to the individual's academic transcript for the exact courses or subjects completed." 25 IDELR at 391.

As to any other modifications, think twice before you call the printer. While not authorized to make prior agency approval a requirement, OCR recommends that "an opinion be obtained in advance from either the [state education agency] or OCR." *Id.*

9. Can a school district categorically deny students with disabilities participating in special education programs an opportunity to graduate with honors?

Generally speaking, no. Denial of a benefit or program participation on the sole basis of disability is illegal discrimination. 34 C.F.R. § 104.4(a), (b)(1), (b)(3), and (b)(4). However, in *Pueblo (CO) City School District #60*, 17 EHLR 535 (OCR, Region VIII 1990) OCR explained in an unusually detailed LOF why a school district may exclude students with mental retardation in a self-contained classroom program from competing for graduation honors.

Unlike class rank, graduation honors were not earned by comparing a student's academic performance to the performance of others. Instead, a student earned graduation honors on the basis of his grade point average (GPA). When a Pueblo City student graduated with honors he had the right to wear a different color at the graduation ceremony and to have his name included in the list of honor graduates published by the local newspaper.

All this being the case, you can understand why the parent of a student enrolled in the limited intellectual functioning — educable and trainable (LIFE/LIFT) program claimed the district's exclusion of LIFE/LIFT program students from competing for graduation honors was disability discrimination. Although her daughter's GPA was 3.667, the student was not allowed to march in the graduation parade with a silver cord. Her name did not appear in the newspaper.

In the course of investigating the parent's complaint, OCR determined that LIFE/LIFT program students were the only students — disabled or nondisabled — who could not graduate with honors. Similarly, they were the only students with unique criteria for graduation. As OCR explained, all other students with IEPs were required to meet the same requirements for graduation as regular education students, i.e., they were expected to successfully complete the same number of credits as other students on the basis of achieving mastery of the same course content. In contrast, students in the LIFE/LIFT program did not have to satisfy the graduation requirements that all other students were expected to achieve. The content of each of the program courses was tailored to each student's ability, as opposed to presented on a uniform basis to all students.

Because the LIFE/LIFT students were not graded on mastery of the same course content as the other students competing for graduation honors, OCR found that the school district had not violated Section 504 by excluding these students from graduation honors. (Legality aside, one might be tempted to conclude that LIFE/LIFT students with qualifying GPAs should have been permitted to wear the cord.) It also noted that the district had notified the parent of the graduation honors exclusion before her daughter was placed in the program. And, to put the icing on the cake, it found that the parent had miscalculated the student's GPA. When recomputed, the student's GPA fell below the 3.4 GPA required for graduation honors. OCR is not entirely clear — and the author is similarly uncertain — about the extent to which the parent's apparent acquiescence to the exclusion was a critical factor.

Endnotes

[1]   We discuss the law governing awarding of regular high school diplomas to students with disabilities in chapter 1.

[2]   The parent filed a motion for stay-put and requested as relief rescission of the student's high school diploma and provision of continued special education services. We discuss rescission as a remedy for denial of FAPE in Question 20 in chapter 9.

[3]   We discuss modification and waiver of graduation requirements for students with disabilities in greater detail in chapter 9.

Appendix

26 IDELR ¶ 573

Elizabeth **GUCKENBERGER**, et al.,

> Plaintiffs

v.

BOSTON UNIVERSITY, et al.,

> Defendants

No. 96-11426-PBS

U.S. District Court, Massachusetts

August 15, 1997

Summary

Until the spring of 1995, students with learning disabilities who sought accommodations at Boston University were required to provide the university's Learning Disabilities Support Services Office with information regarding the need for accommodation, the student's accommodation history, and a medical or psycho-educational evaluation that had been conducted within the last three years. The LDSSO then decided whether to grant the accommodation request or not. Some of the accommodations frequently granted by the LDSSO were: note-takers, taped textbooks, and extra time on examinations. Occasionally, a student was allowed to substitute an approved course for the university's foreign language and/or math requirements. In 1995, the president of the university decided to change the accommodations policy. The changed policy (1995 policy) refused to allow exemptions from foreign language and math classes and required students to provide the university with a diagnostic evaluation performed by a physician, clinical psychologist, neuropsychologist or licensed psychologist which was no more than three years old. A group of students with learning disabilities and/or attention deficit disorders filed a class action suit against the university challenging these modifications as violating Title III of the ADA and the Rehabilitation Act. The complaint further contained a state law breech of contract claim. During the course of the litigation, the university changed its accommodation policy (1997 policy) slightly, expanding who could perform the required evaluation and establishing a procedure to waive the requirement of submitting a complete evaluation every three years.

HELD: for the students, in part.

In examining the students' assertion that the "documentation requirement" of the accommodation policies was discriminatory in that it tended to screen out students with disabilities, the court examined the 1995 and 1997 policies. The court noted that the applicable laws allowed the university to require current documentation, but that the 1995 policy tended to place "significant additional burdens" on students who requested accommodations. The 1997 policy, through the addition of the waiver provision, was appropriate, according to the court. The court also found the "credential" requirement of both the 1995 and the 1997 policies burdensome to students with learning disabilities and attention disorders who had already been diagnosed. This requirement was inconsistently implemented by the university. Turning to whether the challenged portions of the accommodation policies were necessary, the court concluded that the currency requirement, as applied to students with specific learning disabilities, was not required. The evidence failed to demonstrate retesting of these students was required every three years. The court upheld this requirement as applied to students with attention disorders, since the evidence demonstrated this type of disorder could change over time. The qualifications requirement was not necessary with respect to the evaluation of students with learning disabilities, but was necessary with respect to students with attention disorders due to the difficulty in distinguishing between ADD/ADHD and other conditions with similar symptoms.

Next, the court examined the university's procedure for reviewing accommodation requests and determined that the review process, as applied during the 1995-96 school year, violated the ADA and Rehabilitation Act. During that school year, the president of the university and his assistant, despite their lack of experience in the area of learning disabilities, played an active role in determining which accommodation requests would be granted. The judge characterized certain comments made by the president and his assistant as containing "misinformed stereotypes." The current accommodation procedure, in which the president had little to do with deciding whether accommodations were granted was approved by the court. The students' objection to the lack of a formal appeals process to challenge the denial of an accommodation request was rejected, since there was no private right of action under the Section 504 regulations for claims of this type.

Turning to the foreign language and math course requirements, the court concluded that the university was not required to modify degree requirements which would result in a fundamental alternation of its programs as long as the university makes a "diligent, reasoned, academic judgment" that the requirement is essential to the academic program. In this case, the university failed to make a reasoned determination that the requirements were essential and the president based his decision to deny course substitutions on discriminatory stereotypes.

The court determined that three of the student plaintiffs had valid breach of contract claims against the university, due to the students' reliance on representations made by university officials regarding the availability of accommodations. Six students were awarded approximately $30,000 in damages for the university's violations of the ADA, Rehabilitation Act and state law. The university was ordered to stop requiring students with learning disabilities to obtain current evaluations conducted by individuals with medical or doctoral degrees or licensed clinical psychologists. The court also ordered the university to formulate a procedure for determining if allowing exemptions to the foreign language requirement would fundamentally alter the university's program.

Counsel for Plaintiffs: Sidney Wolinsky, Disability Rights Advocates, Oakland, CA.

Counsel for Defendants: Lawrence Elswit.

PATTI B. SARIS, United States District Judge.

Introduction

This is a class action[1] brought by students with Attention Deficit Hyperactivity Disorder ("ADHD"), Attention Deficit Disorder ("ADD"), and learning disorders (collectively "learning disabilities") against Boston University ("BU") under the Americans with Disabilities Act ("ADA"), 42 U.S.C. § 12101 et seq. (1995), the Rehabilitation Act, 29 U.S.C. § 794 (1997), and state law.[2] The class claims that BU discriminates against the learning-disabled by: (1) establishing unreasonable, overly-burdensome eligibility criteria for qualifying as a disabled student; (2) failing to provide reasonable procedures for evaluation and review of a student's request for accommodations; and (3) instituting an across-the-board policy precluding course substitutions in foreign language and mathematics. BU contends that its eligibility criteria are reasonably designed to ensure that a student is entitled to the requested accommodations, that its review procedures are adequate, and that it has the right to require that a student meet certain levels of proficiency in math and foreign language before it confers a liberal arts degree.

Particularly with respect to the issue of course substitution, this class action concerns the interplay between the rights of learning-disabled students to reasonable accommodation and the rights of institu-

tions of higher education to establish and enforce academic standards.

The plaintiff class now seeks injunctive and declaratory relief against the continued implementation of BU's accommodations policy. Moreover, the named individuals[3] request compensatory damages for the harm allegedly caused them by the university's purported violation of federal law, and by its alleged breach of the promotional promise to provide reasonable accommodations for students with diagnosed learning disabilities.

After a two-week bench trial, and an evaluation of the witnesses and evidence in this case, I have made numerous findings of fact and conclusions of law. To assist the reader, the Court's fundamental conclusions are summarized as follows:

1. Federal law prohibits private and public universities, colleges and post-secondary educational institutions from discriminating against students with specific learning disabilities.

2. In the fall of 1995, BU imposed new documentation requirements that required students with learning disabilities to be retested every three years, and that provided that evaluations by persons who were not physicians, clinical psychologists, or licensed psychologists were unacceptable. These new documentation requirements, as initially framed, violated the ADA and the Rehabilitation Act because they were "eligibility criteria" that "screen[ed] out or tended to screen out" students with specific learning disabilities, and because BU did not demonstrate that the requirements were necessary to the provision of educational services or reasonable accommodations.

3. The documentation policies have changed, however, since the start of this litigation. Because BU now permits a student to obtain a waiver of the three-year currency retesting requirement where medically unnecessary, I conclude that the retesting requirement, as currently framed, does not screen out or tend to screen out learning disabled students.

4. BU has also restructured its policy with respect to the qualifications of evaluators by permitting evaluators with doctorates in education (and in "other appropriate specialties") to document students' learning disabilities. Nevertheless, by precluding any evaluations by persons with masters degrees, BU's present policy still unnecessarily screens out or tends to screen out some students with specific learning disorders who have been evaluated by adequately trained professionals. BU has not demonstrated that an evaluator with a masters degree and appropriate training and experience cannot perform the testing for an assessment of learning disability as well as an evaluator with a doctorate. Accordingly, BU has not proven that a doctorate-level of qualification is necessary to the provision of reasonable accommodation with respect to students with learning disorders.

5. However, with respect to students with ADD and ADHD, BU has demonstrated that its "bright

line" policy of requiring current evaluation by a person with a doctorate is necessary because ADD/ADHD is often accompanied by co-existing physical and psychological conditions, is frequently treated by medications, and is a rapidly changing condition that usually remits over the period from adolescence through early adulthood.

6. The administration of BU's new accommodations policy during the 1995-1996 school year violated the ADA and the Rehabilitation Act because it was implemented without any advance warning to eligible students, in such a way as to have the effect of delaying or denying reasonable accommodations. Moreover, BU President Jon Westling and his staff administered the program on the basis of uninformed stereotypes about the learning disabled.

7. However, because BU has recently hired an experienced clinical psychologist to review student accommodation requests, and because President Westling and his assistant Craig Klafter now review recommended accommodations primarily to ensure that they meet academic standards, the university's current procedure for evaluating requests for accommodation submitted by students with learning disabilities does not violate federal law.

8. The plaintiff class has no private right of action to challenge BU's violation of Rehabilitation Act regulations that require a university to adopt grievance procedures that incorporate appropriate due process standards.

9. In general, federal law does not require a university to modify degree requirements that it determines are a fundamental part of its academic program by providing learning disabled students with course substitutions.

10. Here, BU's refusal to modify its degree requirements in order to provide course substitutions, particularly in the area of foreign languages, was motivated in substantial part by clinical psychologist to review student accommodation requests, uninformed stereotypes by the President and his staff that many students with learning disabilities (like the infamous, nonexistent "Somnolent Samantha") are lazy fakers, and that many evaluators are "snake oil salesmen" who overdiagnose the disability.

11. BU failed to demonstrate that it met its duty of seeking appropriate reasonable accommodations for learning disabled students with difficulty in learning foreign languages by considering alternative means and coming to a rationally justifiable conclusion that the available alternative (i.e., a course substitution) would lower academic standards or require substantial program alteration. Rather, the university simply relied on the status quo as the rationale for refusing to consider seriously a reasonable request for modification of its century-old degree requirements.

12. Plaintiffs have failed to demonstrate that a request to modify the degree requirement in mathematics is reasonable in light of the dearth of scientific evidence that any specific learning disability in mathematics (i.e. dyscalculia) is sufficiently severe to preclude any student from achieving sufficient proficiency in mathematics to meet BU's degree requirements with appropriate accommodations.

13. BU breached its contract with three of the named plaintiffs by failing to honor the express representations of its representatives about the students' ability to document their disabilities and to receive accommodations from the university.

Findings of Fact

I. BU's Recruitment of the Learning Disabled

BU is one of the largest private universities in the United States, with 20,000 students, 2,000 faculty members, and fifteen undergraduate and graduate colleges that offer 150 separate degree-granting programs. The College of Arts and Sciences is the largest college in the university. It has longstanding course requirements, including one semester of mathematics and four semesters of a foreign language. Degree requirements at all of BU's colleges are approved by the Provost, the President, and the Board of Trustees.

Before 1995, BU was a leader among educational institutions in seeking to provide comprehensive services to students with diagnosed learning disabilities. The university recruited learning-disabled enrollees by establishing the Learning Disabilities Support Services ("LDSS"), a renowned accommodations program that functioned as a unit within BU's Disability Services office ("DSO"). LDSS was often described as a "model program." Through LDSS, the university declared a commitment to enabling students with learning disabilities to reach their maximum academic potential. For example, LDSS promotional brochures offered learning-disabled students various complimentary accommodations including notetaking assistance, and extended time on examination. For a fee, students who enrolled at BU also had access to comprehensive services such as private tutoring and support groups, while potential enrollees of the university had the option of attending two different summer programs geared toward helping learning-disabled pupils make the transition from high school to college.

Before 1995, not only did LDSS often authorize in-class notetakers, tape-recorded textbooks, and time and one half on final examinations for students with documented learning disabilities (the so-called "vanilla" accommodations),[4] but LDSS staff also occasionally recommended that disabled students receive a course substitution for required mathematics and foreign language classes. For example, students who received an LDSS recommendation for a math substitution were allowed to take classes such as Anthropology 245 ("Anthropology of Money"), Economics 320 ("Economics of Less Developed

Regions"), or Geography 100 ("Introduction to Environmental Science") instead of the required math curriculum. Similarly, learning-disabled students who received a foreign language exemption might opt instead for one of several foreign culture courses including Art History 226 ("Arts of Japan") or History 292 ("African Colonial History").

In developing lists of "approved" course substitutions and recommending waivers of math and foreign language requirements for certain students, LDSS worked with the heads of the various academic departments at the College of Liberal Arts ("CLA") (now called the College of Arts and Sciences) ("CAS"). However, neither LDSS nor CLA notified or sought the approval of the President, Provost, or any other of BU's central administration. Eighty-eight students requested foreign language waivers at CLA during academic years 1992-1993 and 1993-1994.[5] On average, BU granted approximately 10 to 15 requests for course substitutions a year.

Prior to 1995, the process of applying for accommodations, including course substitutions, from BU was relatively straightforward. A learning-disabled student submitted to LDSS a description of her need for accommodation, a statement of her accommodations history, and a current medical or psycho-educational evaluation (one that had been conducted within three years of entering the university). Once the student's documentation was filed, members of the LDSS staff determined whether accommodation was appropriate. In 1995, LDSS was permanently staffed with a full-time director, two assistant coordinators and a secretary, and it also employed several part-time learning disabilities specialists. Several of these administrators had specific training in special education and in the provision of accommodations to post-secondary students with learning disabilities.

If LDSS granted a student's request for accommodation, the student would be notified. An LDSS staff member would also write letters, referred to as "accommodations letters," to the student's faculty members and to the dean of the student's particular school explaining the student's disability and recommending that the student be provided with the listed accommodations. Students were responsible for distributing these letters to their professors, and for meeting with their instructors to arrange the provision of in-class and exam accommodations.

The results of LDSS's "marketing" to students with learning disabilities were pronounced. In academic year 1990-1991, 42 students who self-identified as learning disabled applied, 24 were accepted and two enrolled. Four years later, 348 such students applied, 233 accepted and 94 enrolled. In late 1995, 429 learning-disabled students applied to the university. As its reputation developed, BU was recommended by guidance counsellors and college manuals as a desirable academic setting for the learning disabled. Between 1990 and 1996, hundreds of students with learning disabilities came to BU and registered for academic accommodations and/or comprehensive services through LDSS. By the 1995-1996 school year, BU had approximately 480 learning disabled students.

II. Westling Orders Change

Current BU president Jon Westling became the university's provost (i.e., its chief academic officer) in 1985. A graduate of Reed College and a Rhodes Scholar, Westling has spent a total of 23 years at BU. He has served as both an administrator and as a teacher in the humanities core curriculum at the CLA. Westling holds no graduate degrees.

In the spring of 1995, Provost Westling[6] discovered that LDSS and CLA had been allowing students with learning disabilities to substitute other classes for the mathematics and foreign language coursework that was otherwise a long-standing prerequisite to obtaining a baccalaureate degree in the College of Arts and Sciences.[7] Chagrined that LDSS was facilitating alterations of the core curriculum without university approval, Westling assigned his assistant and troubleshooter, Craig Klafter, a Ph.D in Modern History, to research learning disabilities in general and LDSS's process of granting accommodations in particular. Confronting LDSS-director Loring Brinckerhoff, Klafter sought proof of the existence of a disability that prevented a student from learning a foreign language. Brinckerhoff referred Klafter to a book that he had co-authored concerning learning disabilities in post-secondary education. After reading Brinckerhoff's book and other secondary materials, Klafter determined that there was no scientific proof of the existence of a learning disability that prevents the successful study of math or foreign language.

As a result of Klafter's investigation, in June of 1995 Westling informed W. Norman Johnson, BU's Vice President and Dean of Students, and the College of Liberal Arts that the university was to cease granting course substitutions, "effective immediately." In addition, Westling told Johnson to direct LDSS to send all accommodation letters to the Provost's office for review before they were distributed to the students or faculty. Westling made the decision to end the course substitution practice without speaking to any experts on learning disabilities or to any faculty members on the importance of math and foreign language to the liberal arts curriculum. With the course substitution "bee" in his academic bonnet, Westling decided to become personally involved with the accommodations evaluation process, even though he had no expertise or experience in diagnosing learning disabilities or in fashioning appropriate accommodations.

III. "Somnolent Samantha"

At around the time that Westling ordered the first changes in the accommodations practice at BU, he also began delivering speeches denouncing the zealous advocacy of "the learning disabilities movement." In addresses delivered in Australia and in Washington, D.C., Westling questioned the rapidly increasing number of children being diagnosed with learning disorders, and accused learning-disabilities advocates of fashioning "fugitive" impairments that are not supported in the scientific and medical literature. Although Westling's orations recognized a need to "endorse the profoundly humane goal of addressing the specific needs of individuals with specific impairments," his public addresses resonated with a dominant theme: that "the learning disability movement is a great mortuary for the ethics of hard work, individual responsibility, and pursuit of excellence, and also for genuinely humane social order."

At the beginning of one such speech entitled "Disabling Education: The Culture Wars Go to School," which was delivered on July 22, 1995, Westling introduced a student named Samantha, who was, he said, a freshman in one of his classes at BU. Westling recounted how Samantha approached him on the first day of class and how, "shyly yet assertively," she presented a letter addressed to him from the Disability Services office.

The letter explained that Samantha had a learning disability "in the area of auditory processing" and would need the following accommodations: "time and one-half on all quizzes, tests, and examinations;" double-time on any mid-term or final examination; examinations in a room separate from other students; copies of my lecture notes; and a seat at the front of the class. Samantha, I was also informed, might fall asleep in my class, and I should be particularly concerned to fill her in on any material she missed while dozing.

Westling's speech went on to name the student "Somnolent Samantha" and to label her "an unwitting casualty of the culture wars." To Westling, Samantha exemplified those students who, placated by the promise of accommodation rather than encouraged to work to achieve their fullest potential, had become "sacrificial victims to the triumph of the therapeutic." Throughout his twenty-page address, Westling reiterated the view that, by "seiz[ing] on the existence of some real disabilities and conjuring up other alleged disabilities in order to promote a particular vision of human society," the learning disabilities movement cripples allegedly disabled students who could overcome their academic difficulties "with concentrated effort," demoralizes non-disabled students who recognize hoaxes performed by their peers, and "wreak[s] educational havoc." In closing Westling remarked:

> The policies that have grown out of learning disabilities ideology leach our sense of humanity. We are taught not that mathematics is difficult for us but worth pursuing, but that we are ill. Samantha, offered the pillow of learning disability on which to slumber, was

denied, perhaps forever, access to a dimension of self-understanding.

Westling fabricated the student Samantha to illustrate his point regarding students with learning disorders. Remarkably, at trial, Westling admitted not only that such a student never existed, but that his description of her did not even represent a prototype of the learning-disabled students he had encountered. Rather, "Somnolent Samantha" represented Westling's belief—fuelled mostly by popular press and anecdotal accounts—that students with learning disabilities were often fakers who undercut academic rigor.

As in the speech "Disabling Education," since the spring of 1995, many of Westling's addresses, statements, and letters regarding accommodations for the learning disabled have reflected his opinion that "hundreds of thousands of children are being improperly diagnosed with learning disabilities by self-proclaimed experts who fail to accept that behavioral and performance difficulties exist." Even though Westling has referred to students with learning disabilities as "draft dodgers" and has repeatedly voiced his concern that students without established learning disorders might be faking a disability to gain an educational advantage, to date, there has not been a single documented instance at BU in which a student has been found to have fabricated a learning disorder in order to claim eligibility for accommodations.

IV. The Twenty-Eight Files

By the fall semester of the 1995-1996 academic year, BU was at a bureaucratic impasse. LDSS head Loring Brinckerhoff[8] was ignoring Westling's directives, and LDSS was continuing the practice of approving course substitutions and granting accommodations without Westling's involvement. Although Dean Johnson had specifically conveyed Westling's orders to Brinckerhoff in a memo dated June 29, 1995, LDSS issued 58 accommodations letters (some of which allowed course substitutions) to students between July and September of 1995 without seeking Westling's approval.

Irate that his mandates were being disregarded, in October of 1995, Westling directly ordered that all of the accommodations letters that LDSS had prepared but that had not yet been picked up by the affected students be delivered to his office. At the time, LDSS held 28 such letters. Westling also requested that he be given access to the documentation files for each of the students who were the subject of the 28 letters.

After receiving the letters and files, Westling and his staff reviewed the documentation to determine if the students' evaluations actually supported LDSS's recommended accommodations. Specifically, when reviewing the files, the provost's office looked for current evaluations done by credentialed evaluators, clear diagnoses, an evaluator's recommendation listing specific accommodation, and an LDSS recommendation that was consistent with the recommendations made by the student's evaluator. None of the provost office staff members who were involved in this review had any expertise in learning disabilities.

In a letter dated November 2, 1995, Westling communicated his analysis of the letters and files to Brinckerhoff's supervisor, the director of the Office of Disability Services, William P. ("Kip") Opperman. Of the 28 files, Westling determined that, "[i]n all but a few cases, the requested accommodations [were] not supported by the attached documentation." With respect to several of the students, Westling reached the reasonable conclusion that there was actually "insufficient information" to determine whether or not students were entitled to accommodation because the documentation provided by LDSS was not current, did not support the requested accommodation, or was missing.[9] For example, in regard to one student, Westling states that the testing psychologist "does not say [the student] is incapable of learning a foreign language," only that the student "'has had a history of difficulty with foreign language.'" Rather than authorizing a course substitution as LDSS had done, Westling remarks that the student should be "encouraged to avail himself of the tutoring available to him through the University." With respect to other students, Westling incorrectly determined that the documentation did not support a claim of learning disability.

After describing in detail the perceived shortcomings of each file, Westling's letter to Kip Opperman concludes:

> [I]t is clear to me that the staff of the Learning Disabilities Support Services does not meet any reasonable standard of professional competence in their field. There is also considerable evidence that in addition to being incompetent, the staff has willfully and knowingly undermined University academic standards, distributed false information about University policy, and directly disobeyed University policy. I do not know whether it is possible to make Learning Disabilities Support Services perform its appropriate functions under current management and with its current staff. While I am still considering this issue, I strongly advise you to take the corrective actions indicated in this letter.

Among the "corrective actions" Westling suggests throughout the letter are: (1) that students "be required to provide current evaluations" in light of federal guidelines stating that evaluations that are more than three years old are unreliable; (2) that the

evaluations provide actual test results that support the tester's conclusions; (3) that "[i]ndividuals who provide evaluations of learning disabilities should be physicians, clinical psychologists or licensed psychologists and must have a record of reputable practice"; (4) that all requests for accommodation contain an analysis by LDSS staff, an academic history of the student, and the students academic status at BU; and (5) that LDSS "should not misinform students that course substitutions for foreign language or mathemtics requirements are available." Although Westling had no evidence that learning disabilities changed or abated after students finished high school, he mandated that BU students provide current evaluations (i.e., those that are less than three years old) on the basis of regulations promulgated by the Department of Education for grades kindergarten through twelve. In establishing standards for the credentials of evaluators, Westling relied on consultations with doctors at BU's School of Medicine that Klafter sought in late 1995.

In crafting the November 2, 1995 letter to Opperman, Westling did not intend for LDSS to deny all accommodations to the students whose files he reviewed. Rather, Westling hoped to castigate ODS officials regarding the office's method of approving accommodation requests for students who claimed to have a learning disability, and to obtain better documentation prior to granting a requested accommodation. Nonetheless, as a result of Westling's correspondence, Brinckerhoff sent a letter on behalf of LDSS to most of the 28 students whose files Westling had reviewed, denying the student's request for accommodation and informing the student of his right to appeal the decision to the Provost. For example, in a letter dated December 3, 1995, addressed to named plaintiff Scott Greeley, Brinckerhoff states that Greeley's request for accommodation "was reviewed" and that "the proposed accommodation of requiring the instructor to provide an opportunity to clarify test questions is not supported by the 'educational therapist' who evaluated you." As a further example, in the fall of 1995, plaintiff Michael Cahaly received an accommodation letter from the LDSS office authorizing him to receive up to double time on his exams and to use a notetaker in his classes. However, in December 1995, he received another letter refusing accommodation because his evaluation was not conducted within the past three years. Cahaly had never been informed that there was any problem with the qualifications of his evaluator.

LDSS staff members later told several worried students to disregard Brinckerhoff's letter denying accommodation; however, no formal letter or statement retracting the denial of accommodations was ever issued.

V. Chaos

On December 4, 1995, Brinckerhoff sent a form letter to all BU students who had previously registered with LDSS. The letter, which purported "to inform [students] of recent policy changes at LD Support Services," stated that the following requirements must be fulfilled by January 8, 1996, if students were to remain eligible for accommodations through LDSS:

(1) Students whose documentation was more than three years old "must be reevaluated in order to continue to receive services and accommodations through the LDSS office;"

(2) Students must submit to LDSS documentation of a learning disability that has been prepared by "a licensed psychologist, clinical psychologist, neuropsychologist, or reputable physician;" and

(3) Students seeking accommodations for the spring semester of 1996 must provide LDSS with a high school transcript, a college transcript, and a current BU course schedule including course numbers, course descriptions, and the names and addresses of the professors.

Brinckerhoff distributed the letter to students just prior to final examinations for the fall semester of 1995. He did not forward a copy of the letter to Westlinq for his approval; nor did he check that it accurately conveyed Westling's policy directives. When Westling learned of the letter, he requested that Norm Johnson issue a statement retracting some of the requirements for accommodation that Brinckerhoff had articulated.

On December 22, 1995, approximately three weeks after Brinckerhoff's correspondence, Johnson sent a letter to the learning-disabled students at BU. Johnson's letter notified students that the university was deferring the deadline for submitting current documentation from January 8, 1996—the date set forth by Brinckerhoff—until August 31, 1996. Moreover, it sought "to correct a significant error in Dr. Brinckerhoff's letter" regarding the need for reevaluation. Although Brinckerhoff's letter stated that students with old documentation must be retested if they were to continue to receive assistance from LDSS, Johnson maintained (without explanation) that "[n]o such reevaluation will be necessary in order to continue receiving services from Learning Disability Support Services." Johnson also expressed his "regret" that students "were notified of these proposed changes during the examination period," and he apologized "for any inconvenience."

Throughout the first semester of the 1995-1996 school year, learning-disabled students, parents and professors received mixed and inconsistent messages from university administrators regarding the requirements for seeking and receiving academic accommodations at BU. As a result of the confusing and chaotic climate occasioned by BU's new accommodations policy, there was a substantial reduction in the number of students with self-identified learning disabilities who have attended BU since 1995. Whereas 94 students with self-proclaimed learning disabilities enrolled at BU in 1994, the number of such students had dropped to 71 by the 1996-1997 academic year.

VI. Resignation, Reorganization, and Restructure

Early in 1996, several members of the disability services office resigned, including Brinckerhoff and Opperman, and the Provost's office became the primary decision maker in determining whether a student was to receive an accommodation for a learning disability. In evaluating requests for reasonable accommodations, the Provost's office consulted with specialists like neuropsychologists or the remaining staff at LDSS. With the LDSS office virtually unstaffed, the university undertook to restructure the entire disability services department. Instead of having a self-contained unit within the disability services office to evaluate the accommodations requests of learning disabled students, the new Office of Disability Services ("DS") was structured to manage accommodations for all students with disabilities, whether physical, mental, or in learning. The reconfigured DS staff consisted of a full-time director, an assistant director, a clinical director of learning disability support services, an LD coordinator, a coordinator of interpreter services, and two senior staff assistants. The office was also designed to employ several part-time learning specialists, tutors, interpreters, readers, and notetakers.

On March 25, 1996, BU hired Allan Macurdy, an adjunct assistant professor of law, as the new DS director. Macurdy, a quadriplegic, is a specialist in laws affecting the physically disabled. Soon after his arrival, in the absence of a complete staff, Macurdy personally undertook to review the accommodation requests of students with learning disabilities, even though the student files were in complete disarray (many were inaccurate, incomplete or missing), and neither he nor the other newly-hired DS staff members had any expertise in diagnosing learning disabilities or in fashioning appropriate accommodations.[10]

Between March of 1996 and January of 1997, Macurdy's office reviewed over 80 student files and made recommendations about the requested accommodations. During this time, BU also retained neuropsychologists with expertise in learning disabilities to review student files and make accommodations determinations with regard to learning-disabled students. All recommendations for accommodations made by the DS staff were forwarded to the Provost's office for approval.

By May 31, 1996, the Office of the Provost at BU had reviewed DS recommendations for 77 learning-disabled students. Students whose requests for accommodation were denied by Westling's office were often told to contact the Provost in order to seek reconsideration. However, because there was no established appeal procedure, students and their parents were occasionally not given any information at all regarding further review. As a matter of informal, unwritten policy, the only appeal from the denial of a requested accommodation was to seek reconsideration by the Provost. Students with physical disabilities grieved any denials through the Section 504 procedure handled by the Office of the Dean of Students.

VII.   Present Accommodations Process

In January of 1997, BU hired Dr. Lorraine Wolf as the new clinical director for learning disability support services. Before being appointed, Wolf was a practicing neuropsychologist and an assistant professor of Clinical Psychology at Columbia University. Wolf had also done consulting work for BU since November of 1996.

From early 1997 until the present, Wolf's responsibilities as clinical director have included reviewing the documentation submitted by learning-disabled students and recommendations regarding the accommodations that should be provided to a student on the basis of a learning disability. Although Wolf officially began the clinical director's task of reviewing student files in January, she did so remotely—from her office in New York City[11]—until late May, when she completed her maternity leave and moved to Boston to begin her full-time in-house position.

At present, students with documented learning disabilities at BU may request accommodations such as reduced course loads, use of special computer technology, books on tape, extra time on examinations in a distraction-free environment, and note takers. BU's eligibility requirements for receiving such accommodations are summarized as follows:

(1)   Learning-disabled students must be tested for a learning disorder by a physician, licensed clinical psychologist or a person with a doctorate degree in neuropsychology, educational or child psychology, or another appropriate specialty. The evaluator must have at least three year's experience in diagnosing learning disorders.

(2)   Documentation must be current, as it is recognized by BU for only three years after the date of the evaluation. A learning-disabled student whose documentation is too old at the time he matriculates, or whose documentation

"expires" during his time at BU, must be reevaluated (including retesting). If retesting is deemed unnecessary by the student's evaluator, the evaluator is required to fill in a form explaining why it is not "medically necessary."

The procedure for requesting and receiving an accommodation for a learning disability at BU is as follows. First, a student requesting accommodations submits an application to the DS office.[12] Wolf reviews the submitted documentation and makes a determination regarding the accommodations that are appropriate for the student. Then, the student's file and Wolf's recommendations are forwarded to the President's Office. Klafter reviews each student's documentation for consistency and, when necessary, discusses with university faculty and administrators how the recommended accommodation will affect a particular academic program or course of study. If the President's office accepts Wolf's accommodation recommendations, as is mostly the case, the DS office notifies the student. Generally within two weeks of the request, the DS office also generates accommodations letters to be given to the affected faculty members.

As of April 1997, the President's office endorsed most of Wolf's recommendations for a grant or denial of a request for accommodations due to a learning disability. In several situations, Westling consulted with Wolf and with the relevant department head and denied a requested accommodation where he believed the request was inconsistent with academic standards. For example, Westling rejected a request for a notetaker by a learning-disabled ROTC student in a course on manufacturing engineering; however, he authorized the student's use of a tape-recorder. In other situations, despite initial hesitation, Westling agreed to a notetaker for a student studying social work and a calculator for a student in a math course. In the Wolf era, the interaction between the President's Office and DS in evaluating student files focuses on determining which modifications of academic requirements are appropriate for a given learning-disabled student, rather than on ascertaining the nature and extent of a student's learning disability.

BU admits that it has yet to articulate a single, specific process for students to follow if their request for accommodation is denied. In this litigation, the university takes the position that either the appeal to President Westling or the university's Section 504 grievance procedure is adequate to address student concerns.

VIII.   Impact on Individual Students

The experiences of several of the plaintiffs in attempting to secure accommodations from BU under the new accommodations policy are summarized as follows.[13]

A. Elizabeth Guckenberger

Elizabeth Guckenberger was diagnosed with dyslexia in 1990 during her freshman year at Carleton College. As an undergraduate she received double time on her examinations, exemptions from her language requirements, and the option of a notetaker. Based on her 1990 diagnosis, Guckenberger also received testing accommodations for the LSAT. With these accommodations, Guckenberger was successful enough academically to be accepted to BU's School of Law in the spring of 1993.

Guckenberger enrolled at BU Law School in the fall of 1994. She chose BU in part because her letters of acceptance specifically acknowledged her learning disorder and stated that the university would accommodate her "to the full extent required by law." Guckenberger also spoke to Brinckerhoff before she matriculated about the services provided by LDSS.

To document her disability as required, Guckenberger submitted to LDSS the evaluation that had been prepared in 1990, when she was first diagnosed by a learning disabilities consultant from the Dyslexia Institute of Minnesota. Based an this documentation, LDSS determined that Guckenberger "has problems with both visual and auditory processing," and recommended to the Dean of Academic Affairs at the Law School that she be given notetaking assistance, a reduced course load, priority registration for a section with afternoon classes, and time and one half on exams in a quiet, distraction-free room. During her first year of law school, Guckenberger received these accommodations without incident.

Early in November of 1995, during the first semester of her second year, Guckenberger went to LDSS to verify that she would be receiving accommodations for her fall examinations. Brinckerhoff informed her that, pursuant to the new accommodations policy, she would have to be completely retested for dyslexia before exams began (within the ensuing three weeks) in order to receive acommodations. Stunned, Guckenberger asked for the names of testing specialists who would be acceptable to the school. Brinckerhoff told her that no such list was available.

Confused and upset, Guckenberger arranged a meeting with Kip, Opperman, BU's Director of Disability Services. Opperman told her that she definitely needed to be retested due to the insufficiency of her documentation; however, he could not provide her with a formal statement of the new policy or with the names of any doctors approved by LDSS. Guckenberger then met with Law School Associate Dean Beerman, who told her that accommodations would be made for her pending examinations as long as she made an effort to comply with the new accommodations policy. Over the next few days, Guckenberger contacted two qualified LD specialists; however, neither doctor could evaluate her until the middle of January. Guckenberger notified BU administrators Opperman and Beerman that a reevaluation before the end of the semester would not be possible.

In early December of 1995, Guckenberger received Brinckerhoff's letter stating that she had to be retested by January 6, 1996. At the end of the month, she received, Norman Johnson's letter deferring the retesting deadline until August of the following year.

In the months that followed, Guckenberger and a few of her colleagues met with Klafter to discuss BU's new accommodations policy for students with learning disabilities. Klafter expressed the concern about students who might be "faking" a learning disorder to procure special accommodations. At some point, he referred to licensed, learning-disabilities specialists as "snake oil salesmen." Klafter told her that it was significant that mostly "rich kids" had diagnoses of learning disorders and expressed concern that the diagnoses were not genuine. Then, without clarification, Klafter told the group that not all learning-disabled students with insufficient documentation needed to be completely retested under BU's new policy.

On April 10, 1996, Guckenberger spoke with Carolyn Suissman, an LDSS coordinator, and was told that she must be retested in order to comply with BU's new requirements. Although she was unsure of whether retesting actually was required, to avoid future problems Guckenberger arranged for a complete reevaluation by a licensed clinical psychologist beginning in late April of 1996. The retesting process spanned four days and cost over $800.00. The test results confirmed that Guckenberger had dyslexia, and the psychologist, who had been recommended by BU, suggested the same accommodations that Guckenberger had received during her first and second years of law school.

Guckenberger received all of the accommodations that she had requested throughout her time at BU Law School, including being allowed to take one class less per semester than the average law student. She also received time and one-half on her examinations, a distraction reduced environment in which to take examinations, and the use of a notetaker. Nevertheless, Guckenberger, who has a history of depression, suffered anxiety during the 1995-1996 school year after her accommodations were threatened as a result of BU's new documentation requirements. During the spring semester of 1996, she organized the Law Disability Caucus, a student group that is a co-plaintiff in this class action, to confront the university about its treatment of learning-disabled students seeking reasonable accommodation.

Guckenberger has apparently rebounded well. She is currently completing a joint-degree program, and is working for the office of the United States Attorney in Boston this summer.

B. Avery LaBrecque

A school psychologist identified Avery LaBrecque's language-based learning disability when LaBrecque was in the first grade. The disorder, which impairs her ability to process, memorize, and understand the mechanics of languages, prevented LaBrecque from being successful at reading, mathematics, and spelling. At a very early age, she began a twelve-year odyssey of private tutoring.

LaBrecque took her first foreign language class in the ninth grade. Because of her extremely low performance, her Latin teacher recommended that she be exempted from the high school's language requirement, and be formally tested for a learning disability. In 1990, a neuropsychologist's evaluation revealed that LaBrecque had a language-based learning disorder as well as Attention Deficit Hyperactivity Disorder ("ADHD").

In high school, LaBrecque was placed in a special education program that met once a day. In her regular courses, she received accommodations such as extra time on examinations and a separate testing room. Although she was completely exempted from the foreign language requirement, she nonetheless continued to receive private tutoring for her regular classes.

In 1992, LaBrecque attended BU's "Taste of College" summer program for high school students with learning disorders. During the program, Loring Brinckerhoff informed her that, even though she did not take foreign language in high school, she was still eligible for admission into a competitive university such as BU. Brinckerhoff also discussed the option of substituting cultural courses for BU's foreign language requirement. At the conclusion of the summer program, LaBrecque was retested by a psycho-educational clinician and a school psychologist at the recommendation of support service administrators at LDSS. The specialists confirmed that LaBrecque had a language-based learning disorder and ADHD.

LaBrecque entered the College of General Studies ("CGS") at BU as a freshman in 1993.[14] For her first two years, she received double time on exams in a separate room, a spellchecker for exams, taped lectures, and a note taker. In the fall of 1995, she transferred to the College of Liberal Arts and four semesters of foreign language became a required part of her course of study. Seeking a course substitution through LDSS, LaBrecque submitted an application to LDSS and took a foreign language aptitude test in August of 1995 to determine if she was eligible for a course substitution. When LaBrecque contacted LDSS for the results in September, she was told that her application for accommodations had been forwarded to the Provost's office, along with LDSS's recommendation that she receive a course substitution in lieu of the foreign language requirement.

In October of 1995, LaBrecque was notified that her request for a course substitution for the required four semesters of foreign language was denied. Dismayed that she was not allowed the course substitution in spite of LDSS's recommendation that she receive one, and upset that the denial occurred so late in the semester, LaBrecque took steps to appeal the university's decision. In early November her father contacted the Provost's Office, and in response to expressed concern, Westling reconsidered her documentation. In a letter dated November 10, 1995, Westling approved an exclusion from the written portion of LaBrecque's foreign language courses. The letter stated that the basis for Westling's determination was LaBrecque's evaluator's opinion that, although "Avery is at risk for foreign language learning," "[i]f it is possible for her to deal with foreign language learning only [sic] an oral level, that may be tried."

In subsequent meetings with Professor Robert Richardson of the Department of modern Foreign Languages and Literatures at BU, LaBrecque was told that Swahili was an oral-based language and that Westling had agreed that she should enroll in Swahili because it had no written-component. However, when LaBrecque contacted the Professor of Swahili, John Hutchinson, he informed her that Swahili was indeed a written language, and that her written foreign language abilities would be tested in the class along with her oral language skills.

Devastated by the BU's refusal to accommodate adequately her fully-documented foreign-language learning disorder, LaBrecque decided to transfer to a different college. In May of 1996, during what would have been the end of her junior year at BU, LaBrecque enrolled at Florida State University ("FSU"). LaBrecque withdrew from FSU that fall. Since returning to Boston late in 1996, LaBrecque has sought treatment from both a psychiatrist and a psychologist, and she is still dealing with loss of self-esteem and depression.

C. Benjamin Freedman

Benjamin Freedman was diagnosed with dyslexia as a freshman in high school. Based on his 1989 diagnosis, his high school provided him with a number of accommodations including extra time on exams, a separate examination room, and oral administration of certain tests. As a high school senior, he was retested for dyslexia, and his evaluator, who had a masters in education, found no changes in his learning disability.

Freedman enrolled at BU as a freshmen in 1993. For his first two years in college, Freedman received extended time on his exams, use of a note taker and word processor, and oral examinations for certain courses—accommodations that he learned about prior to deciding to attend BU through independent research and a conversation with a BU admissions representative.

In December of 1995, Freedman received Brinckerhoff's letter regarding the changes in LDSS's accommodations policy. Confused and angered, Freedman contacted Brinckerhoff and Dean David Mansfield, Assistant Dean of Students, about the new policy.

At around the same time, Freedman began to hear and read about the comments that Westling had been making about the learning disabilities movement. Early in 1996, Freedman read one of Westling's speeches, and was upset by its rhetorical reference to learning disorders as "genetic catastrophes." Freedman appeared with Westing on the television show "Good Morning America" and expressed his belief that Westling's derogatory comments discriminated against BU students with learning disabilities.

In the fall of 1996, at the beginning of his senior year of college, Freedman transferred to CW Post, Long Island University in New York, near to his home. At trial, Freedman testified that the tuition at CW Post is approximately half of what he had been paying to attend BU.

D. Jill Cutler

Jill Cutler, now a junior majoring in Early Childhood Education at BU'S School of Education, was first diagnosed with a learning disability when she was in the sixth grade. Evaluations that were conducted when she was in the seventh grade, and again when she was a freshman and a junior in high school, revealed that she has a learning disorder that specifically affects auditory processing, sequencing, and reading comprehension. As a result, throughout high school, Cutler received tutors, untimed examinations, and modified classes. She was also given extended time on her college entrance examinations.

Cutler enrolled at BU's College of General Studies in the fall of 1994, and submitted to LDSS a copy of an evaluation conducted in 1993 in support of her request for special accommodations for her learning disability. During her first two years at BU, BU allowed Cutler to have extended time on her nations and to take the exams in a distraction-free room.

Cutler first became aware of BU's new accommodations policy when her father read about it in the New York Times in February of 1996. Cutler met with LDSS representative Carolyn Suissman before she left Boston for the summer break. Suissman told Cutler that she needed to be completely retested in order to comply with BU's new requirements. Cutler was also informed that she needed to provide the university with a copy of her high school transcript.

In June of 1996, Cutler underwent what she describes as "the humiliating" and "traumatic" ordeal of being retested for a learning disability. She was "frantic" about the retesting because it reinforced her belief that she was not "normal." Over a period of three to four hours and at a total cost of $650.00, a neuropsychologist found that Cutler's learning disorder had remained unchanged since her last evaluation in 1993. The evaluator recommended that Cutler be allowed to retain the accommodations she received during her first two years at BU for the reminder of her education.

E. Scott Greeley

In 1984, Scott Greeley's first grade teacher discovered that he had a problem with sequential processing, i.e., the ability to transfer concepts into a verbal or written form. An assessment by the school psychologist confirmed that Greeley had a learning disorder. In 1991, when Greeley was fourteen, he was formally evaluated by an educational therapist. The therapist tested Greeley and detected that he had an audio-visual learning processing deficit that limits his ability to process basic information quickly.

Throughout high school, Greeley received special accommodations from the school district including extra time to complete tests and assignments. He successfully completed four years of foreign language classes in high school. With the aid of accommodations such as extra time, Greeley performed well academically (even in honors classes), and he received a score of 1210 on the standardized Scholastic Aptitude Test. In 1994, Greeley was re-evaluated by the same educational therapist who conducted his 1991 assessment in order to document further his disability.

In the fall of 1994, during his senior year in high school, Greeley wrote to BU requesting information about university programs for students with learning disabilities. After learning about LDSS and the various accommodations available for learning-disabled students, Greeley decided to apply to BU.[15] BU not only accepted Greeley, the university also gave him a four-year financial scholarship premised on his maintenance of a 3.0 grade point average.

Early in the spring of 1995, Greeley and his father flew to Boston to visit BU and to investigate further the support structure for students with learning disabilities. Greeley and his father met with LDSS representative Carolyn Suissman, who explained the various types of accommodations available and stated that Greeley should have "no problem" in getting accommodations from the university. Greeley got an even better sense of the university's requirements by attending BU's transition summer program for learning-disabled students.

Greeley enrolled as a freshman in BU's College of Arts and Sciences in the fall of 1995. Before classes began, Greeley requested accommodations such as time and one-half on examinations, a note taker, access to books on tape, and the opportunity to clarify test questions.[16] Once the semester began, and Greeley still had not heard from LDSS regarding his requested accommodations, he began to contact the LDSS office regularly. At first, he was told that LDSS was going through changes, that the accommodations letters might have to be revised, and that he should return within the week. One week turned into months. Greeley kept returning to the LDSS office to check on the status of his accommodations and was told time and time again to come back later.

On November 27, 1995, after enduring nearly an entire semester without the requested classroom accommodations, Greeley was told by an LDSS representative that he was ineligible for accommodations under the new guidelines. When he asked for a copy of the guidelines, he was told that none existed. Without LDSS accommodations letters, Greeley had to approach each of his professors, explain his situation, and ask for extra time on his exams. For his first semester at BU, LDSS did not authorize the in-class accommodations that Greeley had requested.

On or about December 3, 1995, Greeley received a letter addressed to him from Loring Brinckerhoff informing him that his request to clarify test questions was not supported by the evaluation that he had submitted as documentation of his learning disability. The letter also indicated that Greeley's evaluator needed to be a physician, clinical psychologist, licensed psychologist or neuropsychologist and must "have a record of reputable practice" in order to be acceptable to the university. At about this time, Greeley also received the form letter from Brinckerhoff describing the changes in LDSS policy.

Early in 1996, prior to the start of the spring semester, Greeley sought clarification from LDSS regarding his eligibility for accommodations in light of the new policy. He was told that he needed to be retested, even though his original documentation had been accepted by the BU summer program. At LDSS's suggestion, Greeley had his test results reviewed by a licensed clinical psychologist who wrote BU a letter confirming Greeley's disability and indicating that his accommodations requests were reasonable. At some point during the spring semester, Greeley was told that the psychologist's report would be valid for that semester only, and that he would have to be retested to receive accommodations for the remainder of his time at BU. At the end of February of 1996, Greeley received his first LDSS approval and accommodations letters.

Greeley suffered extreme stress from the fall of 1995 until February of 1996 during his attempts to get BU to honor his documentation and to provide him with accommodations for his learning disability. As a physical manifestation of his anxiety, Greeley contracted severe acne which he had to treat with a medication that caused him to be drowsy and to gain weight. During his first semester at BU, Greeley's grade point average was a mere 1.67. As a result, he lost his promised academic scholarship and his federal subsidized loans. The increased financial hardship, in turn, contributed to his feelings of stress, low self-esteem, and depression. Although Greeley received accommodations of a notetaker and time-and-a-half on examinations in the fall of 1996, at the beginning of his sophomore year, he still finished the semester with a poor grade point average.

F. Jordan Nodelman

Jordan Nodelman first became aware of his attention problem in 1989, when he was in the eighth grade. At his mother's request, a clinical psychologist administered a battery of tests and discovered that Nodelman exhibited "all the features of a moderate attention deficit disorder ("ADD") with mental rather than physical restlessness." In the spring of 1993, when Nodelman was in the eighth grade, he was evaluated again by an individual with a doctorate in education. The evaluator's diagnosis, which was consistent with the results of an additional review that she conducted nine months later, was that Nodelman had "significant learning discrepancies" that "appear[] to be the result of an attention deficit disorder." Nodelman used this evaluation in order to qualify for such accommodations as an untimed administration of the Scholastic Aptitude Test in a distraction-reduced environment.

During the summer of 1993, between his junior and senior years of preparatory school, Nodelman attended BU's summer transition program for high school students with learning disorders. As a result of the program, Nodelman not only learned about college-level academic requirements, but was also informed that the diversity provided accommodations for ADD. Based on his experience in the summer program and the recommendation of his evaluator, Nodelman decided to apply to BU.

Nodelman matriculated at BU's College of General Studies ("CGS") in the fall of 1994. At the beginning of his freshman year, Nodelman talked with Loring Brinckerhoff about the accommodations that he would need. On the basis of his documentation,[17] Nodelman received all of the accommodations that he asked for including time and one-half on examinations, a distraction-free examination room, and use of a calculator (where warranted) for his first two years at BU. Nodelman performed well with the accommodations he received, making the Dean's List at CGS every semester during his freshman and sophomore years.

Nodelman first became aware of the changes in LDSS policy in 1995, at the end of the first semester of his sophomore year. In early December, he received the letter from Brinckerhoff describing the new requirements, and in late December he received the letter from Dean Johnson modifying Brinckerhoff's correspondence. Concerned about the seemingly conflicting statements of policy, and confused about the effect of the new procedure on his ability to receive accommodations, Nodelman called several LDSS administrators, including Brinckerhoff, for clarification. Brinckerhoff told Nodelman that his documentation was sufficient to support accommodations for his pending examinations.

Early in 1996, Nodelman went to LDSS to apply for accommodations for the spring semester. A few weeks later, Nodelman received accommodations letters from LDSS addressed to his professors recommending the accommodations that he had requested.

Just prior to summer vacation at the end of his sophomore year, Nodelman met with LDSS representative Manju Banerjee to make sure that his documentation fulfilled university requirements so that he could receive accommodations when he returned in the fall. Banerjee told Nodelman that his LD file, which contained copies of his evaluations and test results, was missing and that he would have to supply BU with new information. During the summer of 1996, he sent new copies of the evaluations that had been in his file to the Disability Services Office at the request of new DS director, Allan Macurdy.

Still confused about whether his documentation was adequate under the new accommodations policy, Nodelman spoke with Macurdy during the summer of 1996 to get clarification on the acceptability of his evaluations. Specifically, Nodelman was worried that his evaluator, who had a doctorate in education, would be deemed unqualified under the then existing version of BU's new accommodations policy.[18] Macurdy told Nodelman that, in lieu of being completely retested, he could get the clinical psychologist who conducted his eighth-grade evaluation to review the educational doctorate's report and write a letter stating that the report was adequate. At a cost of $150.00, Nodelman's mother commissioned the psychologist to prepare such a letter.

Nodelman has been successful both academically and socially at BU. In January of 1997, Nodelman left for France to participate in BU's semester-abroad language program.

G. Catherine Hays Miller

Catherine Hays Miller, who testified at trial but is not a named plaintiff in this action, was diagnosed with ADD in the second grade. She also has dyslexia, particularly in foreign language, which was discovered when she flunked one year of Spanish in her sophomore year of high school. Miller enrolled at BU in 1995 because it was reported to have one of the best learning disabilities programs in the country, and because she had been told by BU representatives that BU made course substitutions available for students with documented foreign language learning problems. However, when Miller sought such an exemption, BU refused to allow the requested substitution. Miller took first semester Spanish as required, and with a huge amount of effort, she received a "B" in the class.

Eventually, Miller and her parents convinced Westling to reconsider her request to be exempted from BU's foreign language requirement. After reviewing a report that was completed by a licensed clinical psychologist with a doctorate stating that "Hays appears to have difficulties in the area of auditory processing," Westling approved a waiver of the verbal portion of the foreign language requirement. When the evaluator supplemented his report with a letter clarifying that "Hays' disability will in fact greatly impair her ability to learn a foreign language either verbally or her written instructional methods," Westling declared that "[t]he clinical record presented in support of Hays' claim [for exemption] is, at best contradictory," that "as such, it is insufficient to substantiate the assertion that she is incapable of learning a foreign language." BU continues to require Miller to complete four semesters of a foreign language program emphasizing written instruction.

IX. Learning Disorders, ADD, and ADHD—A Primer

Seven expert witnesses testified at trial about the nature, diagnosis, and accommodations of the conditions known as learning disorders, ADD, and ADHD. In order of appearance, the expert witnesses were: (1) Dean Robert Shaw, Associate Dean and learning disabilities administrator at Brown University; (2) Peter Blanck, Professor of Law, Preventive Medicine, and Psychology at University of Iowa; (3) Sally Shaywitz, M.D., Professor of Pediatrics at Yale University and Co-Director of the NIH-Yale Center from the Study of Learning and Attention; (4) George Hynd, Research Professor of Special Education and Psychology at the University of Georgia and Editor-in-Chief of the Journal of Learning Disabilities; (5) Rachel Klein, Professor of Clinical Psychology at Columbia University's College of Physicians and Surgeons and Director of clinical Psychology at the New York State Psychiatric Institute; (6) Linda Seigel, Professor of Educational Psychology and Special Education at the University of British Columbia in Vancouver, and (7) Richard Sparks, Associate Professor of Education at the College of Mount St. Joseph.[19]

A. The Disabilities

1. Dyslexia

Dyslexia has been traditionally defined as an "unexpected difficulty learning to read despite intelligence, motivation and education."[20] As Professor Seigel pointed out, both Agatha Christie and William Butler Yeats had learning disabilities which created problems in spelling.

Dr. Sally E. Shaywitz, co-director of the Yale Center for the Study of Learning and Attention, and Professor of Pediatrics at the Yale University School of Medicine, describes the disorder as a neurobiological condition that "interfere[s] with a normally intelligent [person's] ability to acquire speech, reading, or other cognitive skills." Id. Dyslexia, the most common learning disorder, is a reading disability that is the result of a phonological processing deficit, or "decoding" problem.[21] A dyslexic's ability to break down written words into their basic linguistic units is impaired. However, her higher-level cognitive comprehension abilities—vocabulary, reasoning, concept formation, and general intelligence—may remain intact despite the deficit in phonological processing. About 80 percent of people with learning disabilities have dyslexia. If an individual has a learning disability that makes phonological processing difficult, that individual will have a difficulty with any aspect of learning that involves language, including the acquisition of proficiency in a foreign language.

2. Attention Deficit Disorder ("ADD")/Attention Deficit Hyperactivity Disorder ("ADHD")

ADD and ADHD, as described in volume four of Diagnostical Statistical Manual of the American Psychiatric Association ("DSM-IV"), have the following diagnostic feature: "a persistent pattern of inattention and/or hyperactivity-impulsivity that is more frequent and severe than is typically observed in individuals at a comparable level of development." An individual who has the chronic disorder classified as ADHD has neurological problem that involve inattention, hyperactivity, and impulsivity. ADD, which is a subtype of ADHD, is manifest only as a problem with attention. The DSM-IV's diagnostic criteria require that some hyperactive, impulsive or inattentive symptoms that caused impairment were present before age 7 years, and that the symptoms are not better accounted for by another mental disorder. Although ADD and ADHD may interfere with a student's ability to perform effectively, they are not technically learning disabilities, in that the person's ability to acquire basic academic skills is not compromised.

Approximately three percent of the young adult population demonstrates symptoms of ADD or ADHD. According to Professor Rachel Klein, who has performed a longitudinal study, ADD and ADHD have a relatively high rate of permanent, spontaneous remission as a person moves from adolescence into adulthood. She concluded that between ages 16 and 18, 40 to 50 percent of students get better, and another 30 to 40 percent improve between the ages of 18 and 20. The study indicates that, although approximately 70 percent of individuals diagnosed with some form of ADHD as children still have symptoms by age 16, once those individuals reach their 30's, only some ten percent are still symptomatic. Another study shows that 40 to 60 percent of students with ADD continue with symptoms into adulthood. Klein also testified that "there are a fair number of instances in which there is considerable question about the accuracy of the diagnosis of ADHD in college-age students."

According to Dr. John Ratey, M.D., of Harvard Medical school, certain medical conditions may mask or simulate ADD. For example, hyperthyroidism also has symptoms like hyperactivity and inattentiveness. Other medical conditions produce symptoms of inattentiveness like brain damage, substance abuse, depression and hormonal problems. Because the vast majority of individuals with ADHD and ADD respond well to medications, psychopharmacological treatment enables seventy percent of individuals to function in the range of normal. According to Dr. Ratey, people that have ADD are in an ongoing process of medical evaluation.

B. The Diagnoses

Over the last decade, there has been a steady growth in the number of students identifying themselves as learning disabled, but this is now flattening out. Some experts attribute this growth to: (1) the enactment of the Individuals with Disabilities Education Act in 1975, which requires public school districts to identify students with learning disabilities; (2) the increasing awareness of the existence of learning disabilities among educators, researchers and the public at large; and (3) the passage of the Americans with Disabilities Act. The number of students with learning disabilities at colleges and universities hovers at about two per cent.

The DSM-IV now has a section on learning disorders which include reading disorders, mathematics disorders, disorder of written expression, and learning disorders not otherwise specified. It states that the prevalence of reading disorders (which accounts for 80 percent of all learning disorders, alone or in combination with other disorders) is estimated at approximately 4 percent of school-age children. The DSM-IV provides: "Learning disorders are diagnosed when the individual's achievement on individually administered, standardized tests in reading, mathematics, or written expression is substantially below that expected for age, schooling, and level of intelligence." The American Psychiatric Association defines "substantially below" as a discrepancy of more than 2 standard deviations between achievement and I.Q. Although some experts are beginning to maintain that I.Q. testing is not essential to diagnosing a learning disability (and is sometimes misleading), I.Q. tests are used in twenty-nine states and two Canadian provinces in evaluating the learning disabled, and universities still require the submission of I.Q. test results. In addition, learning disorders are diagnosed through a battery of standardized tests such as Wechster Individual Achievement Test ("WIAT"), the Wide Range Achievement Test-Revised ("WRAT-R"), and the Woodcock Johnson tests of Cognitive Ability.

By contrast, ADD and ADHD diagnoses involve a clinical evaluation and can include psychological testings that costs up to $1,200. Evaluators make assessments on the individual that take into account behavioral reports from sources such as the person himself, his parents, teachers, spouses, and friends. As a result, ADD/ADHD is both underdiagnosed and overdiagnosed, and normal behavioral problems in children are sometimes misdiagnosed as ADD or ADHD, especially in young boys.

C. Possibility for Change

Once diagnosed, learning disorders and ADD/ADHD have significantly different possibilities of change or remissin. Although ADD/ADHD have a high rate of remission as a person enters adulthood, specific learning disorders do not disappear over time. Some individuals with language-based learning disorders such as dyslexia may learn to overcome their processing problems; however, reading can occur only "at a great cost in time."[22] Other dyslexics may never learn to decode, but may accomplish reading by struggling to recognize words in context. As opposed to individuals with ADHD, after a person with a learning disorder reaches adulthood (age 18), there is no significant change in his cognitive abilities.

D. Professional Guidelines

An ad hoc committee of the Association for Higher Education and Disabilities ("AHEAD"), which consists of an impressive array of experts in post-secondary education,[23] has issued guidelines for "Documentation of a Specific Learning Disability." The Guidelines provide standard criteria for post-secondary personnel to use in verifying learning disabilities in order to: (1) to provide "a conservative—though flexible—approach to minimize the risk of over-diagnosis;" (2) to offer recommendations on how to determine the appropriateness of requests made by individuals with learning disabilities; and (3) provide guidance in "deteremining the necessary qualifications of the evaluator and his/her role in the process."

With respect to documentation, AHEAD states that a complete set of aptitude and achievement test results are required. Actual test scores must be provided because the "assessment must show evidence of discrepancies and intra-individual differences." In addition, the guidelines provide:

> B. Testing must be current.
>
> In most cases, this means testing that has been conducted within the past three years. Because the provision of all reasonable accommodations and services is based upon assessment of the current impact of the student's disabilities on his/her academic performance, it is in a student's best interest to provide recent and appropriate documentation. In the case of adults tested after age 21, testing within a five-year period can be accepted.

With respect to the qualifications of the professional conducting the evaluation, the guidelines state that "[t]he following professionals would generally be considered qualified to evaluate specific learning disabilities provided that they have comprehensive training in learning disabilities: clinical or educational psychologists, neuropsychologists, learning disabilities specialists, and Medical doctors known to specialize in specific learning disability conditions."

Conclusions of Law

I. Discrimination Claims under the ADA and Section-504

The plaintiff class claims that BU discriminates against students with learning disabilities in violation of the Americans with Disabilities Act ("ADA"), and the Rehabilitation Act of 1973 ("Section 504").

A. The Laws

In relevant part, Title III of the ADA provides:

> No individual will be discriminated against on the basis of disability in the full and equal enjoyment of the goods, services, facilities, privileges, advantages, or accommodations of any place of public accommodation by any person who owns, leases (or leases to) or operates a public accommodation.

42 U.S.C. § 12182(a) (1995). The Rehabilitation Act of 1973 ("Section 504"), the venerable ancestor of the ADA makes a similar guarantee:

> No otherwise qualified individual with a disability ... shall, solely by reason of her or his disability, be excluded from the participation in, be denied the benefit of, or be subjected to discrimination under any program or activity receiving Federal financial assistance ... .

29 U.S.C. § 794(a) (1997), as amended by Pub. L. No. 102-569, § 102(p)(32)(1992) (changing "handicap" to "disability"). The ADA and Section 504, which are both applicable to BU,[24] "are frequently read in sync."

"It is the purpose of both the ADA and the Rehabilitation Act to provide a coherent framework and consistent and enforceable-standards for the elimination of discrimination against persons with disabilities." *Thomas v. Davidson Academy*, 846 F.Supp. 611, 620 (M.D. Tenn. 1994) (citing 42 U.S.C. § 12101(b)(1) and (2) and 29 U.S.C. § 701). Section 504, which "was the first broad federal statute aimed at eradicating discrimination against individuals with disabilities," *Helen L. v. DiDario*, 46 P.3d 325, 330 (3d Cir. 1995), cert, denied, 116 S.Ct. 64 (1995), was a "sweeping[ ] statutory attempt to combat all forms of discrimination against the handicapped." *Allen v. Heckler*, 780 F. 2d 64, 66(DC. Cir. 1985). "Through [the ADA], the federal government extended the non-discrimination principles required of institutions

　　APP : 15

receiving federal funds by the Rehabilitation Act to a much wider array of institutions and business." *Easley v. Snider*, 841 F.Supp. 668, 672 (E.D. Pa. 1993) (internal citation omitted), rev'd on other grounds, 36 F.3d 297 (3d Cir. 1994). The ADA thus "represents a major commitment by the federal government to assure adequate projection to Americans with disabilities." *Jacques v. Clean-Up Group, Inc.*, 96 F.3d 506, 515 (1st Cir. 1996)

The ADA and Section 504 specifically prohibit discrimination against the handicapped, not just based on invidious "affirmative animus," but also based on thoughtlessness, apathy and stereotypes about disabled persons. See *Alexander v. Choate*, 469 U.S. 287, 295-297 (1985) (pointing to legislative history that § 504 would prohibit the denial of "special educational assistance" for handicapped children). Congress has found that individuals with disabilities are a "discrete and insular minority" who have been faced with restrictions and limitations "resulting from stereotypic assumptions not truly indicative of the individual ability of such individuals to participate in, and contribute to, society." 42 U.S.C. § 12101(a)(7). The ADA defines discrimination to include: (1) the use of criteria that unnecessarily "screen out" or "tend to screen out" individuals with disabilities from the use and enjoyment of goods and services, (2) the failure to make nonfundamental, reasonable modifications of "policies, practices or procedures" when such modification is necessary to accommodate disabled persons, and (3) the failure to take necessary steps "to ensure that no individual with a disability is excluded, denied services, segregated or otherwise treated differently than other individuals." 42 U.S.C. § 12182(b)(2) (defining "discrimination" under the ADA); see also 34 C.F.R. §§ 104.43-104.44 (implementing Section 504); 28 C.F.R. § 36.103 (stating that the ADA "shall not be construed to apply a lesser standard than the standard to be applied" under Section 504).

These statutes protect individuals who have a "disability," explicitly defined as "a physical or mental impairment that substantially limits one or more of the major life activities of such individual," "a record of such an impairment," or "being regarded as having such an impairment." 42 U.S.C. § 12102(2); accord 29 U.S.C. 5706(8)(B) (defining "handicapped person" for the purpose of the Rehabilitation Act). The regulations that interpret the statutes list "specific learning disabilities" among the physical or mental impairments that may render an individual "disabled" within the meanin of the acts. See 28 C.F.R. § 36.104 (implements the ADA); 34 C.F.R. § 104.3(j)(2)(i)(B) (implementing Section 504)

B.   Documentation Requirements

Plaintiffs argue that BU's new accommodations policy makes it unnecessarily difficult for students to document their learning disabilities when requesting accommodation.[25] Specifically, plaintiffs allege that BU's documentation requirements violate the provision of the ADA that defines discrimination to include:

> the imposition or application of eligibility criteria that screen out or tend to screen out an individual with a disability or any class of individuals with disabilities from fully and equally enjoying any services, facilities, privileges, advantages, or accommodations, unless such criteria can be shown to be necessary for the provision of the goods, services, facilities, privileges, advantages, or accommodations.

42 U.S.C. § 12182(b)(2)(i); 28 C.F.R. § 35.130(b)(8); accord 34 C.F.R. § 104.4(b)(4) (interpreting Section 504); see also *Emery v. Caravan of Dreams, Inc.*, 879 F.Supp. 640, 643-44 (N.D. Tex. 1995) (discussing the statutory term "criteria"). Under federal law, public entities cannot use eligibility criteria that screen out or tend to screen out individuals with disabilities unless they can show that the criteria are necessary. See *Doe v. Judicial Nominating Comm'n*, 906 F.Supp. 1534, 1540 (S.D. Fla. 1995). This tend-to-screen-out concept, which is "drawn from current regulations under Section 504 (see e.g. 45 C.F.R. § 84.13), makes it discriminatory to impose policies or criteria that, while not creating a direct bar to individuals with disabilities, diminish an individual's chances of such participation." *Doukas v. Metropolitan Life Ins. Co.*, 950 F.Supp. 422, 426 (D.N.H. 1996). Plaintiffs need not show discriminatory intent to establish a violation of the ADA's tend-to-screen-out provision. See *Emery*, 879 F.Supp. at 643.

1.   BU's Eligibility Criteria

At present, students who seek reasonable accommodation from BU on the basis of a learning disability are required to document their disability by: a) being tested by a physician, or a licensed psychologist, or an evaluator who has a doctorate degree in neuropsychology, education, or another appropriate field; b) producing the results of testing conducted no more than three years prior to the accommodation request; and c) providing the results of I.Q. tests in addition to the results of the normal battery of tests designed to assess the nature and extent of a learning disability. These requirements are "eligibility criteria," within the meaning of the ADA and Section 504 because they are policies that allow the university to judge which students are eligible for the learning disability services and to tailor reasonable academic accommodations provided by BU. See *Emery*, 879 F.Supp. at 643-44.

2. Screen Out

The ADA permits a university to require a student requesting a reasonable accommodation to provide current documentation from a qualified professional concerning his learning disability. See *Halasz v. Univ. of New England*, 816 F.Supp. 37., 46 (D. Me.1993) ("When a university operates a program specifically for the handicapped, it clearly needs to know about an applicant's handicaps before it can make a decision about admission to the program."); see also *Farley v. Gibson Container Inc.*, 891 F.Supp. 322, 326 (N.D. Miss. 1995) (finding that "Employers should not be expected to recognize a physical impairment solely on an employee's 'say-so'"); *Miller v. Nat'l Cas. Co.*, 61 F.3d 627, 629 (8th Cir. 1995) (quoting 29 C.F.R. app. § 1630.9); *Kalekiristos v. CTS Hotel Management Corp.*, 958 F.Supp. 641, 657 (D.D.C. 1997) (holding that individuals "alleging a disability protected by the ADA [have] the burden of establishing with medical evidence the existence of the alleged disability.") cf. *Grenier v. Cynamid Plastics, Inc.* 70 F.3d 667, 675-76 (1st Cir. 1995) (allowing an employer to ask for medical certification from a treating psychiatrist).

Nevertheless, a university cannot impose upon such individuals documentation criteria that unnecessarily screen out or tend to screen out the truly disabled. 42 U.S.C. § 12182(b)(2)(i); see also 34 C.F.R. § 104.4(b)(4) (interpreting Section 504 so as to prohibit eligibility criteria that "have the purpose or effect of defeating or substantially impairing the accomplishment of the objectives of the recipient's program"). Just as a covered entity is prohibited from defining the offered benefit "in a way that effectively denies otherwise qualified handicapped individuals the meaningful access to which they are entitled," *Alexander*, 469 U.S. at 301, 105 S.Ct. at 720, so too is a university prevented from employing unnecessarily burdensome proof-of-disability criteria that preclude or unnecessarily discourage individuals with disabilities from establishing that they are entitled to reasonable accommodation. Cf. *Coleman v. Zatechka*, 824 F.Supp. 1360, 1366 (D. Neb. 1993) (rejecting "unnecessary" eligibility requirements imposed on disabled students who seek to participate in the school's roommate assignment program).

In determining whether BU's documentation requirements "screen out or tend to screen out" students with learning disabilities, the Court considers separately each of the contested eligibility criteria and takes into account the changes that BU has made to its policies in response to this litigation.

a. Currency Requirement

During the 1995-1996 school year, BU's policy required that a student seeking accommodations on the basis of a learning disability submit documentation that had been completed within three years of the request for accommodation. This meant that students essentially had to be retested every three years. Based on the evidence, I easily find that this initial "currency" requirement imposed significant additional burdens on disabled students. For example, Elizabeth Guckenberger testified that her retesting process took four days and cost $800.00. Jill Cutler's retesting took four hours and cost $650.00. Dean Robert Shaw testified that the evaluations could cost up to $1,000 and involve multiple visits. Cutler's tearful testimony was particularly compelling with respect to the emotional impact of the retesting because it was a poignant reminder that she was not "normal." BU's initial requirement mandating retesting for students with learning disabilities screened out or tended to screen out the learning disabled within the meaning of the federal law.

However, BU's retesting policy at present has been changed substantially to provide for a waiver of the reevaluation requirement. A recent statement of policy provides: Reevaluation is required to ensure that services and accommodations are matched to the student's changing needs. Comprehensive retesting is not required. A student need only be re-tested for his previously diagnosed learning disability. The issue of what specific re-testing is required is in the first instance, left to the discretion of the student's physician or licensed clinical psychologist should write to DS to explain why. Re-testing that is not medically necessary will be waived. (Emphasis omitted). This waiver process was reconfirmed in the procedural pronouncements that BU distributed in March of 1997. Thus, it is clear that the retesting can now be obviated if a qualified professional deems it not medically necessary.

I am not persuaded that BU's current retesting policy tends to screen out disabled students. The university's new waiver position appears consistent with plaintiffs' position that the need for retesting should be examined on a student-by-student basis. This policy permits a qualified professional to evaluate the noncurrent testing data, examine issues of co-morbidity (whether other psychological or physical problem are contributing to the learning problem), and talk with the student to determine whether re-testing is desirable, thereby meting BU's goals without placing an undue burden on the students. In any event, the waiver provision is so new this Court has an insufficient record for determining how this policy is being implemented, and whether it tends to screen out students.

b. Credentials of Evaluators

BU accepts evaluations and test results that document a learning disability only if the student's evaluator has certain qualifications. Plaintiffs appear to concede that a university can require credentialed evaluators; however, they argue that BU's policy of accepting only the evaluations of medical doctors, licensed clinical psychologists, and individuals with doctorate degrees is too restrictive. With respect to BU's narrow definition of the acceptable qualifications of the persons performing an evaluations plaintiffs have proven that, both in its initial and current form, these eligibility criteria tend to screen out learning disabled students.

Many students (e.g., Greeley) with long histories of learning disorders in elementary and high school were tested by trained, experienced professionals whose credentials do not match BU's criteria but were deemed acceptable by the student's secondary school, and are acceptable under the guidelines set forth by the Association for Higher Education and Disabilities ("AHEAD").[26] BU's policy raises a high hurdle because it seemingly requires students with current testing to be retested if the evaluation has not been performed by a person with credentials acceptable to BU. As initially drafted and implemented, the policy tends to screen out students because of the time, expense and anxiety of having to be completely retested, even if their documentation has been recently performed by an evaluator who specialized in learning disabilities and who had a masters degree in education or developmental psychology.

To complicate things further, BU's implementation of the credentials policy has been uneven. It has permitted some students with learning disabilities to fulfill the requirement via the much less expensive route of asking an evaluator with the requisite credentials to review and confirm the evaluator's test results, while other students have been required to undergo a complete reevaluation. For example, plaintiff Jordan Nodelman only spent $150 to obtain a review of his original ADD evaluation from a licensed clinical psychologist, and there is no evidence that he had difficulty procuring the confirmation letter. However, though Scott Greeley was offered a similar concession, BU ultimately refused to accept Greeley's confirmation correspondence. Assuming that the Nodelnan review procedure is unavailable under the current policy for students who have been tested by evaluators with masters degrees, I conclude that plaintiffs have proven that BU's present eligibility criteria concede the credentials of the evaluators tend to screen out some students with learning disabilities.

One caveat. With respect to BU students who have not been tested for a learning disability prior to matriculation at the university, there is no evidence that testing by evaluators with doctorate degrees is significantly more expensive or burdensome than testing by a person with a masters degree. Also, there is no evidence that it is more difficult to locate or to schedule an appointment with a person with credentials acceptable to BU, particularly in an academic mecca like Boston. This court finds that BU's credentials requirement does not tend to screen out students who do not have to bear the burden of being retested in order to satisfy BU's qualifications mandate.

c. I.Q. Tests

Finally, plaintiffs have offered no persuasive evidence that BU's requirement that a student provide his I.Q. test scores tends to screen out any students. Indeed, under the AHEAD guidelines, the diagnostic criteria in the DSM IV, and the standards in 29 states, IQ tests are administered as part of a learning disabilities assessment.

d. BU's Response

BU argues that neither its initial or its current documentation criteria "screen out" the learning disabled within the meaning of federal law because there is no persuasive evidence that its requirements have had the effect of actually preventing students with learning disabilities from getting accommodations from the university. The strongest evidence in support of BU's position is that all of the plaintiffs, after much hassle, eventually received the requested accommodations (except course substitutions) from BU in spite of its new and more burdensome documentation requirements. BU also attempted to present data suggesting that roughly the same number of students are receiving accommodations under the current policy as during the prior LDSS reign.[27]

Contrary to BU's assertions, plaintiffs have demonstrated that BU's initial eligibility criteria actually screened out students. The number of enrolled students who self-identify as learning-disabled 40 Percent between the 1994-1995 academic year and the 1996-1997 academic year. Moreover, as considered in detail, plaintiffs have established that as initially implemented, the currency and qualifications requirements were burdensome and, thus, they at least tended to screen out the disabled students. See *Ellen S. v. Florida Bd. Of Bar Examiners*, 859 F.Supp. 1489, 1494 (S.D. Fla. 1994) (concluding that "a board can discriminate against qualified applicants by placing additional burdens on them and this discrimination can occur even if these applicants are subsequently granted licenses to practice law") (emphasis omitted); *Clark v. Virginia Bd. Of Bar Examiners*, 880 F.Supp. 430, 442 (E.D. Va. 1995) (finding that an unnecessary mental health question on a bar application violates the ADA's prohibition against discriminatory eligibility criteria even though "it is not clear that Question 20(b) 'screens out' potential applicants").

3. Necessity

Documentation requirements that screen out or tend to screen out disabled students—in this case, the qualification criteria and the currency requirement as it was initially imposed—still do not violate the ADA and Rehabilitation Act if BU can demonstrate that the requirement is a "necessary" part of the accommodations process. See 42 U.S.C. § 12182(b)(2)(i) (prohibiting as discriminatory criteria that screen out or tend to screen out the disabled "unless such criteria can be shown to be necessary for the provision of the goods [or] services ... being offered") (emphasis omitted); *Coleman,* 824 F.Supp. at 1368 (considering whether defendants have established that "the additional eligibility requirements ... are 'necessary' to the roommate assignment program"); cf. *Judice, M.D. v. Hospital Serv. Dist. No. 1,* 919 F.Supp. 978, 982 (E.D. La. 1996) (stating that the ADA allows entities to impose different eligibility criteria on the disabled "if necessary for their safe operation") (emphasis omitted). Again, I consider the necessity of the criteria separately.

a. Currency

Because every expert who testified agreed that there is no demonstrable change in a specific learning disorder, such as dyslexia, after an individual reaches age 18, BU has failed to demonstrate that the three-year retesting requirement, as initially written,[28] was necessary for students who had been diagnosed with specific learning disorders.

Professor Shaywitz of Yale University School of Medicine, a physician and medical researcher in the area of dyslexia, has performed a comprehensive longitudinal study of the changes in a large population of dyslexic children over an extended period of time. She testified that dyslexia causes a persistent, life-long deficit in the ability to decode language at the most basic levels of intellectual functioning. This deficit persists after age 18 and does not change. Defendants have produced no peer reviewed literature or scientific testimony that provides evidence for the idea that a person's learning disability will show any change after adulthood, or that a student's test scores will show significant change during the course of their college career. Indeed, there are no peer-reviewed studies about the need for client evaluations in the post-secndary educational environment. Moreover, no other college or university in the United States or Canada requires retesting after age 18,[29] and the AHEAD guidelines call for retesting every five years once an individual reaches adulthood.

To show that learning disabilities change over time, BU relies in part on the testimony of plaintiffs' expert Dean Shaw of Brown University. Shaw testified that approximately 25 percent of the students at Brown University who begin college with accommodations do not need them by the time they graduate. This opinion is consistent with Dr. Shaywitz's research that many so-called "compensated" dyslexics may actually learn to read, even though that the decoding effort remains laborious, tiring and slow. Another defense expert, Professor Hynd, believed that retesting would provide "important insights to a university monitoring co-morbid psychological and physiological conditions (because 30 to 40 percent of all individuals with reading disabilities have a co-morbid condition such as ADHD, depression or anxiety disorders), and that retesting even on a quarterly

or semesterly basis would help an institution to make the most accurate determination of appropriate accommodations."

Nevertheless, Dr. Shaywitz testified credibly that "once a student comes to school diagnosed—with a learning disability, there is no test that is currently available that can determine precisely what accommodations should be provided to a particular student." Professor Hynd's desire for retesting semesterly might be appropriate in an "ideal" world, but few would argue it is "necessary" to do the job. If there is a history of psychological problems in a student, a reevaluation may be appropriate to monitor the co-morbid conditions that Professor Hynd was fairly concerned about; however, the defendants have not proven, as they must, that retesting every three years is "necessary" in adulthood.[30]

On the other hand, BU has presented credible evidence that reevaluation of students with ADD and ADHD is essential because the sysptoms of ADD and ADHD change in different environments, are often treated with medication, and these disorders often remit from adolescence to adulthood. Professor Rachel Klein, one of the foremost authorities in this area, testified credibly about the need for current information.

b. Qualifications Requirements

BU argues that it is necessary to set a high standard for the qualifications of evaluators in order to prevent overdiagnoses for learning disabilities like dyslexia, and to ensure proper documentation of conditions such as ADD and ADHD. To support its assertion that a master's degree does not meet its quality litmus test, it argues in its legal briefs that "[a] doctorate degree is more likely to bring an evaluator into contact with new research and changes in the field. Evaluators with lower degrees tend not to have the sophistication necessary to properly evaluate people with attention deficit disorders and learning disabilities." BU points to the research of Associate Professor Richard Sparks, who believes that overdiagnosis of learning disabilities for students seeking foreign language waivers or substitutions is a problem in the field, and to testimony that between twenty and thirty percent of college students seeking accommodations due to a learning disability provide insufficient documentation. Klafter testified that although there was a large number of potential evaluators, he wanted only the "best evaluations available."

To begin with, BU has produced no evidence that its initial policy in effect from November of 1995 through March of 1997, which required that learning disabled students could only submit evaluations prepared by physicians and licensed clinical psychologists, was necessary to ensure proper documentation and prevent overdiagnosis. Under this initial policy, two of BU's experts at trial who had doctorates in education—Professors Sparks and Hynd—would have been precluded from providing evaluations of learning disabled students. Accordingly, the initial policy flunks the necessity test because BU failed to show the need to preclude evaluators with doctorates in education from providing evaluations.

The post-March 1997 policy is a tougher question because it uses a doctorate degree as the proxy for quality. There is an intuitive appeal to this bright line because evaluators with doctorates generally do have more training and a better education than those with only a masters degree. However, BU's burden is a heavy one because it must show that the more stringent eligibility criterion is "necessary" to achieve its goal of ensuring proper documentation. The record is sparse on the point. While concerns about improving the quality of documentation of learning disabilities are valid, there is no evidence that reports or testing by those evaluators with masters degrees are worse than those by Ph.D.'s, nor is there evidence that a Ph.D. gets better training than a person with a masters in the specific standardized testing that must be conducted to diagnose learning disabilities. Indeed, the AHEAD guidelines list "educational psychologists" and "learning disabilities specialists" among the professionals who may have the experience that qualifies them to diagnose learning disabilities.

The best argument advanced in support of a doctorate requirement is that an evaluator with a lesser level of education may be too focused on learning disabilities and have insufficient training to pick up other "co-morbid" causes for poor academic performance (like medical or psychological problems). However, this myopia concern could be alleviated with a waiver policy akin to the one followed for Nodelman which required an evaluator with a doctorate to evaluate the prior testing to determine its adequacy. In short, BU bears the burden of proving a complete reevaluation by a person with doctorate degree or a licensed psychologist is "necessary" to accomplish its goal of improving the quality of evaluations. Because it has not met its burden, the Court concludes that the blanket policy requiring students to be retested if the prior evaluator has only a masters degree violates federal law.

On the other hand, BU has met its burden of proof with respect to the credentials necessary to evaluate ADD and ADHD. These conditions are primarily identified through clinical evaluations rather than through at standardized testing, and a well-trained eye is essential for proper diagnosis. Defendants' expert Professor Klein testified credibly that an evaluator with a Ph.D. or an M.D. is more likely to distinguish between ADD/ADHD, and medical or psychological conditions that present comparable symptoms. The Court is persuaded that, in regard to ADD/ADHD, a doctorate level of training is "necessary" within the meaning of the federal law.

c. BU's Evaluation Procedure

Plaintiffs contend that BU's process for evaluating accommodation requests is discriminatory because Westling and Klafter, who actively participate in closed-door evaluations of student files, have no expertise in learning disabilities and are motivated by false stereotypes about learning disabled students. Moreover, the class contends that BU's evaluation process is insufficiently "interactive" and that students with learning disabilities have been denied the right to due process (as guaranteed by Section 504 regulations) because BU has failed to provide a neutral grievance procedure when a student's requests for accommodations has been denied.[31]

i. Process for Reviewing Accommodation Requests

The ADA and Section 504 forbid both intentional discrimination against learning disabled students and "methods of administration" that "have the effect of discriminating on the basis of disability." See 42 U.S.C. § 12182(b)(1)(D); see also 34 C.F.R. § 104.4(b)(4). In considering these allegations, the Court distinguishes between the review process that existed during the 1995-1996 school year, when the policy was first implemented, and the procedure that exists at present.

The concerns about the nitty-gritty involvement of Westling and Klafter in the accommodations process during the 1995-1996 school year are well founded. There is no dispute that Westling and Klafter, who have no expertise in learning disabilities and no training in fashioning reasonable accommodations for the learning disabled, were actively involved in the process of approving accommodation requests at that time. Worse still, during that year, these administrators expressed certain biases about the learning disabilities movement and stereotypes about learning disabled students. Westling and Klafter indicated repeatedly that many students who sought accommodations on the basis of a learning disability were lazy or fakers (e.g.,"Somnolent Samantha"), and Klafter labeled learning disabilities evaluators "snake oil salesman." If not invidiousness, at the very least, these comments reflect misinformed stereotypes that, when coupled with Westling and Klafter's dominant role in the implementation of BU's accommodations policy during the 1995-1996, school year, conflicted with the university's obligation to provide a review process "based on actual risks and not on speculation, stereotypes, or generalizations about disabilities." H.R. Rep. No. 101-485, pt. II, at 105 (1990), reprinted 1990 U.S.C.C.A.N. 267, 388; see also *Mantolete v. Bolger*, 767 F.2d 1416, 1422 (9th Cir. 1985) (finding that Congress's intent in enacting the Rehabilitation Act was "to prevent employers from refusing to give much needed opportunities to handicapped individuals on the basis of misinformed stereotypes").

BU's internally-contentious, multi-tiered evaluation process involving evaluators who were not only inexperienced but also biased caused the delay and denial of reasonable accommodations and much emotional distress for learning disabled students. The court concludes that the implementation of BU's initial accommodations policy violated the ADA and Section 504 during the 1995-1996 academic year.

The issue for purposes of the requested declaratory injunctive relief, however, is whether the current procedure is propelled by discriminatory animus or has the effect of discrimination on the basis of disability. See *Anderson v. University of Wisc.*, 841 F.2d 737, 741 (7th Cir. 1988) ("[T]he Rehabilitation Act requires only a stereotype-free assessment of the person's abilities and prospects rather than a correct decision."). This Court concludes that it does not.

At present, Lorraine Wolf, a highly trained professional, makes the initial evaluation as to whether the student is learning disabled and whether the requested accommodations are reasonable. Plaintiffs do not claim she is a wolf in lamb's clothing. They do not challenge her credentials or good faith. While she does forward all recommendations for accommodations to Westling's office, there is no evidence that her professional judgements have been second-guessed or that Klafter does anything other than "rubberstamp" her impartial recommendations. Although BU has occasionally refused a student's request to abrogate a substantial academic requirement since Wolf's arrival, there is no evidence to suggest that the decision not to modify that degree requirement was unreasonable or discriminatory. In sum, plaintiffs have not proven that the present method of administering the learning disability program has the effect of discrimination on the basis of disability, or is tainted by impossible stereotypes.

The plaintiffs also make the argument that the ADA and Section 504 require BU to engage in an "interactive" process in fashioning accommodations for students with learning disabilities, and that BU's review process fails to meet that obligation. In the employment context, courts have held that "[a]n employee's request for reasonable accommodation requires a great deal of communication between the employee and the employer." *Bultemeyer v. Fort Wayne County Schs.*, 100 F.3d 1281, 1285 (7th Cir. 1996). Although a disabled employee must first make his limitations known, see *Taylor v. Prinicipal Financial Group, Inc.*, 93 F.3d 155, 165 (5th Cir. 1996), *cert. denied*, 117 S.Ct. 586 (1996), "the employer has at least some responsibility in determining the necessary accommodation" by engaging in "an interactive process." *Beck v. University of Wisc. Bd. of Regents*, 75 F.3d 1130, 1135 (7th Cir. 1996) (quoting 29 C.F.R. § 1630.2(o)(3) (1995)); *accord Mantolete v. Bolger*, 767 F.2d at 1423 ("[A]n employer has a duty under the Act to gather sufficient information from the applicant and from qualified experts as needed to determine what accommodations are necessary to enable the applicant to perform his job safely."); see also *Feliberty v. Kemper Corp.*, 98 F.3d 274, 280 (7th Cir. 1996) ("The determination of a reasonable accommodation is a cooperative process in which both the employer and the employee must make reasonable efforts and exercise good faith."). However, engaging in a specific give-and-take procedure is not always essential in fashioning the appropriate reasonable accommodation. *Jacques v. Clean-Up Group, Inc.*, 96 F.3d 506, 514 (1st Cir. 1996).

During much of the 1995-1996 academic year, the administration of the learning disability program miserably failed to achieve any measure of interactivity. The president's office did not communicate directly with LDSS or vice versa. Learning disabled students desperately seeking information concerning the status of their reasonable accommodations requests received conflicting information from university officials, wrong information, or no information at all. When accommodations were denied, inadequate explanations of the documentation deficiencies were provided, and parental inquiries were fruitless. While DS head Macurdy did his best in March of 1996 to handle the problem, he was inadequately staffed and trained.

BU's administrative methods during 1995-1996 were also not sufficiently interactive to the extent that unwary students were ambushed by the new, unwritten requirements for accommodation, and the multi-tiered process for reviewing student files was not clearly developed or disclosed. For example, by Westling's insistence that the new policy on course Constitutions be implemented "effective immediately"—without giving students any notice or time to adjust—and Brinckerhoff's precipitous letter requesting retesting at exam time, BU failed to communicate effectively its new accommodation mandates. Westling and Klafter point the finger at Brinckerhoff for much of the insensitivity, delays, poor communication, and bad timing at LDSS. Even if Brinckerhoff fairly shoulders the blame, he, too, is a university official. As a result of BU's representatives' poor implementation of the policy, many students who applied for accommodations at the beginning of the fall semester were not given the requested assistance or even told of the reason for the delay so that documentation deficiencies could be remedied until some time in November—long after classes had begun. At least one student was not accommodated until the following semester.

For the purposes of prospective relief, however, the bleak picture has brightened. No doubt as a result of this litigation, the university has now formulated harmonious written statements of policy that have been authorized by the relevant academic officials. Moreover, the university has hired a professional evaluator who, at trial, promised that she will meet with students and address their concerns as she assesses their need for accommodation.

This Court finds that BU's client review process—now that Wolf is back from maternity leave and the office is staffed up—is sufficiently interactive to withstand the attack under the ADA and Section 504. Plaintiffs have submitted no evidence that students requesting personal meetings do not get them, that phone calls are not returned, that misinformation is generated, or that accommodations requests are not timely handled. Even though BU no longer works as closely with students as it did under Brinckerhoff, this court has no evidence that, as revamped, the administration of the current learning disabilities review procedure has the effect of discriminating against students.

Since 1995, President Westling (or his staff) has reviewed the initial accommodation recommendations generated by LDSS (and now by Wolf), and in addition, Westling has served as the administrative officer who decides a learning-disabled student's specific appeal or denial. At the summary judgement stage of this litigation, plaintiffs urged this Court to find that such an appellate procedure fails to "incorporate appropriate due process procedures" as mandated by 34 C.F.R. § 104.7(b). In relevant part, 34 C.F.R. § 104.7 provides:

> (b) Adoption of grievance procedures. A recipient that employs fifteen or more persons shall adopt grievance procedures that incorporate appropriate due process standards and that provide for the prompt resolution of complaints alleging any action prohibited by this part.

34 C.F.R. § 104.7. The weight of the evidence at trial supports the plaintiffs' contention that BU offers no meaningful "appellate" review of a decision to reject a requested accommodation. Many students have been informed in writing and verbally that they must ask Westling, who had made the initial determination, to reconsider their denials.

Although BU now contends that the student handbook provides a Section 504 grievance procedure that involves appeal to an independent compliance officer, the Court is not persuaded that such an avenue is a realistic alternative for learning disabled students seeking accommodations for essentially four reasons. First, the Lifebook (a student handbook), refers only to the grievance procedures in cases of alleged discrimination by reason of "physical disability" and does not mention requests for grievances by students with learning disabilities. Second, the evidence showed that no student seeking reconsideration for a denial of an accommodation was ever advised orally or in writing to use the 504 procedure. Third, it seems dubious that the dean of students or the head of the DS office, who purportedly handle Section 504 griev-

ances, would have the authority (or the chutzpah) to review and reverse the determination of the boss, BU's president. Finally, most of the relevant officials (including Klafter and Westling) were seemingly unaware of this avenue of appeal as a means of rectifying improper denials of reasonable accommodation.

Although plaintiffs may have a strong argument on the merits of their challenge to BU's weak appeals/grievance procedure, no private cause of action exists to enforce this regulatory due process provision. The traditional analysis that governs a court's evaluation of whether there is an implied private right of action to enforce a statute supports the Court's conclusion. See *Cort v. Ash* 422 U.S. 66, 95 S.Ct. 2080 (1975). Some courts have found analysis factors are useful when courts seek to determine whether there is a private right of action to sue under administrative enactments as well. See, e.g., *Roberts v. Cameron-Brown*, 556 P.2d 356, 360 (5th Cir. 1977) (applying the *Cort* analysis to decide whether an implied private cause of action exists to enforce the provisions of a H.U.D. handbook).

The *Cort* factors are: (1) whether the plaintiff is a member of the class for whom the statute was created, (2) whether there is an indication of legislative intent either to create or deny a private remedy, (3) whether a private right of action is consistent with the purposes underlying the legislative scheme, and (4) whether the cause of action is traditionally relegated to state law. See id. at 78.

Of the four *Cort* factors, only one strongly supports plaintiff's position that a private right of action to enforce 34 C.F.R. § 104.7 should be implied. Under the first factor, the plaintiffs here are, indeed, a part of the class that is intended to benefit from grievance procedures that comport with traditional due process standards. However, since the due process provision appears only in the administrative regulation, there is no evidence whatsoever of the second *Cort* factor—that Congress intended to give private parties the right to a private remedy against institutions that fail to provide adequate grievance procedures. The only explicit statements relating to § 104.7 emanate from the Department of Education, see 34 C.F.R. § 104, app. A, at 358, and the intent of an administrative agency in drafting a regulation cannot be the conclusive basis for finding that Congress desired to provide a private right of action. See 34 C.F.R. § 104, app. A, at 357; *Touche Ross & Co. v. Reddington 94*, 442 U.S. 560, 568 (1979). If anything, the fact that the ADA, which was enacted well after Section 504 and its regulations, is silent regarding whether the disabled have a right to grievance procedures that incorporate due process standards suggests a legislative intent not to use the federal antidiscrimination laws as a vehicle for guaranteeing due process rights.

Other courts have similarly declined to recognize private rights of action under other administrative regulations that go beyond the substantive authorization of Section 504. See *Dopico v. Goldschmidt,* 687 F.2d 644, 651 (2d Cir. 1982) (holding that even though there was an implied right of action to maintain a suit directly under Section 504,[32] there was no right to enforce the underlying regulations when they appeared to exceed the substantive scope of the statute.); see also *Stewart v. Bernstein,* 769 P.2d 1088, 1093 n. 6 (5th Cir. 1985) (rejecting plaintiff's claim that she could sue a private nursing home for violating Medicare regulations, and noting that "federal regulations cannot themselves create a cause of action").

The recent decision of *Cooper v. Gustav Adolophus College,* 957 F.Supp. 191 (D. Minn. 1997), is most instructive. In *Cooper,* a professor who had been dismissed by the college for violating its sexual harassment policy claimed that he had been denied the right to fair dismissal proceedings under the regulations that enforce Title IX.[33] Like the regulations implementing Section 504, the regulations under Title IX require educational institutions in receipt of federal to adopt grievance procedures that provide for "prompt and equitable resolution of student and employee complaints."[34] The *Cooper* court dismissed the professor's claim because, "even if … Title IX requires that any grievance process be fair to an accused employee, [the plaintiff] has failed to demonstrate that such a right may be enforced through a private cause of action." Id. at 194. It concluded that "alleged flaws in a sexual harassment procedure were not actionable in the absence of a 'particularized allegation relating to a causal connection between the flawed outcome and gender bias.'" Id. (quoting *Yusuf v. Vasssar College,* 35 F.3d 709, 715 (2d Cir. 1994)).

Like the court in *Cooper,* I find that a student has no cause of action to enforce the Section 504 regulations guaranteeing due process because "there is no statutory due process right separate from a right to be free from discrimination." Id.

d.   Course Substitutions

i.   The Competing Contentions

Plaintiffs claim that BU's blanket refusal to authorize course substitutions for students with learning disabilities amounts to a failure to modify the university's practices to prevent discrimination as required by federal law. Specifically, the class argues that, because many learning-disabled students have extreme difficulty in taking and passing courses in mathematics and foreign language, allowing course substitutions for those class members is a reasonable accommodation, and, thus, BU's refusal to authorize such a modification is discriminatory.

BU asserts that its refusal of course substitutions is consistent with the law because exemptions of this nature would amount to a fundamental alteration of its academic liberal arts program, a course of study that has been in place for over a century. Also, BU emphasizes that it provides special programs for students with foreign language and math difficulties (like an oral enhancement program and one-on-one tutoring) in addition to the classroom accommodations that are available in any other course.

ii.   The Legal Framework

"An accommodation is generally any change in the work (or school) environment or in the way things are customarily done that enables an individual with a disability to enjoy equal opportunities." *Thomas v. Davidson Academy,* 846 F.Supp. 611, 616 (M.D. Tenn. 1994) (citing 29 C.F.R. § 1630.2(o)); *accord Burch v. Coca-Cola Co.,* No. 95-10990, at *7 (5th Cir. July 30, 1997) ("In all cases a reasonable accmomdation will involve a change in the status quo, for it is the status quo that presents the very obstacle that the ADA's reasonable accommodation provision attempts to address."). The ADA specifically defines discrimination to include:

> a failure to make reasonable modifications in policies, practices or procedures, when such modifications are necessary to afford such goods, services, facilities, privileges, advantages, or accommodations to individuals with disabilities, unless the entity can demonstrate that making such modifications would fundamentally alter the nature of such goods, services, facilities, privileges, advantages, or accommodations.

42 U.S.C. § 12182(b)(2)(A)(ii). The regulations implementing Section 504 also require an educational institution that receives federal funding to make such modifications to its academic requirements as are necessary to ensure that such requirements do not have the effect of discriminating, on the basis of handicapped applicant or student. 34 C.F.R. § 104.44 (entitled "Academic Adjustments"). However, the regulations further explain that "academic requirements that the recipient can demonstrate are essential to the program of instruction being pursued by such student … will not be regarded as discriminatory within the meaning of this section." Id.

Significantly, with regard to academic institutions, the regulations interpreting Section 504 provide that reasonable modifications "may include changes in the length of time permitted for the completion of degree requirements, substitution of specific courses required for the completion of degree requirements, and adaptation of the manner in which specific courses are conducted." 34 C.F.R. § 104-44 (emphasis omitted) See *Alexander,* 469 U.S. at 302 n.21 (pointing to a similar regulation in discussing the "view that reasonable adjustments in the nature of the benefit offered must at times be made to assure meaningful access"). The appendix to the regulations elaborates:

Paragraph (a) of § 104.44 requires that a recipient make certain adjustments to academic requirements and practices that discriminate or have the effect of discriminating on the basis of handicap. This requirement, like its predecessor in the proposed legislation, does not obligate an institution to waive course or other academic requirements. But such institutions must accommodate those requirements to the needs of individual handicapped students. For example, an institution might permit an otherwise qualified handicapped student who is deaf to substitute an art appreciation or music history course for a required course in music appreciation or could modify the manner in which the music appreciation course is conducted for the deaf student. It should be stressed that academic requirements that can be demonstrated by the recipient to be essential to its program of instruction or to particular degrees need not be changed.

34 C.F.R. § 104, app. A 31 (emphasis omitted). In interpreting these regulations, the Office of Civil Rights ("OCR"), the federal agency reliable for investigating complaints of disability discrimination, has consistently maintained that, though an educational institution must modify its academic requirements to accept a disabled student, an institution need not waive academic requirements that are essential to its program or course of study. See, e.g., Bennett College, 7 Nat'l Disability L. Rep. 26 (1995); Northern Ill. Univ., 7 Nat'l Disability L. Rep. 39 (1995); City Univ. of N.Y., 3 Nat'l Disability L. Rep. 104 (1992); Cabrillo College, 2 Nat'l Disability L. Rep. 78 (1991).

Besides these legislative and administrative pronouncements, several federal courts have also addressed specifically the obligation of an educational institution under the ADA and Section 504 to accommodate disabled students by making reasonable modifications of academic requirements. In *Southeastern Community College v. Davis*, 442 U.S. 397, 99 S.Ct 2361 (1979), the Supreme Court decided whether Section 504 required a college to make substantial changes to its nursing program for a student with hearing loss. Refusing to admit the student, the College claimed that "[the] modifications that would be necessary to enable safe participation would prevent her from realizing the benefits of the program." Id. at 401-402. The Court concluded that Section 504 "does not compel educational institutions to disregard the disabilities of handicapped individuals or to make substantial modifications in their program to allow disabled persons to participate." Id. at 405. Although the student argued that the statute and its regulations required the College to take affirmative steps to ensure that she could participate (e.g., individual

supervision, an exemption from clinical coursework), the Court maintained that "[s]uch a fundamental alteration in the nature of a program is far more than the 'modification' regulation requires." Id. at 410. Justice Powell wrote:

> it is undisputed that respondent could not participate in Southeastern's nursing program unless the standards were substantially lowered. Section 504 imposes no requirement upon an educational institution to lower or to effect substantial modifications of standards to accommodate a handicapped person.

Id. at 413.

In retrospect, the Supreme Court has observed that its opinion in *Davis* "struck a balance between the statutory rights of the handicapped to be integrated into society and the legitimate interests of federal grantees in preserving the integrity of their programs." *Alexander,* 469 U.S. at 300, 105 S.Ct. at 720. The lesson of *Davis* (and its progeny) is that "while, a grantee need not be required to make 'fundamental' or 'substantial' modifications to accommodate the handicapped," under Section 504 and the ADA "it may be required to make 'reasonable' ones." Id.; see, e.g., *McGregor v. Louisiana State Univ. Bd of Supervisors,* 3 F.3d 850, 860 (5th Cir. 1993) (finding that a disabled law student is requested accommodation would force the school to "lower its academic standard" or "compromise the reasonable policy of its academic program" and that "Section 504 did not require this much,"); *Doherty v. Southern College of Optometry,* 862 F.2d 570, 574-75 (6th Cir. 1988) (holding that federal law imposes on colleges a "limited obligation to make reasonable accommodations to handicapped individuals," and that, under the circumstances, "[w]aiver of a necessary requirement would have been a substantial rather than rarely a reasonable accommodation") (emphasis omitted). It is clear from the cases interpreting Section 504 and the ADA that "[a]n educational institution is not required to accommodate a handicapped individual by eliminating a course requirement which is reasonably necessary to proper use of the degree conferred at the end of a course of study." *Doherty,* 862 F. 2d at 570.

In the reasonable modifications context, the plaintiff has the initial burden of proving "that a modification was requested and that the requested modification is [generally] reasonable," that is, "in the run of cases." *Johnson v. Gambrinus Co.,* 116 F.3d 1052, 1059 (5th Cir. 1997). One circuit court has ruled that the plaintiff's burden, at least with regard to reasonable modification in the workplace, is only a "burden of production" and, as such, it "is not a heavy one." *Borkowski v. Valley Cent. Sch. Dist.,* 63 F.3d 131, 138 (2d Cir. 1995) (finding that "[i]t is enough for the plaintiff to suggest the existence of a plausible accommodation, the costs of which, facially, do not clearly exceed its benefits"). "If the plaintiff meets this burden, the defendant must make the requested modification unless the defendant pleads and meets its burden of proving that the requested modification would fundamentally alter the nature of the public accommodation." *Johnson*, 116 F.3d at 1059; see also *Wagner v. Fair Acres Geriatric Ctr.*, 495 F.3d 1002, 1009 (3rd Cir. 1995) ("[I]f there is no factual basis in the record demonstrating that accommodating the individual would require a fundamental modification ... then the handicapped person is otherwise qualified.") (citation omitted)

iii. The Analysis

Turning to the instant case, the Court must first consider whether plaintiffs have met their burden of establishing that course substitutions in math and foreign language are, generally, "reasonable" accommodations.

The plaintiffs are aided substantially in satisfying their initial burden by the mere fact that the administrative regulations interpreting Section 504 and the ADA specifically provide that modifying academic requirements to allow course substitutions may be a reasonable means of accommodating the disabled. See 34 C.F.R. § 104, app. A 31. In addition, plaintiffs offered evidence at trial to support their contention that a course substitution is reasonable, at least in regard to BU's foreign language requirements. Even though the experts disagreed as to whether a language disability made acquisition of a foreign language literally impossible for some students, and plaintiffs' experts conceded there are no peer-reviewed scientific studies which indicate that it is impossible for some students with a learning disability to learn a foreign language, the weight of the evidence supports plaintiffs' arguments that students with learning disorders such as dyslexia have a significantly more difficult challenge in becoming proficient in a foreign language than students without such an impairment. The only evidence to the contrary was the testimony of defendants' expert, Professor Sparks, who has recently concluded that difficulties in learning foreign languages are not necessarily attributable to learning disabilities. However, Sparks conceded that his research was "preliminary." Although another defense expert, George Hynd, testified that most students had the potential to learn with appropriate accommodations, he agreed that persons with learning disabilities may have difficulty learning a foreign language because of neurological deficits. On all of the evidence, the Court is persuaded that plaintiffs have demonstrated that requesting a course substitution in foreign language for students with demonstrated language disabilities is a reasonable modification.

With respect to math course substitutions, however, I conclude that there was no scientific evidence introduced at trial to support plaintiffs' claim that a course substitution is a plausible alternative for a learning disability in mathematics (i.e., dyscalculia). Dyscalculia is specifically listed in the DSM-IV as a learning disorder; however, none of the named testifying plaintiffs had dyscalculia, and the record documents that only two students in CLA requested a course substitution in mathematics. Moreover, plaintiffs' witness, Dean Robert Shaw of Brown University, who is an Associate Professor of Education and the coordinator of the learning disability program, testified that he never met a student with a disability that prevented her from learning math. Professor Seigel, an expert called by the defense, found one student (out of the twenty-eight files) who she claimed had a severe case of "dyscalculia" entitling him to accommodations; however, Professor Seigel testified that "with the appropriate accommodations," a student should be able to fulfill BU's mathematics requirements. Moreover, with regard to the one student whose file she reviewed, Seigel never said that the condition was so severe that a course substitution was needed. Essentially, the evidence at trial concerning dyscalculia was sketchy at best. Accordingly, plaintiffs have not demonstrated that a request for a course substitution in mathematics is a reasonable modification of BU's degree requirements.

Because plaintiffs have established that the request for a course substitution in foreign language is reasonable, the burden, now shifts to BU to demonstrate that the requested course substitution would fundamentally alter the nature of its liberal arts degree program.

Fortunately, in determining which modifications amount to a "fundamental alteration," the Court does not write on a clean blackboard. Two related First Circuit cases provide invaluable assistance in evaluating a university's burden of supporting its conclusion that a requested modification by a learning disabled student of an academic requirement would fatally alter the nature of the program. See *Wynne v. Tufts Univ. Sch. of Med.*, 932 F.2d 19 (1st Cir. 1991) (en banc) (hereinafter "Wynne I"); *Wynne v. Tufts Univ. Sch. of Med.*, 976 F.2d 791 (1st Cir. 1992) (hereinafter "Wynne II"). Both *Wynne* opinions, which arise out of a single student's efforts to get Tufts' Medical School to change its testing policy to accommodate his learning disability, bear discussion at length.

Stephen Wynne was admitted to Tufts Medical School in 1983. After experiencing extreme difficulty with the multiple-choice format of his first year examinations, and after failing eight out of fifteen first-year courses, Wynne underwent a neuropsychological evaluation at the expense of the medical school. The evaluation revealed that Wynne had serious processing difficulties indicative of a learning disability. It was later discovered that, in particular, Wynne had difficulty interpreting the type of multiple choice questions that were characteristic of medical school examinations.

Wynne brought suit in federal court claiming that the school's failure to offer an alternative to written multiple choice examinations violated his rights under Section 504. *Wynne I*, 932 F.2d at 22, The *Wynne I* court concluded that, "in determining whether an individual meets the "otherwise qualified" requirement of section 504, it is necessary to look at more than the individuals ability to meet a program's present requirements." *Wynne I*, 932 F.2d at 22 (considering *Alexander v. Choate*, 469 U.S. 287, 105 S. Ct. 712 (1985)). The Court stressed that, while deference need be given to the institutional decisionmakers in deciding whether an accommodation is possible, "there is a real obligation on the academic institution to seek suitable means of reasonably accommodating a handicapped person."

Id. at 25. Specifically, it found that

> [i]f the institution submits undisputed facts demonstrating that the relevant officials within the institution considered alternative means, their feasibility, cost and effect on the academic program, and came to a rationally justifiable conclusion that the available alternative would result either in lowering academic standards or requiring substantial program alteration, the court could rule as a matter of law that the institution had met its duty of seeking reasonable accommodation.

Id at 26. The *Wynne I* Court remanded the case for a determination of whether Tufts had met its burden "of demonstrating that its determination that no reasonable way existed to accommodate Wynne's inability to perform adequately on written multiple-choice examinations was a reasoned, professional academic judgment, not a mere ipse dixit." Id. at 27.

On appeal after remand, the First Circuit decided whether, in fact, Tufts had reached "a rationally justifiable conclusion that accommodating plaintiff would lower academic standards or otherwise unduly affect its program." *Wynne II*, 976 F. 2d, at 793. The Court considered voluminous documents that Tufts produced after remand which discussed, among other things, why biochemistry is important to a medical school curriculum, why multiple choice testing was the fairest means of evaluating the subject matter, "what thought [the university] had given to different methods of testing proficiency in biochemistry," and "why it eschewed alternatives to multiple-choice testing, particularly with respect to make-up examinations." Id. at 794. The First Circuit concluded that, through evidence of this nature, Tufts had successfully "demythologized the institutional thought processes" leading to its determination that it could not deviate from its wanted format to accommodate Wynne's professional disability. Id. Tufts met its burden of proving fundamental alteration because it

showed that its officials had decided "rationally, if not inevitably, that no further action could be made without imposing and undue (and injurious) hardship on the academic program." Id. at 796.

Even more than the dispute over the format of a test in the *Wynne* cases, the degree requirements that are at issue in the instant litigation go to the heart of academic freedom. Universities have long been considered to have the freedom to determine "what may be taught, how it shall be taught, and who may be admitted to study." *Sweezy v. New Hampshire*, 354 U.S. 234, 263 (1957) (Frankfurter, J., concurring) *Carlin v. Trustees of Boston*, 907 F.Supp. 509, 511 (D. Mass. 1995) (Boston University has absolute authority to render an academic judgment, but that decision must be a genuine one).

Based on a review of the relevant cases, I conclude that a university can refuse to modify academic degree requirements even course requirements that students with learning disabilities cannot satisfy—as long it undertakes a diligent assessment of the available options, *Wynne II*, 976 F. 2d at 795, and makes "a professional, academic judgement that reasonable accommodation is simply not available." *Wynne I*, 932 F. 2d at 27-28. That is to say, neither the ADA nor the Rehabilitation Act require a university to provide course substitutions that the university rationally concludes would alter an essential part of its academic program. Accordingly, plaintiffs' front-line of attack against any across-the-board policy precluding course substitutions under the ADA and Rehabilitation Act fails.

iv. Westling's Ipse Dixit[35]

As a fallback, the plaintiff class argues: (1) that in the circumstances of this case, BU's refusal to modify its liberal arts degree requirements flunks the Wynne-test because Westling was motivated by discriminatory animus in declining to modify the academic standards in question, cf. *Alexander*, 469 U.S. at 301 (indicating that an entity way not set its standards intentionally to deprive qualified disabled individuals of access), and (2) that BU refused to modify its math and foreign language requirements as an accommodation for the learning disabled without making a diligent, reasoned, academic judgment.

Based on my review of the record, plaintiffs prevail on both of these arguments. A substantial motivating factor in Westling's decision not to consider degree modifications was his unfounded belief that learning disabled students who could not meet degree requirements were unmotivated (like "Somnolent Samantha") or disingenuous. Although Westling was also inspired by a genuine concern for academic standards, his course substitution prohibition was founded, in part, on uninformed stereotypes. Relying only on popular press accounts that suggested learning disabilities were being unfairly exaggerated and misdiagnosed, Westling provided no concrete evidence that any BU student faked a learning disability to get out of a course requirement.

Even though Westling may have had a good faith (even passionate) belief in the value of foreign languages to a liberal arts program, the Court finds that he did not dispassionately determine whether the benefits of attaining that proficiency are outweighed by the costs to the learning disabled student.

Westling made the decision not to modify the mathematics and foreign language requirements for students with learning disabilities without consulting any experts on learning disabilities. Nor did Westling discuss the importance of foreign language to BU's liberal arts curriculum with any of the relevant BU department heads, professors or officials. Indeed, the only deliberation that took place regarding academic adjustments as accommodations for the learning disabled was Westlings consultation with Klafter about whether scientific evidence supports the existence of a learning disability that prevents foreign language proficiency. Westling's reliance on discriminatory stereotypes, together with his failure to consider carefully the effect of course substitutions on BU's liberal arts program and to consult with academics and experts in learning disabilities, constitutes a failure of BU's obligation to make a rational judgement that course substitutions would fundamentally alter the course of study. Although BU ultimately has the right to decline to modify its degree requirements—and that decision will be given great deference—it must do so after reasoned deliberations as to whether modifications would change the essential academic standards of its liberal arts curriculum.

II. Discrimination Claims Under Article 114

Article 114 of the Massachusetts constitution ("Article 114"),[36] was derived from and modeled after Section 504 of the Rehabilitation Act of 1973. See *Layne v. Superintendent of Mass. Correctional Inst.*, 406 Mass. 156, 159, 546 N.E.2d 166, 168 (Mass. 1989). Because "assistance in construing art. 114" is to be found in the case law that interprets Section 504, id., this Court finds that its conclusions with regard to the plaintiffs' discrimination claims would be no different under Article 114 than under the ADA and Section 504 as determined above.

III. Breach of Contract

Lastly, the named plaintiffs argue that BU is liable for a breach of contract based on binding promises made to them regarding the accommodations that the university would provide for their learning disabilities. In the alternative, they seek relief under the doctrine of promissory estoppel.[37]

A. The Legal Landscape

"To state a claim for breach of contract under Massachusetts law, a plaintiff must allege, at a minimum, that there was a valid contract, that the defendant breached its duties under its contractual agreement, and that the breach caused the plaintiff damage." *Guckengerger v. Boston Univ.*, 957 F.Supp. 306, 316 (D. Mass. 1997) (citing *Compagnie de Reassurance d'Ille de France v. New England Reinsurance Corp.*, 825 F.Supp. 370, 380 (D. Mass. 1993)). Even in the absence of consideration to support a binding contractual agreement between the parties, a party reasonably relying on a praise may prevail under a theory of promissory estoppel. See *Loranger Constr. Corp. v. R.F. Hauserman Co.*, 376 Mass. 757, 384 N.E.2d 176 (1978) (citing Restatement (Second) of Contracts, § 89B(2) (1973)). A claim in promissory estoppel is essentially a claim in breach of contract; however, the plaintiff must prove reasonable reliance on a promise, offer, or commitment by the defendant rather than the existence of consideration. See *Rhode Island Hosp. Trust Nat'l Bank v. Varadian*, 419 Mass. 841, 850, 647 N.E.2d 1174, 1179 (1995).

Under Massachusetts law, the promise, offer, or commitment that forms the basis of a valid contract can be derived from statements in handbooks, policy manuals, brochures, catalogs, advertisements, and other promotional materials. *Salve Regina College*, 890 F.2d 484, 488 (1st Cir. 1989), *rev'd on other grounds*, 499 U.S. 225, 11 S.Ct. 1217 (1991) and reinstated on remand, 938 F.2d 315 (1st Cir. 1991) (looking at "various catalogs, manuals, handbooks, etc." to determine the terms of a contractual agreement; see also *Hannon v. Original Guinite Aquatech Pools, Inc.*, 385 Mass. 813, 822, 424 N.E.2d 611, 617 (1982) (finding that "express warranties can be created by an advertising brochure"). So long as the promise is "definite and certain so that the promisor should reasonably foresee that it will induce reliance," *Santoni v. Fed. Deposit Ins. Corp* 677 F.2d 174, 179 (1st Cir. 1982), and reliance occurs, a party can maintain an action for breach, see *Rhode Island Hosp. Trust Nat'l Bank*, 419 Mass. At 848-850.

It is well-established that, although "[t]he relationship between a university and a student is contractual in nature," see *Corso v. Crieghton*, 731 F.2d 529, 531 (8th Cir. 1984), as far as contract actions go, "courts should be slow to intrude into the sensitive area of the student-college relationship, especially in areas of curriculum and discipline." *Russell v. Salve Regina College*, 890 F.2d at 489 (upholding jury verdict where nursing school forced student out because she was obese after admitting her with full knowledge of her weight condition because under these circumstances, the "unique" position of the college as educator is "less compelling"). Even though "some elements of the law of contracts are used and should be used in the analysis of the relationship between [student] and the university," because "[t]he student-university relationship is unique," contract law need not be "rigidly applied." *Lyons v. Salve Regina College*, 565 F.2d 200, 202 (1st Cir. 1977) (quoting *Slaughter v. Brigham Young Univ.*, 514 F.2d 622, 626 (l0th Cir. 1975))(internal quotation marks omitted).

B. BU's Brochures

The plaintiffs base their breach of contract claim in large part on BU's promotional materials describing the services that the university makes available to students with learning disabilities. In brochures promoting the university's LDSS office, for example, BU touted a "highly trained staff," the option of "reasonable accommodations in testing and coursework" (including course substitutions, and the chance to attend a specialized comprehensive summer orientation program. None of these LDSS brochures contained a disclaimer. A now obsolete LDSS pamphlet explains that, although students must complete a diagnostic evaluation to receive LDSS services initially, once accommodations had been authorized, "these services will be available through the student's academic career."

BU asserts that, because of the nature of the university student relationship, as a matter of law, a University cannot be deemed to have breached a "contract" with its students when it exercises its inherent right to change the nature of its academic programs. Moreover, BU contends that its admissions office actually did not distribute the primary brochure upon which the breach of contract claim is based, and that, in light of the disclaimer that appears in many of BU's catalogs and brochures,[38] the university had no reasonable expectation that the students would depend upon its promotional materials.

Even assuming arguendo that statements in a university's promotional materials can form the basis of a binding contractual agreement with its students, the concludes that at best, only one of the plaintiffs (Scott Greeley) entered into such an agreement in this case because he is the only one who testified he received and relied on the brochure. None of the other plaintiffs have testified that they relied on these brochures' general representations of policy in deciding to matriculate at BU. There being no proof of an offer (based on the brochures), acceptance, or of detrimental reliance, these other plaintiffs have failed to prove a breach of contract (or, alternatively, promissory estoppel claim) arising out of statements that the university may have made in its materials promoting the disability services program.

C. Express Promises

Three of the named plaintiffs persuasively explained at trial that they were induced to attend BU in reliance on specific promises made to them personally regarding their ability to receive certain accommodations.

Plaintiff Avery LaBrecque credibly described in detail conversations that she had had with LDSS director Loring Brinckerhoff before she began at BU during which he promised her a course substitution for foreign language in light of her history of difficulty with foreign language learning. When plaintiff Scott Greeley and his father flew from California to Boston to investigate BU's support for students with learning disabilities in deciding whether to attend, LDSS coordinator Carolyn Suissman assured Greeley that, with his accommodations history and documentation, he would have "no problem" getting the assistance that he needed. Greeley was the only plaintiff who testified he had received the LDSS brochure prior to matriculating. Similarly, one of the letters that Elizabeth Guckenberger received from the director of admissions at BU Law School, which purported to describe what "is considered reasonable for documentation," explained that students with learning disabilities needed to submit an evaluation that had been prepared by "a professional qualified to diagnose a learning disability, including but not limited to a licensed physician, learning disability, or psychologist." (Emphasis omitted). The letter also stated that the evaluation needed to be "dated no more than three years prior to the date of the application, unless the documentation was completed during the [student's] undergraduate education." (Emphasis omitted).

BU made specific promises to these three individual students and, during the 1995-1996 school year, BU reneged on its representations. Rather than the promised course substitution for her foreign language obligation, BU required LaBrecque to take Swahili, a language that had both an oral and a written component. Greeley labored from August until December of his freshman year without LDSS support and, just prior to finals, he was informed that his request for exam accommodations had been denied because of inadequate documentation. When Guckenberger sought to submit her learning disabilities specialist's evaluation so that she could get exam accommodations during her second year of law school, she was told that she would have to be completely retested for dyslexia within the three weeks prior to exams.

The Court concludes that there was an enforceable contractual agreement between BU and Avery LaBrecque, Scott Greeley, and Elizabeth Guckenberger based on specific statements made by BU officials that were relied upon by these students, and that BU breached these express promises to their detriment.

IV. Damage Claims of the Named Plaintiffs[39]

The Court considers now whether and to what extent the named plaintiffs are entitled to damages on the basis of BU's discriminatory actions and contract breach. See *Jacques v. Clean-Up Group, Inc.*, 96 F.3d

506, 511 (1st Cir. 1996) (finding that, in an employment discrimination claim under the ADA, plaintiff must show that she has actually been discharged or has suffered "an adverse employment action" as a result of her disability); *Katz v. City Metal Co., Inc.* 87 F.3d 26, 30 (1st Cir. 1996) (same); *Doherty v. Soutern College of Optometry,* 862 F.2d 570, 573 (6th Cir. 1988) (finding that among the elements of a Section 504 claim is proof that plaintiff actually is "being excluded from participation in, being denied the benefits of, or being subject to discrimination" on the basis of his handicap); *D'Amico v. New York State Board of Law Examiners,* 813 F.Supp. 217, 221 (W.D.N.Y. 1993) (stating that in order to prevail on an ADA claim, a plaintiff must show "(1) that she is disabled, (2) that her requests for accommodation are, reasonable, and (3) that those requests have been denied"). Compensatory damages are not available to private parties under Title III of the ADA. See 42 U.S.C. § 12188; see generally Mary L. Topliff, Annot., Remedies Available Under Americans with Disabilities Act, 136 A.L.R. Fed. 63, 95 14-16 (1996). In contrast, compensatory damages under a private cause of action are available under Section 504. See e.g., *W.B. v. Matula,* 67 F.3d 484, 494 (3d Cir. 1995) (citing *Franklin v. Gwinnett County Pub. Sch.,* 503 U.S. 60, 66 (1992) (concerning monetary damages under Title IX)); *Rodgers v. Magnet Cove Public Schs.,* 34 F.3d 642, 645 (8th Cir. 1994); *Wood v. President & Trustees of Spring Hill College,* 978 F.2d 1214, 1218 (11th Cir. 1992).

To state a claim for damages under the Rehabilitation Act, a plaintiff must prove the following elements:

> (1) The plaintiff is a "handicapped person" under the Act; (2) The plaintiff is "otherwise qualified" for participation in the program; (3) The plaintiff is being excluded from participation in, being denied the benefit of, or being subjected to discrimination under the program solely by reason of his handicap; and (4) The relevant program or activity receiving is Federal financial assistance.

Doherty v. Southern College of Optometry, 862 F.2d 570, 573 (6th Cir. 1988). To award damages, a court must find intentional discrimination because "good faith attempts to pursue legitimate ends are not sufficient to support an award of compensatory damages under Section 504." *Wood,* 978 F.2d at 1219 (collecting cases).

BU does not appear to dispute that any of the named plaintiffs are disabled individuals who are otherwise qualified within the meaning of Section 504. Because I have found that BU's conduct during the 1995-1996 school year rejected many students to discrimination, in violation of the ADA and the Rehabilitation Act and also amounted to a breach of contract in certain instances, I focus here on the manner and the extent to which the individual plaintiffs have been harmed by BU's indiscretions.

1. Elizabeth Guckenberger has proven that BU violated the ADA, 42 U.S.C. § 12182 (b)(2)(i) and the Rehabilitation Act, 29 U.S.C. § 794 by requiring her to be entirely retested for dyslexia under unnecessary eligibility criteria. This violation caused her $800 in economic wages, the amount of the retesting. She has also proven that the method of administering the program for providing reasonable accommodations was discriminatory in violation of the ADA, 42 U.S.C. § 12182(a) and (b)(1)(D) and 29 U.S.C. § 794 because BU officials intentionally did not give students timely or sufficient advance notice of the new policy in order to enable them to meet the requirements before upcoming examinations. Although BU eventually postponed the effective date of the new policy, the discriminatory administration of the program in the 1995-1996 academic year caused her emotional distress. I award $5,000 for the emotional distress.

Guckenberger also proved that BU breached its contract with her when it failed to honor its written, pre-enrollment promise that documentation completed during a student's undergraduate education by a learning disabilities specialist would be accepted. The breach of contract caused Guckenberger $800 for retesting. The total amount of damages is $5,800.

2. Avery LaBrecque has proven that BU violated the ADA, 42 U.S.C. §§ 12182(a),(b)(1)(D), and b(2)(A)(ii) and the Rehabilitation Act, 29 U.S.C. § 794 by unreasonably delaying action on her request for a reasonable accommodation for a well documented language-based learning disability, and by not notifying her in a timely way as to the change in policy regarding course substitutions.

Even though I find that accommodation eventually provided by President Westling (i.e., that she be required to learn the oral component of a language) was reasonable in light of the documentation provided, her request for an accommodation was made early in the semester in September, but was not provided until November. I find that BU's initial denial of any effective accommodation in October was based in part on an impermissible, discriminatory stereotype that any learning disabled students are lazy and can meet the degree requirements if they try hard enough without accommodation. The portion of the evaluator's report referenced in Westling's November 10, 1995 letter was initially presented to him as part of the 28 files on October 5, 1995. Dr. Seigel testified there was "good justification for accommodations." In part, the initial denial resulted from the administration of the program which had the effect, here, of discriminating against LaBrecque by intentionally failing to give her timely notice of the basis of the denial, or the change in policy regarding course substitutions.

LaBrecque has proven that she suffered emotional distress as a result of the discriminatory method of administering the program, which resulted in her dropping out of school and psychiatric treatment. The court awards $5,000 for emotional distress, and $8,000 for psychiatric bill for a total of $13,600.

LaBrecque has also proven that BU breached its oral agreement with her that she would be afforded course substitutions in foreign language, but has not proven that any damages were proximately caused by that breach.

3.   Benjamin Freedman has not proven that any accommodations were delayed or denied, that any promises were broken, or any unnecessary tests taken. Accordingly, I award him $1.00 in nominal damages.

4.   Jill Cutler has proven that BU violated 42 U.S.C. § 12182 (b)(2)(i) and 29 U.S.C. § 794 by requiring her to entirely retested for dyslexia under unnecessary eligibility criteria at a cost of $650.00. However, Cutler's accommodations were not denied or delayed, and the administration of the program did not have a discriminatory effect on her. Because I do not find that the design of the eligibility criteria was substantially motivated by an intent to discriminate against learning disabled students but rather primarily to improve the quality of documentation, I do not award damage for Cutler's emotional distress resulting from the re-testing.

5.   Scott Greely has proven that BU violated 29 U.S.C. § 794 and 42 U.S.C. § 12182 (b)(2)(i) by requiring him to be retested under unnecessary eligibility criteria. This also constituted a breach of contract. However, there is no evidence in the record as to the cost of the retesting. He has also proven that the method of administering the program for providing reasonable accommodations was discriminatory in violation of 42 U.S.C. § 12182(a) and (b)(1(D) because BU officials intentionally failed to give him timely or sufficient advance notice of the new policy in order to enable him to meet the requirements before upcoming examinations, intentionally delayed in providing him any decision regarding his request for reasonable accommodations, failed for six months to provide him with reasonable accommodations in violation of 42 U.S.C. § 12182 (b)(2)(A)(ii) and 29 U.S.C. § 794. Most importantly, BU intentionally discriminated against Greeley by initially denying him any accommodations. In the November 2, 1995 letter, Westling writes:

> The proposed accommodation of requiring the instructor to provide an opportunity to clarify test questions is not supported by the educational therapist who evaluated Mr. Greeley.

While Westling was fairly concerned about this unusual accommodation, other standard accommodations had also been recommended: Time and one-half to complete exams, use of a notetaker and/or tape recorder for class lectures, and use of books-on-tape as necessary. Dr. Seigel testified that reasonable accommodations were appropriate, but agreed she had never seen the opportunity to clarify test questions before as an accommodation. Rather than simply denying the clarification accommodation, BU denied all accommodations. As a result of BU's discriminatory policy, Greeley suffered extreme emotional anxiety and depression, conditions that had physical manifestations (e.g. severe acne and weight gain) and economic ramifications (e.g. loss of his scholarship). I award Greeley $10,000 for emotional distress.

6.   Jordan Nodelman has not demonstrated that he has suffered any uncompensated harm resulting from any of BU's actions during the initial implementation of its accommodations policy, and I award him only nominal damages.

Order of Judgment

1.   The Court orders BU to cease and desist implementing its current policy of requiring that students with learning disorders (not ADD or ADHD) who have current evaluations by trained professionals with masters degrees and sufficient experience be completely retested by professionals who have medical degrees, or doctorate degrees, or licensed clinical psychologists in order to be eligible for reasonable accommodations.

2.   The Court orders BU to propose, within 30 days of the receipt of this order, a deliberative procedure for considering whether modification of its degree requirement in foreign language would fundamentally alter the nature of its liberal arts program. Such a procedure shall include a faculty committee set up by the College of Arts and Sciences to examine its degree requirements and to determine whether a course substitution in foreign languages would fundamentally alter the nature of the liberal arts program. The faculty's determination will be subject to the approval of the president, as university by-laws provide. As provided in *Wynne*, BU shall report back to the Court by the end of the semester concerning its decision and the reasons. In the meantime, the university shall process all requests for a reasonable accommodation involving a course substitution in foreign language, and shall maintain records of such students, BU is not required to grant such a course substitution in the area of foreign language until its deliberation process is complete.

3.   The Court orders entry of judgment for plaintiffs in the following amounts:

a.   Elizabeth Guckenberger: $5,800.
b.   Avery LaBrecque: $13,000.
c.   Benjamin Freedman: $1.00
d.   Jill Cutler $650.00.
e.   Scott Greeley $10,000.
f.   Jordan Nodelman $1.00

---

[1]   The plaintiff class consists of all students with learning disabilities and/or attention deficit disorder who are currently enrolled at BU. See *Guckenberger v. Boston Univ.*, 957 F.Supp. 306, 327 (D.

Mass. 1997). The Court certified a class pursuant to Fed. R. Civ. P. 23(b)(2) only with respect to declaratory and injunctive relief for alleged violations by the ADA and the Rehabilitation Act. The court did not certify a class with respect to individual claims for compensatory damages, or the breach of contract claims.

[2] Counts I and II of the complaint allege discrimination in violation of the ADA and the Rehabilitation Act respectively; Count III alleges violation of Article 114 of the constitution of the Commonwealth of Massachusetts, and Count V alleges breach of contract.

[3] Elizabeth Guckenberger, MacLean Ports Bishop, Avery LaBrecque, Andrea Schneider, Benjamin Freedman, Jill Cutler, Scott Greeley, Michael Cahaly, and Jordan Nodelman. As the parties were notified, this Court will only be assessing damages with respect to students who testified in court or via videotaped deposition.

[4] This term was dubbed by plaintiff's expert witness, Dean Robert Shaw of Brown University.

[5] The evidence at trial suggest that there were only two requests for math substitutions, but the record is unclear on the point.

[6] Westling assumed the office of university president on June 1, 1996.

[7] Other schools at Boston University, like the Metropolitan College, do not have a language requirement.

[8] In fairness to Brinckerhoff, I hasten to mention that neither side called him as a witness to present his version of events.

[9] These concerns about the adequacy of documentation were confirmed in part by Linda Seigel, Ph.D., defendant's expert in learning disabilities. However, Seigel also disagreed with several of Westling's conclusions.

[10] BU hired Carrie Lewis, a former executive assistant to the superintendent in Chelsea, Massachusetts, as the assistant director of disability services, and Judith Zafft, a former high school special education teacher, as the coordinator of learning disability services. The new DS staff was 'hand-picked' by Westling, and Zafft had expressed to Westling her belief that "there is too much abuse in the granting of accommodations" prior to her consideration for the job.

[11] Members of the DS staff sent student applications and documentation from Boston to New York by express mail. Wolf would review the student files, make her recommendations, and then send the materials back to BU. Dr. Wolf reviewed 38 files in this manner between January and mid-April.

[12] The application form has two parts. Part I requires the student to provide a specific description of the requested accommodations, a list of the classes for which accommodations are requested a copy of the student's course Registration, and transcripts from high school and any post-secondary school course of study. Part II is a form to be completed by the student's evaluator. In sum, the form requires a specific diagnosis, test results, and specific recommendations for accommodation. BU requires that the students evaluation be conducted by a physician, licensed clinical psychologist, or a qualified Ph.D with at least three years experience in diagnosing learning disorders. A student who seeks academic accommodations for semester-long courses must submit Part I of the application form (without the transcripts) at the beginning of each semester.

[13] Court considers only the claims for damages of those named plaintiffs whose testimony was presented in person or was admitted by affidavit or deposition transcript during the two-week bench trial.

[14] The College of General Studies at BU provides a two-year course of study.

[15] Greeley also applied to (and was accepted at) the University of Illinois, the University of California-Davis, California Polytech, Sonoma State, and the University of Puget Sound.

[16] This was not a standard accommodation and was suggested by an LDSS staff member.

[17] To be eligible for accommodation during the summer transition program, Nodelman had submitted to LDSS the 1989 evaluation conducted by the clinical psychologist and the two evaluations done in 1993 and 1994 by the Ed.D.

[18] During the 1996-1997 school year, BU amended its policy regarding the credentials of evaluators in order to allow testing done not only by medical doctors and licensed or clinical psychologists, but also by individuals with doctorates in neuropsychology, educational or child psychology, or "in another appropriate specialty."

[19] The parties also submitted transcripts of the deposition testimony of three additional experts: John J. Ratey, M.D., a clinical assistant professor at Harvard Medical School, Michael Gordon, a professor in the unit of Psychiatry at the State University of New York Health Science Center, and Kenneth Kavale, a professor of Special Education at the University of Iowa.

[20] Sally E. Shaywitz, Dyslexia, Scientific America (November, 1996).

[21] The human language system consists of several hierarchical modules or components. The upper levels of the hierarchy are concerned with higher-order thought processes such as semantics, syntax, discourse, and overall comprehension. The lowest level contains the phonological module, the component that enables a reader to break down a word into its basic phonetic units so that it can be identified. The English language has 44 phonemes, defined as the smallest meaningful segment of language. For example, the word "cat" has three phonemes: C-A-T.

[22] Sally Shaywitz, Jack Fletcher, and Bennett Shaywitz, A conceptual model and definition of dyslexia: findings emerging from the Connecticut Longitudinal Study, in Language, Learning and Behavior Disorders 199 (Joseph H. Beichtman, et al., eds.).

[23] The following individuals are members of the Ad Hoc Committee on Learning Disabilities: Loring Brinckerhoff, Chair, Higher Education Consultant, Learning Outcomes of Greater Boston; the Manager of the Law School Admissions Test; the Director of the University of Memphis Student Academic Support Services; Test Accommodation Specialist, National of Board of Medical Examiners; Director, University of Connecticut for College Students with Learning Disabilities; Chairperson, Committee for People with Disabilities, Educational Testing Service; Coordinator, Academic Skills Center, Dartmouth College; Director, Student Disabilities Resource Center, Harvard University.

[24] The term "place of public accommodation" for the purpose of Title III of the ADA specifically includes a "nursery, elementary, secondary, undergraduate or postgraduate private school, or other place of education." 42 U.S.C. § 12183(7)(J). Section 504 of the Rehabilitation Act applies on its face to "any program or activity receiving Federal financial assistance," 29 U.S.C. § 794, and the regulations implementing the statute recognize its applicability to post-secondary education. See 34 C.F.R. § 104.41.

[25] Plaintiffs also contend that BU's documentation requirements are discriminatory to the extent that they apply to students with learning disabilities and not to students with physical or mental disabilities. Because it is fairly well established that "the ADA does not mandate equality between individuals with different disabilities," *Parker v. Metro, Ins.,* (6th Cir. 1997)(citing *Traynor v. Turnage Co.,* 485 U.S. 535, 549, 108 S.Ct. 1372 (1988)), this assertion fails.

[26] As discussed previously, an ad hoc committee of AHEAD has developed guidelines designed to serve as "standard criteria for verifying learning disabilities and attention deficit disorders (ADHD)" The Court gives great weight to the disinterested recommendations of the committee's authorities regarding the appropriateness of accommodations requests and the documentation that students should be required to provide.

27 Testimony regarding these statistics was excluded from the trial as essentially unreliable. At any rate, such data is only partially helpful because it does not compare the specific accommodations requested with those that the students actually received.

28 The Court has found that, because of the waiver option, BU's present policy does not tend to screen out students with learning disabilities within the meaning of the federal law.

29 Although the Court has considered evidence regarding the policies and practices of other educational institutions, it should be noted that I did not rely on Professor Blanck's survey, which was offered by the plaintiffs as evidence of the documentation criteria used by schools other than BU, because it did not have sufficient indicia of trustworthiness and reliability. See *Toys "R" Us, Inc. v. Carnarsie Kiddie Shop, Inc.*, 559 F.Supp. 1189, 1205 (E.D.N.Y. 1983) (finding that among other things, the subject of the survey must be representative sample of a properly-defined universe, the questions must be clear and precise, and the interviewers must be unbiased). Among other things, the telephone survey was conducted in preparation for this litigation by at least two research assistants—one of whom worked for the advocacy group representing the plaintiffs in this action and the other was entirely unknown to Professor Blanck. To compound the problem of the potential bias of the interviewer, the questions that were asked were imprecise.

30 BU has persuasively demonstrated that it is necessary to have current documentation through the twelfth grade. The Department of Education requires reevaluation of children with learning disabilities every three years during elementary and secondary school, and none of plaintiff's experts testified that such testing throughout adolescence was unnecessary. However, as Dr. Shaywitz says, these regulations are not applicable to post-secondary education, in part, because younger school age children have a different growth rate than adults.

31 As a procedural matter, the parties have agreed that I can consider evidence submitted in support of the motions for summary judgment as well as the bench trial to evaluate these claims.

32 Accord *Pandazides v. Virginia Bd. of Ed.*, 13 F.3d 823, 828 (4th Cir. 1994); *Pushkin v. Regents of the Univ. of Colo.*, 658 F.2d 1372, 1377-78(10th Cir. 1981)(citing cases).

33 In relevant part, Title IX provides:

> No person in the United States shall, on the basis of sex, be excluded from participation in, be denied the benefits of, or be subjected to discrimination under any education program or activity receiving Federal financial assistance.

20 U.S.C. § 1681(a)(1988).

34 These regulations are not entirely analogous to the provisions at issue here, for the regulations under Section 504 mandate that, in addition to being prompt and equitable, a school's proceedings "incorporate appropriate due process procedures." 34 C.F.R. § 104.7(b).

35 According to Black's Law Dictionary (5th ed. 1979), "ipse dixit" means: "He himself said it; a bare assertion resting on the authority of an individual."

36 Article 114 provides:

> No otherwise qualified handicapped individual shall, solely by reason of his handicap, be excluded from the participation in, denied the benefits of, or be subject to discrimination under any program or activity within commonwealth.

Mass. Const. amend. art. CXIV.

37 In *Guckenberger v. Boston Univ.*, 957 F.Supp. 306, 317-18 (D. Mass. 1997), this Court dismissed the promissary estoppel count in the plaintiff's complaint as essentially moot based on BU's representation that under a standstill agreement that was reached after the initiation of this litigation, BU agreed to honor all documented promises made to a learning disabled student enrolled at the university. "The dismissal was without prejudice to plaintiff's reliance claims, if the breach of contract count ultimately should fail." Id. at 318.

38 For example, BU's Viewbook and Application for 1996/97 states:

> The University reserves the right to change course content, fees, program requirements, plans of study, class schedules, and the academic calendar, or to other changes deemed necessary or desirable, giving advance notice of change where possible.
>
> Similarly, the catalog for the College of General Studies provides:
>
> Boston University reserves the right to change the policies, fees, curricula, or any other matter in this publication without prior notice and to cancel programs and courses. This publication is to be read neither as part of a contractual agreement nor as a guarantee of the classes, courses, or programs described herein.

39 In addition to prospective, injunctive relief as members of the class, some of the named plaintiffs seek damages as a result of BU's past conduct in the administration of its accommodations policy for students with learning disabilities.

Table of Regulations

34 C.F.R. § 300.19(a)(2), 2:17
34 C.F.R. § 300.29, 3:5, 12, 18n
34 C.F.R. § 300.121, 9:1; 10:4
34 C.F.R. § 300.121(e), 4:7; 9:14
34 C.F.R. § 300.122, 3:4; 9:1, 7; 10:4
34 C.F.R. § 300.122(a)(3), 9:8, 9
34 C.F.R. § 300.122(a)(3)(i), 3:5; 9:1, 3, 6, 10, 11
34 C.F.R. § 300.122(a)(3)(ii), 9:1, 6
34 C.F.R. § 300.122(a)(3)(iii), 9:1, 6, 7, 9, 10, 12
34 C.F.R. § 300.138, 6:15; 7:2, 3, 4, 5
34 C.F.R. § 300.138(a), 6:4, 7; 7:5
34 C.F.R. § 300.138(b), 7:1
34 C.F.R. § 300.138(b)(1), 7:1, 2
34 C.F.R. § 300.138(b)(2), 7:1
34 C.F.R. § 300.138(b)(3), 7:3
34 C.F.R. § 300.139(b), 6:8
34 C.F.R. § 300.306(a), 10:3, 4
34 C.F.R. § 300.306(b), 10:4
34 C.F.R. § 300.345, 5:6
34 C.F.R. § 300.346, 9:1
34 C.F.R. § 300.346(a)(2), 4:12
34 C.F.R. § 300.346(a)(5), 4:10
34 C.F.R. § 300.347, 3:5; 9:1
34 C.F.R. § 300.347(a)(2), 4:11; 5:3; 9:2
34 C.F.R. § 300.347(a)(2)(i), 4:6, 7, 9, 10, 11
34 C.F.R. § 300.347(a)(2)(ii), 4:11; 5:3
34 C.F.R. § 300.347(a)(3), 1:7; 9:2
34 C.F.R. § 300.347(a)(5), 6:5, 14, 15; 7:1, 2, 3, 4; 9:2
34 C.F.R. § 300.347(a)(5)(i), 6:3, 5
34 C.F.R. § 300.347(a)(5)(ii), 7:2
34 C.F.R. § 300.347(a)(7), 5:4
34 C.F.R. § 300.347(a)(7)(i), 5:2
34 C.F.R. § 300.347(a)(7)(ii), 5:1, 2, 3, 4, 6
34 C.F.R. § 300.347(a)(7)(ii)(A), 5:2
34 C.F.R. § 300.347(a)(7)(ii)(B), 5:2
34 C.F.R. § 300.347(b), 3:12
34 C.F.R. § 300.347(b)(1), 9:2
34 C.F.R. § 300.347(b)(2), 9:2
34 C.F.R. § 300.401(b), 6:14
34 C.F.R. §§ 300.450-300.462, 9:7
34 C.F.R. §§ 300.500-300.517, 5:6
34 C.F.R. § 300.500(b)(2), 6:19n
34 C.F.R. § 300.503, 9:7, 8, 9, 11
34 C.F.R. § 300.503(b)(1), 9:8
34 C.F.R. § 300.503(b)(2), 9:8
34 C.F.R. § 300.503(b)(3), 9:8
34 C.F.R. § 300.503(b)(4), 9:8
34 C.F.R. § 300.503(b)(5), 9:8
34 C.F.R. § 300.503(b)(6), 9:8
34 C.F.R. § 300.503(b)(7), 9:8

Table of Regulations and Statute Cross-References

INDIVIDUALS WITH DISABILITIES EDUCATION ACT

[The 1999 IDEA Regulations]

Regulations: 34 C.F.R. §	Title: 20 U.S.C.	Statute: §
300.1	Purposes	1400
300.2	Applicability of this part to State, local, and private agencies	1412
300.3	Regulations that apply	1221e-3(a)(1)
300.4	Definitions used in this part: Act	1400(a)
300.5	Definitions used in this part: Assistive technology device	1401(1)
300.6	Definitions used in this part: Assistive technology service	1401(2)
300.7	Definitions used in this part: Child with a disability	1401(3)(A), (B); 1401(26)
300.8	Definitions used in this part: Consent	1415(a)
300.9	Definitions used in this part: Day; business day; school day	1221e-3
300.10	Definitions used in this part: Educational service agency	1401(4)
300.11	Definitions used in this part: Equipment	1401(6)
300.12	Definitions used in this part: Evaluation	1415(a)
300.13	Definitions used in this part: Free appropriate public education	1401(8)
300.14	Definitions used in this part: Include	1221e-3
300.15	Definitions used in this part: Individualized education program	1401(11)
300.16	Definitions used in this part: Individualized education program team	1221e-3
300.17	Definitions used in this part: Individualized family service plan	1401(12)
300.18	Definitions used in this part: Local educational agency	1401(15)
300.19	Definitions used in this part: Native language	1401(16)
300.20	Definitions used in this part: Parent	1401(19)
300.21	Definitions used in this part: Personally identifiable	1415(a)

	Submission of information	
300.261	Secretary of the Interior-Eligibility: Public participation	1411(i)
300.262	Secretary of the Interior-Eligibility: Use of Part B funds	1411(i)
300.263	Secretary of the Interior-Eligibility: Plan for coordination of services	1411(i)(4)
300.264	Secretary of the Interior-Eligibility: Definitions	1401(9), (10)
300.265	Secretary of the Interior-Eligibility: Establishment of advisory board	1411(i)(5)
300.266	Secretary of the Interior-Eligibility: Annual report by advisory board	1411(i)(6)(A)
300.267	Secretary of the Interior-Eligibility: Applicable regulations	1411(i)(2)(A)
300.280	Public hearings before adopting State policies and procedures	1412(a)(20)
300.281	Notice	1412(a)(20)
300.282	Opportunity to participate; comment period	1412(a)(20)
300.283	Review of public comments before adopting policies and procedures	1412(a)(20)
300.284	Publication and availability of approved policies and procedures	1412(a)(20)
300.300	Provision of FAPE	1412(a)(1); 1411(i)(1)(C)
300.301	FAPE-methods and payments	1401(8); 1412(a)(1)
300.302	Residential placement	1412(a)(1), 1412(a)(10)(B)
300.303	Proper functioning of hearing aids	1412(a)(1)
300.304	Full educational opportunity goal	1412(a)(2)
300.305	Program options	1412(a)(2); 1413(a)(1)
300.306	Nonacademic services	1412(a)(1)
300.307	Physical education	1412(a)(25), (a)(5)(A)
300.308	Assistive technology	1412(a)(12)(B)(i)
300.309	Extended school year services	1412(a)(1)
300.311	FAPE requirements for students with disabilities in adult prison	1412(a)(1); 1414(d)(6)
300.312	Children with disabilities in public charter schools	1413(a)(5)
300.313	Children experiencing developmental delays	1401(3)(A), (B)
300.320	Initial evaluations	1414(a), (b), (c)
300.321	Reevaluations	1414(a)(2)
300.340	Definitions related to IEPs	1401(11); 1412(a)(10)(B)
300.341	Responsibility of SEA and other public agencies for IEPs	1412(a)(4), (a)(10)(B)
300.342	When IEPs must be in effect	1414(d)(2)(A), (B)

300.751	Annual report of children served: information required in the report	1411(d)(2); 1418(a), (b)
300.752	Annual report of children served: certification	1411(d)(2); 1417(b)
300.753	Annual report of children served: criteria for counting children	1411(d)(2); 1417(b)
300.754	Annual report of children served: other responsibilities of the SEA	1411(d)(2); 1417(b)
300.755	Disproportionality	1418(c)
300.756	Acquisition of equipment; construction or alteration of facilities	1405

Table of Cases

Index

W